THE GLORY OF

THE GLORY OF THEIR TIMES

OVERLEAF   The Boston Red Sox in spring training at Hot Springs, Arkansas, in 1915. The Red Sox became the World Champions that year, so perhaps the steamroller on which they are posing is appropriate. (Germany Schaefer was not on the Red Sox—he just happened to be in town.)

In the photo are: (1) *A fan,* (2) *Forrest Cady,* (3) *Chet Thomas,* (4) *Groundkeeper,* (5) *Smoky Joe Wood,* (6) *Carl Mays,* (7) *Germany Schaefer,* (8) *A fan,* (9) *Vean Gregg,* (10) *A fan,* (11) *A fan,* (12) *George Dauss,* (13) *Dutch Leonard,* (14) *Babe Ruth,* (15) *George Foster,* (16) *Guy Cooper,* (17) *Charlie Flanagan,* (18) *Heinie Wagner,* (19) *Ray Collins,* (20) *Ray Haley,* (21) *Rip Hagerman,* (22) *Joe Lannin (owner),* (23) *Bill Carrigan (manager),* (24) *Bill Sweeney,* (25) *Ernie Shore.*

THEIR TIMES

The Story of

the Early Days of Baseball

Told by the Men

Who Played It

LAWRENCE S. RITTER

NEW ENLARGED EDITION

WILLIAM MORROW AND COMPANY, INC.

New York   1984

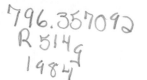
New Preface and Chapters 5, 15, 20, and 25 copyright © 1984 by Lawrence S. Ritter
Remainder copyright © 1966 by Lawrence S. Ritter

Acknowledgment is gratefully made to the following copyright holders for permission to
reprint from previously published materials:

A. S. Barnes and Company, Inc., for permission to use excerpts from *My Baseball Diary*,
by James T. Farrell. Copyright © 1957 by A. S. Barnes and Company, Inc.

Charles Scribner's Sons for permission to use excerpts from: *Of Time and the River*, by
Thomas Wolfe. Copyright 1935 by Charles Scribner's Sons; "Polo Grounds" (which first appeared in *The New Yorker*, Copyright 1942 by Rolfe Humphries) from *The Summer Land-
scape*, by Rolfe Humphries; *The Great Gatsby*, by F. Scott Fitzgerald. Copyright 1925 by
Charles Scribner's Sons, renewal copyright 1953 by Frances Scott Fitzgerald Lanahan.

Irving Shepard for permission to use an excerpt from *The Apostate*, by Jack London. Copyright 1911 by The Macmillan Company.

Boosey and Hawkes, Ltd., for permission to use an excerpt from "The Kerry Dance," by
J. L. Molloy.

Wesleyan University Press for permission to reprint "The Base Stealer" by Robert Francis.
Reprinted from *The Orb Weaver* by Robert Francis, copyright 1948 by Wesleyan University
Press.

St. Martin's Press, Inc., for permission to use excerpts from *The Brooklyn Dodgers: A
Pictorial History*, by Donald Honig, copyright © 1981.

Harcourt Brace Jovanovich, Inc., for permission to reprint "Hits and Runs" from *Corn-
huskers* by Carl Sandburg, copyright 1918 by Holt, Rinehart and Winston, Inc.; copyright
1946 by Carl Sandburg.

Edgar A. Guest, Jr., and Contemporary Books, Inc., Chicago, Illinois, for permission to
reprint "Speaking of Greenberg" by Edgar A. Guest, copyright 1934.

Mrs. R.W. Marquard for permission to reprint the letter from Rube Marquard.

Library of Congress Catalog Card Number: 84-61113

ISBN: 0-688-03901-4

Printed in the United States of America

First Morrow Edition

1 2 3 4 5 6 7 8 9 10

THIS BOOK IS DEDICATED TO THE MEN

WHO LIVE WITHIN ITS PAGES

All these were honored in their generation,
And were the glory of their times.

Ecclesiasticus 44:7

Contents

NOTE: Dates in brackets indicate years played in the major leagues

Preface to the
New Enlarged Edition

THIS NEW enlarged edition of *The Glory of Their Times* contains the complete text and all the photographs that were in the original book, published in 1966, plus for the first time the first-person stories of four additional major-league players—George Gibson, Babe Herman, Specs Toporcer, and Hall of Famer Hank Greenberg.

The original tapes from which *The Glory of Their Times* was written are now themselves in the Baseball Hall of Fame in Cooperstown, New York. Indeed, it has even been suggested that publication of the book helped some of the men in it get elected to the Hall, because it stimulated renewed interest in the early days of the game and in the men who played then.

Goose Goslin, Stanley Coveleski, Rube Marquard, and Harry Hooper were all elected to the Hall of Fame after the book was published—the Goose in 1968, Stan Coveleski in 1969, and Rube Marquard and Harry Hooper in 1971. On the other hand, Sam Crawford, Edd Roush, and Paul Waner were Hall of Famers well before the book appeared.

Whether the book helped or not is questionable, but there is no doubt about the fact that Rube Marquard was the first Hall of Famer to learn of his election while on the high seas aboard the *Queen Elizabeth* 2. Rube was elected on January 30, 1971, by the Committee on Veterans, which bestowed on me the honor of communicating the good news to him. It took a while before the shore-to-ship phone was free, but eventually I got in touch with the QE2 and asked for Mr. Marquard. Rube wrote me about it on the following day:

Dear Larry:

I was the happiest and most surprised man in the world when I heard your voice yesterday telling me that I was voted into the Hall of Fame. The reason I didn't say anything for so long was that I couldn't. I was all choked up and tears were running down my cheeks.

Yesterday evening, a few hours after you called, everybody was dancing and having a good time and suddenly the Captain of the ship stopped the music and said he wanted to make an important announcement. He said they had a very prominent man on board who had just been elected to the Baseball Hall of Fame. His name is Rube Marquard and he is right here dancing with his wife.

Well, all hell broke loose, people yelling and clapping, and the band played "Take Me Out To The Ball Game." I was so happy and Jane just loved it too. When we go to Cooperstown this summer, please come with us and be my guest.

Goose Goslin's experience was somewhat less rapturous. The Goose was elected to the Hall of Fame by the Committee on Veterans in January of 1968. The Cooperstown induction was scheduled for Monday morning, July 22, and the Goose joyously made plans for his big day. "You be sure to be there," he said to me on the phone. "We'll have a wonderful time."

Both of us arrived at Cooperstown on Sunday evening, the day before the ceremonies, the Goose accompanied by some relatives and close friends from home in southern New Jersey. He and his party happily established themselves in several beautiful rooms at the Otesaga Hotel, a few blocks from the Hall of Fame, and all of us enjoyed a bountiful meal, with many toasts, as we awaited the day of days.

Monday dawned warm and beautiful. A large crowd was already on hand as we arrived at the Hall of Fame at ten in the morning. At the appropriate time, General William D. Eckert, then the Commissioner of Baseball, introduced the Goose and presented him with a replica of the plaque that would stand forever in his honor, in close proximity to those of Babe Ruth, Ty Cobb, and Walter Johnson.

The Goose, his eyes wet, tried to maintain his composure. "I want to thank God, who gave me the health and strength to compete with those great players," he said. Then he started to cry and couldn't continue, until the gentle hand of the commissioner and the applause of the crowd restored his self-control. "I will never forget this moment," he concluded. "I will take the memory of this day to my grave."

Finally, we made our way back to the hotel, where a buffet luncheon had been prepared for the new inductees and their guests. Although the lunch was excellent, the Goose could hardly eat because of his exhilaration, not to mention the steady stream of interruptions by congratulatory old friends and autograph seekers.

After lunch we returned to the room and began to make plans for the afternoon and evening. "I think I'll take a nap for an hour or so," the Goose said. "Then let's all walk back to the Hall and take a good look at it."

Before anyone could answer, however, the phone rang. It was the room clerk. "You'll have to vacate your rooms within the hour, Mr. Goslin," he said. "We have a convention arriving and people are already waiting in the lobby for your rooms."

"What are you talking about?" the Goose protested. "I'm not leaving until tomorrow. It's a long drive home and I'm tired. We expected to stay overnight."

"I'm sorry," said the clerk. "But when we wrote you several months ago we told you that we had reserved your rooms for Sunday night only, and that if you or any of your party wanted to stay longer you'd have to let us know. Since we never heard from you, we assigned your rooms to someone else for tonight."

The Goose was stunned. He phoned Ken Smith, the Hall of Fame's director, Paul Kerr, its president, and everyone else he could think of. But no one, not even Commissioner Eckert, could help. There simply were no vacancies in the Otesaga, or in any other hotel or motel within 20 miles. The Goose had no choice. He had to leave Cooperstown.

And so it happened that on his great day, July 22, 1968, Leon Allen Goslin was honored, acclaimed, and applauded in the morning—and unceremoniously ejected from his hotel room that same afternoon. *Sic transit gloria mundi!*

To do the interviews for *The Glory of Their Times*, I traveled 75,000 miles searching for the heroes of a bygone era. They were not easy to find. The teams they played for had lost track of them decades ago, and there was no central source of information. Modern players are relatively easy to locate. Since they are entitled to pension benefits, the Players Association keeps track of their whereabouts. But there were no pensions for those I was seeking, and often no Social Security either.

In desperation, I consulted old baseball record books, which usually contained information on date and place of birth. Then I went to the New York Public Library's collection of up-to-date municipal telephone directories. I reasoned that many of these men might well have returned to their home towns after their playing days were over, and even if they hadn't, relatives might still be living there who could help me.

Surprisingly, this worked. More often than not the home-town telephone book had a listing for the last name of the person I was looking for, and generally it was a close or distant relative of the old ballplayer. If they didn't know where he was, they at least knew some other member of the family who did.

Not that it was any bed of roses from there on in. Far from it. As a case in point, for example, consider the tracking down of Sam Crawford, the top long-ball hitter of the early 1900's. I was told that Sam lived in Los Angeles, but when I arrived at the address, his wife, somewhat startled, said he hadn't been there in months. Sam didn't like big cities, she said, so she seldom saw him. Well, then, where could I find him? Oh, she couldn't tell me that; he'd be furious. Sam loved peace and quiet . . . and, above all, he wanted privacy.

After I pleaded for hours, Mrs. Crawford relented somewhat. She wouldn't tell me exactly where he was, but there was probably no harm in giving me "one small hint." If I drove north somewhere between 175 and 225 miles, I'd be "warm." Oh yes, she inadvertently dropped one more clue—Sam Crawford, the giant who had once terrorized American League pitchers, enjoyed two things above all: tending his garden and watching the evening sun set over the Pacific Ocean.

A long drive and inquiries at post offices, real-estate agencies, and grocery stores placed me, two days later, in the small town of Baywood Park, California, halfway between Los Angeles and San Francisco. For the next two days, however, I made no further progress. On the morning of the fifth day, frustrated and disappointed, I took some wash to the local Laundromat and disgustedly sat watching the clothes spin. Seated next to me was a tall, elderly gentleman reading a frayed paperback. Idly, I asked if he had ever heard of Sam Crawford, the old ballplayer.

"Well, I should certainly hope so," he said, "bein' as I'm him."

I sometimes wonder what could have prompted me to embark on such a strange crusade, searching the highways and byways of America for old ballplayers, a quest that preoccupied me for the better part of six years. For a long time I thought my travels had been inspired by the death of Ty Cobb in 1961 and that I was pursuing a social goal, recording for posterity the remembrances of a sport that had played such a significant role in American life in the early years of the twentieth century.

But now, on reflection two decades later, I don't think my journey had much to do with social purposes. Deep down, it was a quest of a more personal nature. It so happens that my own father died at about the same time as Ty Cobb. Still vivid in my memory is the day, when I was nine years old, that my father took me by the hand to my first big-league baseball game. It seems to me now that I was trying to recapture that unforgettable ritual of childhood and draw closer to a father I would never see again—and I think that, through *The Glory of Their Times*, I somehow succeeded.

LAWRENCE S. RITTER
1984

Original Preface

THIS IS A book about the early days of baseball. It is a book about what it was like and how it felt to be a baseball player at the turn of the century and in the decades shortly thereafter. At least that was my intent when I began working on the book five years and 75,000 miles ago. But now that it has been completed, I am not so sure.

Without implying comparison, I am reminded of Melville's *Moby Dick*. What is *Moby Dick* about? Is it a book about whaling in the nineteenth century? Indeed it is. It probably contains more information on the subject than any learned treatise written before or since. Nevertheless, any schoolboy knows that *Moby Dick* is not *really* about whaling. It is about man's hopes, his struggles, his triumphs, and his failures. It is about trying to attain the unattainable—and sometimes making it. And, on its own terms, that is also what this book is about.

So is this a book about the early days of baseball, or isn't it? It most assuredly is. It is about Ed Delahanty running away from home in 1887, about Honus Wagner playing third base with a first baseman's glove in 1898, about Ty Cobb coming up from the South with a chip on his shoulder in 1905. It is about Walter Johnson and Christy Mathewson, Babe Ruth and Rube Waddell, John McGraw and Frank Chance, Home Run Baker and Wee Willie Keeler.

But it is about much more as well, because what baseball was like in the early days is told here by the players themselves, by the men who —wearing tiny gloves, wielding heavy bats, attired in uniform shirts with upturned collars and sleeves below the elbows—were playing in major-league baseball games 50, 60, and almost 70 years ago. These are their life stories, told in their words. And in recalling those days, in remembering what their teammates and their opponents were like, in reminiscing about their victories and their defeats, they re-create with dramatic impact the sights and sounds, the vigor and the vitality, of an era that can never return. Here is what it felt like to be young and a big leaguer in a high-spirited country a long time ago.

The narratives contained in this book are chronicles of men who chased a dream and, at least for a time, caught up with it and lived it. They were pioneers, in every sense of the word, engaged in a pursuit in which only the most skilled, the most determined, and, above all, the most rugged survived. They entered an endeavor which lacked social respectability, and when they left it, it was America's National Game. They are proud of what they did, and they talk of it with enthusiasm in their voices and happiness in their eyes.

This is also the story of America at the turn of the century and prior to World War I. Jacques Barzun, the distinguished Columbia University philosopher, wrote that "whoever wants to know the heart and mind of America had better learn baseball." Here, illustrated in microcosm, is the exuberance and unbounded optimism of a nation confident of its ability to shape the future to its will and mold its own destiny. In the days of Teddy Roosevelt a man's fate was seen as his own doing, and individual initiative and hard work were viewed as the pathways to success. At that time the words "welfare state," "corporate image," and "organization man" were not even a part of the language. So it was in baseball as in America at large.

Most history, whether of baseball or of war, is written many years after the event by outsiders desperately trying to reconstruct the way things were. This book has been written by the participants themselves. For them, yesterday, their day of glory, has more immediacy than today. They do not have to reconstruct. All they have to do is recollect. They do not have to try to imagine what it would have been like. They were there. They do not have to try to analyze yesterday from the perspective of today. To them, today is strange and different, and the way it used to be is the natural way. They are more used to analyzing today from the vantage point of yesterday.

Of course, this book was really not "written" at all. It was spoken. And, as spoken literature, it is characterized by the simplicity and directness of the spoken word as contrasted with the written word. My role was strictly that of catalyst, audience, and chronicler. I asked and listened, and the tape recorder did the rest.

I first thought of this book back in 1961, when Ty Cobb died in Atlanta, Georgia, at the age of seventy-four. It seemed to me then that someone should do something, and do it quickly, to record for the future the remembrances of a sport that has played such a significant role in American life. Ty Cobb symbolized America from the turn of the century to World War I perhaps better than any other single figure, just as Babe Ruth symbolized America between the wars and, in so many ways, Mantle, Mays, and Koufax do today.

It seemed obvious that there was only one way to go about this, and that was to take a tape recorder and go and talk to as many old-time ball players as one could find and ask them what it was like. Of course, there are not very many men still alive today who played major-league baseball as long ago as about 1910. A twenty-five-year-old in 1910 would be over eighty today. Furthermore, I did not know where they were, what kind of people they would be, or how they would receive me, a person who had never been professionally involved in baseball in any way.

Since then I have traveled over 75,000 miles throughout the United States and Canada, and have spent countless hours reliving the legend that baseball in the early decades of the century has come to be. We talked in modest, middle-class homes, in elegantly furnished mansions, and in run-down shacks. We talked on farms and in cities. We talked in 100° heat and in 10° below zero cold. We talked for two hours and we talked for twelve: and although I had no idea what to expect when I started out, what I found was a group of friendly and intelligent men who were not only delighted to talk about their experiences, but who were also able to articulate them in such a way as to bring them vividly alive today, often half a century or more after the fact. They re-created their lives and those of their contemporaries with warmth, insight and compassion. They told their stories with pride and with dignity, and also with joy.

They talked not only about what it was like to be a baseball player in the early days, but also about what it was like just to be alive then; about how they got started, and about how they felt when, at the age of thirty-five or so, they found that they were too old to continue playing; about what their contemporaries were like as ballplayers, and what they were like as human beings—all with a sense of drama and urgency that could not have been surpassed had it been about this morning's headlines.

These autobiographies are reproduced here as they were told to me between 1962 and 1966. I had feared that the presence of a tape recorder would be inhibiting, but it was not. It was always placed in an inconspicuous spot where neither of us could see it, and invariably it was soon forgotten. I was quite surprised that not one person objected to its being there.

In preparing these interviews for publication I have done very little editing of the tapes. I have eliminated my questions and comments and have selected and rearranged the material to make it more comprehensible than the verbatim transcript of a six-hour conversation could possibly be. Also, because of space limitations and inevitable repetitions, I have deleted a good deal of material in order to reduce hundreds of hours of tape to manageable proportions and to improve the readability of the book as a whole. By and large, however, the editing has been minor, and I do not believe it in any way diminishes the authenticity of what remains. This is their story, told in their own way, and in their own words.

The reader may wonder at the detail contained in these narrations, the near total recall of events that took place a half century or more ago. If so, he can join me in that wonderment. The memory of man is a remarkable storehouse indeed. Many of the people I talked to had to think longer to get the names of all their great-grandchildren straight than they did to run down the batting order of the 1906 Chicago Cubs. Psychologists assure me, however, that it is not at all unusual as one gets older for the more distant past to be remembered more clearly than what happened three weeks ago, especially if the distant past was particularly memorable.

Initially skeptical, I spent weeks checking a great deal of what was told me. I pored through record books and searched out old newspapers and other primary sources to verify a fact or an incident. But almost without exception I found that the event took place almost precisely as it had been described. And in those instances where something had been added, the embellishments invariably were those of the artist: they served to dramatize a point, to emphasize a contrast, or to reveal a truth.

This, then, is the way it was.

Listen!

LAWRENCE S. RITTER
1966

Oh, the days of the Kerry dancing,
Oh, the ring of the piper's tune,
Oh, for one of those hours of gladness,
Gone, alas, like our youth, too soon. . . .

1 *Rube Marquard*

After twilight had gone, in the first darkness of the night, a freight train rumbled into the station. When the engine was switching cars on the sidetrack, he crept along the side of the train, pulled open the side door of an empty boxcar, and awkwardly and laboriously climbed in. He closed the door. The engine whistled. He was lying down, and in the darkness he smiled.

—Jack London, *The Apostate*

M Y NICKNAME being what it is, you probably automatically assume I must have been a country boy. That's what most people figure. But it's not so. Fact is, my father was the Chief Engineer of the city of Cleveland, and that's where I was born and reared.

Then how come I'm called "Rube"? Well, I'll get to that. But let me tell you about my father first. Like I say, he was the Chief Engineer of the city of Cleveland. As far as he was concerned, the only important thing was for me to get a good education. But as far back as I can remember all I could think of, morning, noon, and night, was baseball.

"Now listen," Dad would say, "I want you to cut this out and pay attention to your studies. I want you to go to college when you're through high school, and I don't want any foolishness about it. Without an education you won't be able to get a good job, and then you'll *never* amount to anything."

"I already have a job," I'd say.

"You've got a job? What are you talking about?"

"I'm going to be a ballplayer."

"A ballplayer?" he'd say, and throw his hands up in the air. "What do you mean? How can you make a living being a ballplayer? I don't understand why a grown man would wear those funny-looking suits in the first place."

"Well," I'd answer, "you see policemen with uniforms on, and other people like that. They change after they're through working. It's the same way with ballplayers."

"Ha! Do ballplayers get paid?"

1

"Yes, they get paid."

"I don't believe it!"

And round and round we'd go. We'd have exactly the same argument at least once a week. Sometimes my grandfather—my father's father—would get involved in it. He liked baseball and he'd take my side.

"Listen," he'd say to my father, "when you were a youngster I wanted you to be something, too. I wanted you to be a stonecutter, same as I was when I came over from the old country. But no, you wouldn't listen. You wanted to be an engineer. So you became an engineer. Now Richard wants to be a baseball player. He's so determined that nothing is going to stop him. Let's give him a chance and see what he can do."

But Dad would never listen. "Ballplayers are no good," he'd say, "and they never will be any good."

And with that he'd slam the door and go outside and sit on the porch, and not talk to either my grandfather or me for the rest of the evening.

The thing is, I was always very tall for my age. I had three brothers and a sister, and my sister was the shortest of the five of us. She grew to be six feet two. So I was always hanging around the older kids and playing ball with them instead of with kids my own age. When I was about thirteen I used to carry bats for Napoleon Lajoie and Elmer Flick and Terry Turner and a lot of the other Cleveland Indians. They weren't called the Indians then. They were called the Cleveland Bronchos and then the Naps, after Napoleon Lajoie. After the regular season was over, a lot of them would barnstorm around the Cleveland area, and sometimes I'd be their bat boy.

Then later I even pitched a few games for Bill Bradley's Boo Gang. Bill Bradley was the Cleveland third baseman—one of the greatest who ever lived—and he also barnstormed with his Boo Gang after the season was over. So by the time I was only fifteen or sixteen I knew a lot of ballplayers, and I had my heart set on becoming a Big Leaguer myself.

One of my friends was a catcher named Howard Wakefield. He was about five years older than I was. In 1906 he was playing for the Waterloo club in the Iowa State League, and that summer—when I was only sixteen—I got a letter from him.

"We can use a good left-handed pitcher," the letter said, "and if you want to come to Waterloo I'll recommend you to the manager." I think Howard thought that I was at least eighteen or nineteen, because I was so big for my age.

I wrote Howard that my Dad didn't want me to play ball, so I didn't think he'd give me the money to go. If I asked him, he'd probably hit me over the head with something. Except for that, I was ready to go. Now if they could possibly arrange to send me some money for transportation. . . .

Well, pretty soon I got a telegram from the Waterloo manager. He said: "You've been recommended very highly by Howard Wakefield. I'd like you to come out here and try out with us. If you make good, then we'll reimburse you for your transportation and give you a contract."

Of course, that wasn't much of an improvement over Howard's letter. So I went upstairs to my room and closed the door and wrote back a long letter to the manager, explaining that I didn't have any money for transportation. But if he sent me an advance right now for transportation, then I'd take the next train to Waterloo and he could take it off my salary later on, after I made good. I didn't have the slightest doubt that I would make good. And, of course, I didn't mention that I was only sixteen years old.

I mailed the letter to Iowa, and then I waited on pins and needles for an answer. Every day I had to be the first one to get at the mail, because if anyone else saw a letter to me from the Waterloo ball club that would have been enough to alert Dad to what was going on and I'd have been sunk. So every day I waited for the first sight of the mailman and tried to get to him before he reached the house.

As it turned out, I could have saved myself a lot of worrying. Because no letter ever came. Three weeks passed and still no answer. I couldn't understand what had gone wrong. Maybe it was against the rules to send transportation money to somebody not yet under contract? Maybe they didn't know how good I really was? Maybe this and maybe that.

Finally, I just couldn't stand it anymore. I gave some excuse to my folks about where I was going—like on an overnight camping trip with the Boy Scouts—and I took off for Waterloo, Iowa, on my own.

From Cleveland, Ohio, I bummed my way to Waterloo, Iowa. I was sixteen years old and I'd never been away from home before. It took me five days and five nights, riding freight trains, sleeping in open fields, hitching rides any way I could. My money ran out on the third day, and after that I ate when and how I could.

Finally, though, I arrived at my destination. It was early in the evening of the fifth day. The freight slowly drew into the Illinois Central station at Waterloo, Iowa, and just before it stopped I jumped off and went head over heels right in front of the passenger house. I hardly had time to pick myself up off the ground before the stationmaster grabbed me.

"What do you think you're doing?" he growled. "Come on, get out of here before I run you in."

"No," I said, "I'm reporting to the Waterloo ball club."

"You're what?" he says. "My God, did you ever wash your face?"

"Yes I did," I said, "but I've been traveling five days and five nights and I'm anxious to get to the ball park. Where do the ballplayers hang around?"

The railroad station at Waterloo, Iowa, in 1906: "I jumped off the train and went head over heels right in front of the passenger house."

"At the Smoke Shop," he said, "down the street about half a mile. If you walk down there probably whoever you're looking for will be there."

So I thanked him and told him I'd see that he got a free pass to the ball game as soon as I got settled, and started off for the Smoke Shop. It turned out that two brothers owned the Smoke Shop, and they also owned the ball club. One of them was behind the counter when I walked in. He took one look at me and let out a roar.

"What are you doing in here?" he yelled. "This is a respectable place. Get out of here."

"Wait a minute," I said. "I've got a telegram from the manager of

the ball club to report here, and if I make good I'll get a contract."

"Are you kidding?" he said. "Who in the world ever recommended you?"

"Howard Wakefield did."

"Well," he said, "Wakefield is in back shooting billiards. We'll soon settle this!"

"I'd like to go back and see him," I said.

"Don't you go back there," he shouted. "You'll drive everybody out. Did you ever take a bath?"

"Of course I did," I said, "but I've bummed my way here and I haven't had a chance to clean up yet."

So he called to the back and in a minute out came Howard. "Holy Cripes!" he said. "What happened to you?"

I was explaining it to him when in came Mr. Frisbee, the manager, and I was introduced to him. "I received your telegram," I said. "I didn't have enough money to come first class or anything like that, but here I am."

"Keokuk is here tomorrow," he said, "and we'll pitch you."

"Tomorrow? You don't want me to pitch tomorrow, after what I've been through?"

"Tomorrow or never, young fellow!"

"All right," I said. "But could I have $5 in advance so I can get a clean shirt or something?"

"After the game tomorrow," he said, and walked away.

So Howard took me to his rooming house, and I cleaned up there and had something to eat, and they let me sleep on an extra cot they had.

The next day we went out to the ball park and I was introduced to the players and given a uniform that was too small for me. The Keokuk team was shagging balls while I warmed up, and they kept making comments about green rookies and bushers and how they'd knock me out of the box in the first inning. Oh, I felt terrible. I had an awful headache and I was exhausted. But I was determined to show them that I could make good, and I went out there and won that game, 6–1.

With that I felt sure I'd be offered a contract. So after the game I went to Mr. Frisbee and said, "Well, I showed you I could deliver the goods. Can we talk about a contract now?"

"Oh," he said, "Keokuk is in last place. Wait until Oskaloosa comes in this weekend. They're in second place. They're a tough team, and if you can beat them then we'll talk."

"Can't I get any money, any advance money, on my contract?" I asked him.

"You haven't got a contract," he said.

"All right," I said, and I didn't say another word.

That evening I didn't say anything to anybody. But when it got dark I went down to the railroad station, and the same stationmaster was there.

"Hey," he said, "you pitched a fine game today. I was there and you did a great job. What are you doing back here? Did you come to give me that free ticket you promised me?"

"No, I'm sorry," I said. "I'm going back home to Cleveland, and I want to know what time a freight comes by." And I explained to him everything that had happened.

He was very nice to me, and after we talked awhile he said, "Look, this train comes in at one o'clock in the morning and the engine unhooks and goes down to the water tower. When it does, you sneak into the baggage compartment, and meanwhile I'll talk to the baggage man before the engine gets hooked up again. Then when the train pulls out and is about five miles out of town he'll open the baggage door and let you out."

So that all happened, and when we were five miles out of town the door opened and the baggage man appeared. I talked with him all the way to Chicago, and as we got close to the yards he said to me, "OK, you better get ready to jump now. There are a lot of detectives around here and if you're not careful they'll grab you and throw you in jail. So once you get on the ground, don't hesitate. Beat it away from here as fast as you can."

The baggage man must have told the engineer about me, because we slowed down to a crawl just before we approached the Chicago yards, and off I jumped. I got out of there quick and took off down the street. I don't know what street it was, and I'm not sure where I was headed, but I do remember that I was awfully tired. It was the middle of the morning and I had hardly slept a wink the night before.

I'd walked about three or four blocks when I passed by a fire engine house. Evidently all the firemen were out at a fire, because the place was empty. I was tired, so I went in and sat down. Well, they had a big-bellied iron stove in there, and it was warm, and I guess I must have fallen asleep, because the next thing I knew a couple of firemen were shaking me and doing everything they could to wake me up. They called me a bum and a lot of other names, and told me to get out of there or they'd have me thrown in jail.

"I'm no bum," I said, "I'm a ballplayer."

"What, you a ballplayer! Where did you ever play?"

So I told them: Cleveland, around the sandlots, and in Waterloo, Iowa, too. And I told them all about it.

They still didn't really believe me. They asked me did I know Three-Fingered Brown, Tinker, Evers, Chance, and all those fellows.

"No," I said, "I don't know them. But some day I'll be playing with them, or against them, because I'm going to get in the Big Leagues."

"Where are you going now?" they asked me.

"Back home to Cleveland."

"Have you got any money?"

"No."

So they got up a little pool of about $5 and said, "Well, on your way. And use this to get something to eat."

I thanked them, and as I left I told them that some day I'd be back. "When I get to the Big Leagues," I said, "I'm coming out to visit you when we get to Chicago."

And home I went. I played around home all the rest of that summer, and then the next summer, 1907, I got a job with an ice-cream company in Cleveland. I made $25 a week: $15 for checking the cans on the truck that would take the ice cream away, and $10 a Sunday, when I pitched for the company team. It was a good team. We played the best semipro clubs in the Cleveland area, and I beat them all. I was only seventeen, but I hardly lost a game.

Then one day I got a postal card from the Cleveland ball club, asking me to come in and talk to them. Mr. Kilfoyl and Mr. Somers, the owners of the club, wanted to see me.

My Dad saw the card. "I see you still want to be a ballplayer," he said.

"Yes, I do. And I'm going to be a great one, too. You wait and see. Some day you're going to be proud of me."

"Yeah," he said, "proud of nothing."

But I went to the Cleveland club's office anyway, and Mr. Kilfoyl and Mr. Somers were both there.

"I received your card," I said. "You know, you got me in a little jam. My dad doesn't want me to be a ballplayer."

"Don't you worry," Mr. Kilfoyl said, "after you sign with us and get into the Big Leagues he'll think differently about it."

"Well," I said, "I'm not signing with you or anybody else until I hear what you're offering. I've been taken advantage of before, and it's not going to happen again. I know a lot of ballplayers and they always tell me not to sign with anybody unless I get a good salary. They all tell me you better get it when you're young, 'cause you sure won't get it when you're old."

"That's a lot of nonsense," Mr. Kilfoyl said. "Don't you worry. We'll treat you right. We'll give you $100 a month. That's a wonderful offer."

"I think he'll be overpaid," Mr. Somers says.

"I don't think that's so wonderful," I said. "And as for being overpaid, I get that much right now from the ice-cream company, and in addition I get to eat all the ice cream I want."

They wouldn't increase their price, and I wouldn't reduce mine, so I left and went home. On the way home, though, I stopped in this sporting-goods store at 724 Prospect Avenue. It was owned by Bill Bradley and Charlie Carr, and was a popular hangout for ballplayers. Bill Bradley, of course, played third base for Cleveland, and Charlie Carr managed and played first base for Indianapolis in the American Association.

When I walked in the door Bill Bradley said, "Hello, Big Leaguer, I understand the boss wants to sign you up."

"Not me," I said, "he wouldn't pay me as much as I already make with the ice-cream company."

"You know, I manage the Indianapolis club," Charlie Carr said.

"I know that."

"How would you like to sign with me?"

"You're in the minor leagues," I said. "If a major-league club won't pay me what I want, how could you do it?"

"How much do you want?"

I took a deep breath. "Two hundred a month."

"Wow! You want all the money, don't you!" he said.

"No, but you want a good pitcher, don't you?"

"Yes."

"Well," I said, "I'm one."

And darned if he didn't agree to it. So right then and there I signed my first professional contract, with Indianapolis of the American Association.

When I got home that night I had to tell my Dad about it, because I was to leave for Indianapolis the next day. Oh, that was a terrible night. Finally, Dad said, "Now listen, I've told you time and time again that I don't want you to be a professional ballplayer. But you've got your mind made up. Now I'm going to tell you something: when you cross that threshold, don't come back. I don't ever want to see you again."

"You don't mean that, Dad," I said.

"Yes I do."

"Well, I'm going," I said, "and some day you'll be proud of me."

"Proud!" he said. "You're breaking my heart, and I don't ever want to see you again."

"I won't break your heart," I said. "I'll add more years to your life. You wait and see."

So I went to Indianapolis. They optioned me out to Canton in the Central League for the rest of the 1907 season, and I won 23 games with them, which was one-third of all the games the Canton club won that year.

Next year—that would be 1908—I went to spring training with the Indianapolis club. We went to French Lick Springs, Indiana. After three weeks there we went back to Indianapolis and played a few exhibition games before the season opened. Well, believe it or not, the first club to come in for an exhibition game was the Cleveland team: Napoleon Lajoie, Terry Turner, Elmer Flick, George Stovall, and the whole bunch that I used to carry bats for. When they came on the field I was already warming up.

"Hey, what are you doing here?" a couple of them yelled at me. "Are you the bat boy here?"

"No," I said, "I'm a pitcher."

"You, a pitcher? Who do you think you're kidding?"

"Just ask Bill Bradley. He was there when I signed my first contract. You'll see, I'm going to pitch against you guys today, and I'm going to beat you, too."

"Beat us! Busher, you couldn't beat a drum!"

So then Bill Bradley came over and said hello. As he was leaving he said, "Richard, you're a nice boy, so I want to give you some advice before today's game. Be careful of the Frenchman." He meant Napoleon Lajoie. He said, "The Frenchman is very sharp and he's been hitting terrific line drives this past week. He's almost killed three of our own

Rube Marquard

pitchers in practice, so there's no telling what he'll do in a real game, even if it is just an exhibition game."

I thanked him, of course, and went back to warming up. Well, I pitched the whole nine innings and beat them, 2–0. Lajoie got two hits off me, and I think George Stovall got a couple, but I shut them out— and I wasn't killed, either.

That night Charlie Carr called me over. "You know," he said, "a funny thing just happened. Mr. Somers, the owner of the Cleveland club, just came over to my hotel room and wanted to buy you. He offered me $3,500 for your contract with the understanding that you'd stay here all season, to get more experience, and then you would join the Cleveland club next year."

"Charlie," I said, "if you sell me to Somers I'm going right back to the ice-cream company. He had first chance to get me, and he wouldn't give me what I deserved. I won't play for Cleveland, no matter what."

"OK," he said, "don't worry. I won't sell you. Later on I'll be able to sell you for a lot more, anyway."

On opening day Kansas City was at Indianapolis, and I pitched the opening game. I won, 2–1, and that evening the story in the Indianapolis *Star* read like this: "The American Association season opened up today, and it was a beautiful game between two fine teams. Each had great pitching, with an eighteen-year-old right-hander pitching for Kansas City and an eighteen-year-old left-hander for the home team. The right-hander with Kansas City looks like he's going to develop into a great pitcher. They call him Smoky Joe Wood. But we have a left-hander with Indianapolis who is going places, too. He resembles one of the great left-handed pitchers of all time: Rube Waddell." And from that day on they nicknamed me "Rube."

I had a wonderful season that year with Indianapolis. I pitched 47 complete games, won 28 of them, led the league in most strikeouts, least hits, most innings pitched, and everything. Occasionally what I'd do would be reported in the Cleveland papers, and friends of mine would tell me that they'd pass by the house and see Dad sitting on the porch.

"Well, Fred," they'd say—that was my Dad's name, Fred—"did you see what your son Rube did yesterday?"

"Who are you talking about?" he'd say. "Rube who?"

"Your son, Richard."

"I told him baseball was no good," my Dad would reply. "Now they've even gone and changed his name!"

Anyway, I had a terrific year with Indianapolis, like I said. Late in the season we went into Columbus, Ohio, and Charlie Carr came up to me before the game.

"Rube," he said, "there are going to be an awful lot of celebrities here at the game today. The American and National Leagues both have an off-day, and they're all coming to see you pitch. If you pitch a good game I may be able to sell you before the night is out."

"For how much?" I asked.

"I don't know," he said, "but a lot. It depends on what kind of game you pitch."

"Will you cut me in?"

"No, I won't," he said. "You're getting a good salary and you know it."

"OK," I said, "I was only kidding anyway."

"I don't want you to get nervous today," he said.

"Nervous? Have I ever been nervous all season?"

"No," he said. "I've been in baseball a long time and I never saw anything like it. I never saw a kid like you, who can beat anybody and is so successful."

"Well," I said, "the reason I'm so successful is because I can beat anybody."

I went out there that day and I pitched one of those unusual games: no hits, no runs, no errors. Twenty-seven men faced me and not one of them got to first base. And that evening in Columbus they put me up for sale, with all the Big-League clubs bidding on me, like a horse being auctioned off. The Cleveland club went as high as $10,500 for my contract, but the Giants went to $11,000, and I was sold to them. At that time that was the highest price ever paid for a baseball player.

I reported to the New York Giants in September of 1908, as soon as the American Association season was over. I was eighteen years old and I was in the Big Leagues!

I came up too late in the season to make a trip to Chicago with the Giants that year, but the next season we made our first trip to Chicago the second week in June. And the first thing I did, as soon as I got there, was to make a beeline for that firehouse.

The only one there when I first got there was the lieutenant. I walked up to him and said, "Lieutenant, do you remember me?"

"Never saw you before in my life," he said.

"Well, remember about three years ago you caught me sleeping back of that stove there?"

"Oh, are you the kid from Cleveland that said he's a ballplayer?"

"Yes. Remember me? My name is Marquard, Richard Marquard."

"Of course. What are you doing here?"

"I'm in the Big Leagues," I said. "I told you when I got to the Big Leagues I was coming out to visit you."

"Well, I'll be darned," he said. "Who are you with?"

"Why, I'm with the New York Giants."

And boy, for years after that, whenever the Giants would come to Chicago I'd go out to that firehouse. I'd sit out front and talk for hours. The firemen would have all the kids in the neighborhood there . . . and all the families that lived around would stop by . . . and it was really wonderful. Everybody was so nice and friendly. Gee, I used to enjoy that. It was a great thrill for me.

Actually, every single day of all the years I spent in the Big Leagues was a thrill for me. It was like a dream come true. I was in the Big

Leagues for eighteen years, you know, from 1908 through 1925. I was with the Giants until 1915, with the Dodgers for five years after that, with Cincinnati for one year, and then with the Boston Braves for four. And I loved every single minute of it.

The best years of all were those with the Giants. I don't mean because those were my best pitching years, although they were. In 1911 I won 24 games and lost only 7, and in 1912 I won 26. That's the year I won 19 straight—I didn't lose a single game in 1912 until July 8!

Actually, I won 20 straight, not 19, but because of the way they scored then I didn't get credit for one of them. I relieved Jeff Tesreau in the eighth inning of a game one day, with the Giants behind, 3-2. In the ninth inning Heinie Groh singled and Art Wilson homered, and we won, 4-3. But they gave Tesreau credit for the victory instead of me. Except for that it would have been 20 straight wins, not 19. Well, at any rate that record has stood up for a long time now. Over fifty years.

And, of course, I had other great years with the Giants, too. In 1914 I beat Babe Adams and the Pirates in a 21-inning game, 3-1. Both of us went the entire distance that day, all 21 innings. And in 1915 I pitched a no-hitter against Brooklyn and beat Nap Rucker, 2-0.

But that isn't why I remember my years with the Giants best. Maybe it's because that was my first club. I don't know. Whatever the reason, though, it was wonderful to be a Giant back then, from 1908 to 1915.

Take Mr. McGraw. What a great man he was! The finest and grandest man I ever met. He loved his players and his players loved him. Of course, he wouldn't stand for any nonsense. You had to live up to the rules and regulations of the New York Giants, and when he laid down the law you'd better abide by it.

I'll never forget one day we were playing Pittsburgh, and it was Red Murray's turn to bat, with the score tied in the ninth inning. There was a man on second with none out. Murray came over to McGraw—I was sitting next to McGraw on the bench—and he said, "What do you want me to do, Mac?"

"What do I want you to do?" McGraw said. "What are you doing in the National League? There's the winning run on second base and no one out. What would you do if you were the manager?"

"I'd sacrifice the man to third," Murray said.

"Well," McGraw said, "that's exactly what I want you to do."

So Murray went up to the plate to bunt. After he got to the batter's box, though, he backed out and looked over at McGraw again.

McGraw poked his elbow in my ribs. "Look at that so-and-so," he said. "He told me what he should do, and I told him what he should do, and now he's undecided. I bet he forgot from the bench to the plate."

Now, in those days—and I guess it's the same now—when a man was up there to bunt the pitcher would try to keep the ball high and tight. Well, it so happened that Red was a high-ball hitter. Howie Camnitz was pitching for Pittsburgh. He wound up and in came the ball, shoulder high. Murray took a terrific cut at it and the ball went over the left-field fence. It was a home run and the game was over.

Back in the clubhouse Murray was happy as a lark. He was first into the showers, and out boomed his wonderful Irish tenor, singing "My Wild Irish Rose." When he came out of the shower, still singing, McGraw walked over and tapped him on the shoulder. All of us were watching out of the corner of our eyes, because we knew The Little Round Man—that's what we used to call McGraw—wouldn't let this one go by without saying *something*.

"Murray, what did I tell you to do?" McGraw asked him.

"You told me to bunt," Murray said, not looking quite so happy anymore. "But you know what happened, Mac. Camnitz put one right in my gut, so I cow-tailed it."

"Where did you say he put it?"

"Right in my gut," Murray says again.

"Well," McGraw said, "I'm fining you $100, and you can try putting that right in your gut, too!" And off he went.

Oh, God, I never laughed so much in my life! Murray never did live that down. Years later something would happen and we'd yell to Murray, "Hey Red, is that right in your gut?"

There were a lot of grand guys on that club: Christy Mathewson and Chief Meyers, Larry Doyle and Fred Snodgrass, Al Bridwell and Bugs Raymond. Bugs Raymond! What a terrific spitball pitcher he was. Bugs drank a lot, you know, and sometimes it seemed like the more he drank the better he pitched. They used to say he didn't spit on the ball: he blew his breath on it, and the ball would come up drunk.

Actually, there was very little drinking in baseball in those days. Myself, I've never smoked or taken a drink in my life to this day. I always said you can't burn the candle at both ends. You want to be a ballplayer, be a ballplayer. If you want to go out and carouse and chase around, do that. But you can't do them both at once.

Of course, when we were on the road we had a nightly eleven o'clock bed check. At eleven o'clock we all had to be in our rooms and the trainer would come around and check us off. We'd usually have a whole floor in a hotel and we'd be two in a room. I always roomed with Matty all the while I was on the Giants. What a grand guy he was! The door would be wide open at eleven o'clock and the trainer would come by with a board with all the names on it. He'd poke his head in: Mathewson, Marquard, check. And lock the door. Next room, check, lock the door.

As far as I was concerned, I never drank a drop even when I was in show business. In 1912 I made a movie with Alice Joyce and Maurice Costello, and then I was in vaudeville for three years, Blossom Seeley and I. That's when she was my wife. It didn't work out, though. I asked her to quit the stage. I told her I could give her everything she wanted.

"No," she said, "show business is show business."

"Well," I said, "baseball is mine." So we separated.

How did I feel when I was traded from the Giants to the Dodgers? Well, not too bad. See, I traded myself. I didn't seem to be able to get going in 1915 after I pitched that no-hitter early in April, and late in the season McGraw started riding me. That was a very bad year for the Giants, you know. We were favored to win the pennant, and instead we wound up last. So McGraw wasn't very happy. After I'd taken about as much riding as I could stand, I asked him to trade me if he thought I was so bad.

"Who would take you?" he said.

"What do you mean?" I said. "I can still lick any club in the league." Heck, I wasn't twenty-six years old yet.

"Lick any club in the league?" McGraw said. "You couldn't lick a postage stamp."

"Give me a chance to trade myself, then," I said. "What would you sell me for?"

"$7,500," he answered.

"OK," I said, "can I use your phone?"

"Sure," he said. We were both pretty mad.

So I got hold of the operator and asked her to get me Wilbert Robinson, manager of the Brooklyn club. See, Robbie had been a coach with us for years before he became the Dodger manager in 1914. After a while she got Robbie on the phone.

"Hello," he says.

"How are you, Robbie?" I said.

"Fine," he said. "Who is this?"

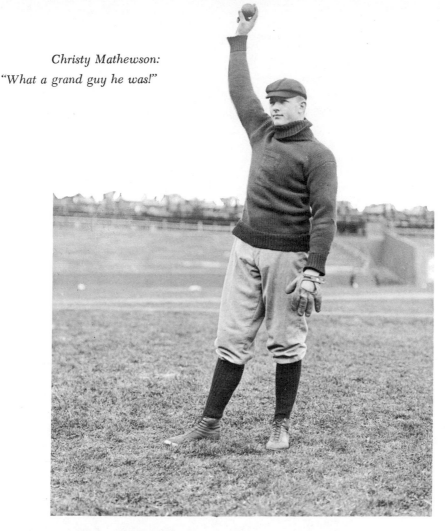

"How would you like to have a good left-handed pitcher?"

"I'd love it," he said. "Who is this? Who's the man? Who are you going to recommend?"

"I'm going to recommend myself."

"Who are you?"

"Rube Marquard."

"Oh, what are you kidding around for, Rube?" he said. "I have to go out on the field and I don't have time to fool around."

"No, I'm serious," I said. "McGraw is right here and he says he'll sell me for $7,500. Do you want to talk to him?"

"Of course I do," Robbie said. And right then and there I was traded from the Giants to the Dodgers.

And, of course, we—the Dodgers, that is—won the pennant the next

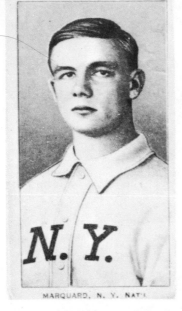

MARQUARD, N. Y. NAT'L

year, and I had one of the best years I ever had. I think I had an earned run average of about 1.50 in 1916. And then we won the pennant again in 1920. So everything worked out pretty well.

One day when I was pitching for Brooklyn I pitched the first game of a double-header against Boston and beat them, 1–0. I was in the clubhouse during the second game, taking off my uniform, when the clubhouse boy came in.

"Rube," he said, "there's an elderly gentleman outside who wants to see you. He says he's your father from Cleveland."

"He's not my father," I said. "My father wouldn't go across the street to see me. But you go out and get his autograph book and bring it in, and I'll autograph it for him."

But instead of bringing in the book, he brought in my Dad. And we were both delighted to see one another.

"Boy, you sure are a hardhead," he said to me. "You know I didn't mean what I said ten years ago."

"What about you, Dad?" I said. "You're as stubborn as I am. I thought you never wanted to see me again. I thought you meant it."

"Of course I didn't," he said.

After we talked a while, I said, "Did you see the game today?"

"Yes, I did," he said.

"Where were you sitting?" I asked him.

"Well, you know the man who wears that funny thing on his face?"

"You mean the mask? The catcher?"

"I guess so. Well, anyway, I was halfway between him and the number one—you know, where they run right after they hit the ball."

"You mean first base?"

"I don't know," he said. "I don't know what they call it. I was sitting in the middle there."

"How many ball games have you seen since I became a ballplayer, Dad?"

"This is the first one," he said.

Well, he stayed in New York with me for a few weeks, and we had a great time. Finally, he had to go back to Cleveland. After he'd left, the newspapers heard about my Dad and they wanted to know his address back home. So I gave it to them, and doggone if they didn't send reporters and photographers to Cleveland to interview him.

They took his picture and asked him a lot of questions. One of the things they asked him was whether he had ever played very much baseball himself.

"Oh, of course I did, when I was younger," he told them. "I used to love to play baseball. I used to be a pitcher, just like my son Richard —I mean like my son Rube."

"Are you proud of your son?" they asked him.

"I certainly am," Dad said. "Why shouldn't I be? He's a great baseball player, isn't he?"

2 *Tommy Leach*

We used no mattress on our hands,
No cage upon our face;
We stood right up and caught the ball,
With courage and with grace.
　　　　　　　—GEORGE ELLARD, 1880's

L ISTEN, when you say the name Wagner to me, you better say *Honus* Wagner. Anybody else, you mention Wagner to them and they know right off who you're talking about. But not me. That very confusion resulted in me almost pulling one of the biggest boners of my whole life.

It happened in 1898. I was a skinny twenty-year-old kid, only 135 pounds, playing third base for the Auburn Club of the New York State League. About a month before the end of the season the owner of the club sent down word that he wanted me to come in and see him. "Uh-oh," I thought, "what the dickens is coming now?"

"I told you I was going to sell you to a Big League club before the season was over," he said, "and I've got a chance to do just that. Two National League clubs want you, and I'm going to let you make the choice. Where would you rather go, Washington or Louisville?"

"Well," I said, "I'd like to talk to the manager first, before I make a decision, if you're really going to let me make it. I don't know anything about those clubs, and I'd like to go where I have the best chance."

"That's all right," he said. "You won't go until our season is over, anyway. And then you'll report to whichever club you pick."

So I went to the manager. He was a real old-timer. I don't know whatever became of him. He was a drinking man, and they let him go soon after.

I put it to him: "I just want you to tell me where I'll have the opportunity to show what I can do," I said. "I'd like to go where I'll have the best chance to play third base, because I know that's my best position."

"I'll tell you," he said, "knowing what I know, I'd say take Louisville.

If you go to Washington, they have a man there who's a darned good third baseman. His name is Wagner."

Well, I didn't know Wagner from beans. So, naturally, I chose Louisville. Our season at Auburn ended a month before the Big League season was over, so in late August of 1898 I reported to the Louisville club.

I hardly had time to get settled before it hit me that this guy the Louisville club had at third base was practically doing the impossible. I'm sitting on the bench the first day I reported, and along about the third inning an opposing batter smacks a line drive down the third-base line that looked like at least a sure double. Well, this big Louisville third baseman jumped over after it like he was on steel springs, slapped it down with his bare hand, scrambled after it at least ten feet, and fired a bullet over to first base. The runner was out by two or three steps.

I'm sitting on the bench and my eyes are popping out. So I poked the guy sitting next to me, and asked him who the devil that big fellow was on third base.

"Why, that's Wagner," he says. "He's the best third baseman in the league."

And when I heard that, did I ever groan. I'm sure it was loud enough to be heard the whole length of the bench. "What chance does a tiny guy like me have here, anyway?" I thought to myself. "Wagner isn't with Washington, he's *here*."

Do you know what happened? There was a Wagner with Washington, all right. But it was *Al* Wagner, Honus' brother. Honus himself was right there in Louisville.

Well, it all turned out for the best, of course, but until it did you can bet I was pretty sore at that Auburn manager for giving me the benefit of his wisdom. It turned out for the best because I wound up in Pittsburgh on one of the greatest teams that ever played. We won the pennant four times in the next ten years or so, and beat Ty Cobb and the Tigers in the World Series the last time.

You see, after the 1899 season the National League cut back from twelve to eight clubs. Louisville was one of the four clubs cut out, but Barney Dreyfuss, who owned the Louisville club, bought the Pittsburgh Pirates and transferred a dozen of us who were with Louisville over to Pittsburgh. So the Pittsburgh club that started the season in 1900 was mostly the same team as the Louisville club that had ended the 1899 season.

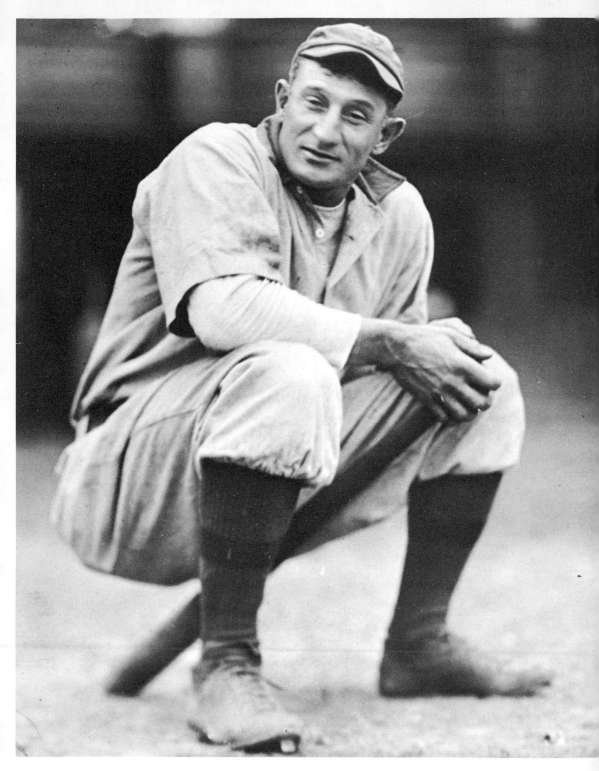

Honus Wagner: "He isn't with Washington, he's here"

And it also turned out that while Honus was the best third baseman in the league, he was also the best first baseman, the best second baseman, the best shortstop, and the best outfielder. That was in fielding. And since he led the league in batting eight times between 1900 and 1911, you know that he was the best hitter, too. As well as the best base runner.

But to get back to that day in 1898 when I first reported to Louisville. I got into uniform and the manager, Fred Clarke, told me to go up and take some batting practice. My own bat hadn't arrived yet, so I just went over and picked out one I liked and went up to hit. After I was through, I hardly had time to lay the bat down before somebody grabbed me and I heard this strange voice say something like, "What are you doing with my bat?" Scared the dickens out of me.

I looked up, and it was a deaf mute. We had a deaf mute playing center field, Dummy Hoy. His real name was Bill Hoy. You probably read of his living to be ninety-nine years old.

I roomed with Dummy in 1899, and we got to be good friends. He was a real fine ballplayer. When you played with him in the outfield, the thing was that you never called for a ball. You listened for him, and if he made this little squeaky sound, that meant he was going to take it.

He married a deaf-and-dumb girl named Anna Maria, who was a teacher at a deaf-and-dumb school in Cincinnati, which is where they both came from. They could read lips so well they never had any trouble understanding anything I said. They could answer you back, too, in a little squeaky voice that usually you could understand once you got used to it. We hardly ever had to use our fingers to talk, although most of the fellows did learn the sign language, so that when we got confused or something we could straighten it out with our hands.

I was just a utility player with the Louisville club for what remained of that '98 season. In those days, they didn't take extra players on the road, so when the team went on a trip they left me behind in Louisville. I was supposed to keep in condition in case something happened and they sent for me.

Well, I was the only utility player, so I had to try to keep in shape all by myself. What I'd do was every day I'd go out to the ball park and take the ball and bounce it up against the grandstand and run back and forth, back and forth, playing catch with myself. I did that for hours every day. Of course, I got no hitting practice. But I did keep in condition.

When the team came back home, Fred Clarke said, "How about you? Would you like to get in?"

"Sure," I said, "I'd like to see what I can do."

So Fred put me in at third base, with Honus moving over to first. That reminds me, did you know that when Honus played third he played it with a first baseman's mitt? I don't know why, but he did. Anyway, I got two hits in that game, which surprised me as much as anybody.

I only weighed about 135 pounds then. I never weighed over 150 in my life, and I'm only 5 feet 6 inches tall, so it took me a long time before I learned how to be a decent hitter. In Pittsburgh later on, you know, I was Wee Tommy Leach, like Willie was Wee Willie Keeler.

I still remember in 1896 when I was playing semipro ball with Hanover, Pennsylvania, in the Cumberland Valley League. I couldn't hit a lick on earth. One day I struck out four straight times. Some fellow got a piece of wood about half a foot wide and four or five feet long from someplace—that's when they used to have those rail fences—and when I came up for the fifth time he presented it to me at home plate. I didn't even have enough sense to laugh. I never dreamed that day that I'd wind up playing nineteen years in the Big Leagues and get over 2,000 hits. The odds against it looked pretty big. Way bigger than me.

So after I got those two hits in that first game I felt pretty good. I went home that night sitting on top of the world. The next day I didn't know whether or not I'd play again, but as I got dressed in uniform that afternoon I really had my hopes up.

While I was dressing, I went over to the end of the clubhouse and, doggone it, there was my bat, sawed into three pieces. Boy, was I ever sore. That was my only bat, and nobody would ever let you borrow theirs. Besides, my bat was something special: a kid had made it in school for me and given it to me as a present. I challenged that whole ball club. All 135 pounds of me. I swore I'd rip whoever did a thing like that into a thousand pieces. And while I was jumping up and down I happened to look over at the manager, and there he was, Fred Clarke, laughing his head off!

I never did find out for sure who did that, but on the basis of the way he acted I still suspect it was Fred himself. He never admitted it. though.

Do you know who joined us on that Louisville club in 1899? Rube Waddell! He came up from Grand Rapids in the Western League late in 1899 and spent the rest of that season with us in Louisville, and then part of the 1900 season with us in Pittsburgh. But he jumped the team in 1900 and went home to a place called Punxsutawney, Pennsylvania. I still remember that name. Connie Mack finally got him to leave there and made him into the terrific pitcher he later became with the Athletics.

I roomed with that crazy character for a while. If they thought he was nutty later, they should have seen him then. He was just an overgrown boy. It was a riot. I remember one time he called the outfield in and pitched an inning without any outfielders. It happened in an exhibition game during spring training, coming up from the South. It was an Easter Sunday, and somebody in the stands threw an egg at him and hit him right on top of the head. You couldn't faze that guy, though. He's the only guy I know who appreciated a thing like that. So he showed them how good he was by calling in the outfield and striking out the side.

I used to stand there at third base and watch him throw. I wasn't playing, I was watching! "How can a man throw that hard?" I used to wonder to myself. He had a terrific curve ball, too, and great control.

Anyway, when the 1899 season opened I was still that extra utility man. Pretty soon after the season began, though, the shortstop got hurt and they put me in there. Well, in my very first game I made five errors. So right after that they sent me back to the minors—they loaned me to Wooster—with the understanding that I'd play shortstop. Third base was where I belonged; I knew that all the time. But who was I to argue about it?

I'd been playing at Wooster for about two weeks, when about ten o'clock one night I got a wire to report back to Louisville. Well, I didn't have any money, so I went to show the wire to the manager of the Wooster club. It took me an hour or so before I could find him.

"How much money have you got?" he says.

"I don't have any," I said.

"Well, then," he says, "you're not going to Louisville. If you come to me thinking the club is going to pay your railway fare, you're wrong. You're going to stay here. I need you."

"But I have to report back there," I said. "I'm just here on loan, and they want me back."

"That's too bad," he says.

"Well," I said, "I guess there isn't anything I can do about it, so I might as well go home and go to bed." And that's exactly what I did.

The next morning, though, he came around and handed me the

ticket. "It might be your big chance," he said, "so I'm not going to stand in your way. Good luck."

And back I went to Louisville. Pretty soon after that I became the regular third baseman, and I got in over 100 games that year. Hit a respectable .290, too, if I remember correctly. My salary that year was $5 a day—$150 a month, for the season.

The next year—that would be 1900—we moved from Louisville to Pittsburgh. We had a little trouble getting started that year, and in June we were in last place. Then we started playing the way we should, and we almost won the pennant. Brooklyn beat us out by only a couple of games, even after our bad start.

But we did win it the next three years, in 1901, 1902, and 1903. In 1902 we won the National League pennant by 27½ games over the second-place team. Even in all the years that have passed since then no club in either major league has ever finished that far out in front. That was the year, believe it or not, that I led the league in home runs. I really did. I had six. The next year I did even better: I hit seven. But Jimmy Sheckard beat me out with nine.

Of course, I wasn't a home-run hitter like you see today. The fields were big then, and if you hit a ball between the outfielders and were fast enough, you had a home run. None of those I hit went over the fence.

In 1902, like I said, we won the pennant by 27½ games, and do you know that our starting pitcher pitched the *complete* game in something like 130 out of the 140 games we played that season? Just think of that, and compare it with today. It's hard to believe, isn't it? We had four pitchers, and they just took their regular turn, day after day, and went the distance almost every time: Jack Chesbro, Deacon Phillippe, Sam Leever, and Jesse Tannehill. Four of the best pitchers in baseball!

In 1903 we won the pennant again, the third year in a row, and that was the year we were in the first World Series ever played. The very first there ever was. The American League had started in 1901, but the two leagues couldn't get together to play each other until 1903. I hit four triples in that Series, but it didn't help, because the Boston Red Sox beat us anyway. I think they were called the Boston Pilgrims then, by the way.

That was probably the wildest World Series ever played. Arguing all the time between the teams, between the players and the umpires, and especially between the players and the fans. That's the truth. The fans were *part* of the game in those days. They'd pour right out onto the field and argue with the players and the umpires. Was sort of hard to keep the game going sometimes, to say the least.

I think those Boston fans actually won that Series for the Red Sox. We beat them three out of the first four games, and then they started singing that damn *Tessie* song, the Red Sox fans did. They called themselves the Royal Rooters and their leader was some Boston character named Mike McGreevey. He was known as "Nuf Sed" McGreevey, because any time there was an argument about anything to do with baseball he was the ultimate authority. Once McGreevey gave his opinion that ended the argument: nuf sed!

Anyway, in the fifth game of the Series the Royal Rooters started singing *Tessie* for no particular reason at all, and the Red Sox won. They must have figured it was a good-luck charm, because from then on you could hardly play ball they were singing *Tessie* so damn loud.

Tessie was a real big popular song in those days. You remember it, don't you?

> Tessie, you make me feel so badly,
> Why don't you turn around.
> Tessie, you know I love you madly,
> Babe, my heart weighs about a pound.

Yeah, that was a real humdinger in those days. Like *The Music Goes Round and Round* in the 'thirties. Now you surely remember *that* one?

Only instead of singing "Tessie, you know I love you madly," they'd sing special lyrics to each of the Red Sox players: like "Jimmy, you know I love you madly." And for us Pirates they'd change it a little. Like when Honus Wagner came up to bat they'd sing:

> Honus, why do you hit so badly,
> Take a back seat and sit down.
> Honus, at bat you look so sadly,
> Hey, why don't you get out of town.

Sort of got on your nerves after a while. And before we knew what happened, we'd lost the World Series.

That year, 1903, was also the year Honus became a full-time shortstop. Up until 1903 he played almost every position on the team, one day at short, the next day in the outfield, the day after at first base. He didn't look like a shortstop, you know. He had those huge shoulders and those bowed legs, and he didn't seem to field balls the way we did. He just ate the ball up with his big hands, like a scoop shovel, and when he threw it to first base you'd see pebbles and dirt and everything else flying over there along with the ball. It was quite a sight! The greatest shortstop ever. The greatest *everything* ever.

We never finished out of the first division the next five years, but we didn't win again until 1909. That year we evened it up with the American League by beating the Tigers in the World Series. They had a good team, too: Ty Cobb, Sam Crawford, Davy Jones, Donie Bush, George Moriarty, and all that bunch.

That was a mighty rough World Series in 1909, you know. Almost as rough as that first one in 1903. There was a lot of bad blood between us and Detroit, especially with that George Moriarty, the Detroit third baseman. He was a tough character.

It so happened that right about that time I started to get bald. Terrible feeling. I was only about thirty years old then. Well, somebody told me that I could stop my hair from falling out if I'd shave it off completely and rub this liniment on my head. I think it was some kind of horse liniment, to tell the truth. So that's exactly what I did, just before the Series started. It was foolishness, but I did it anyway.

Well, in one of the games of the Series—I forgot just which one— I got a single and went to third on a hit by Honus. I'm standing there on third base, not thinking about anything in particular, when this Moriarty suddenly comes over and kicks me in the shin. Just like that.

I looked at him in surprise, and asked him what was the meaning of such a thing. He just walked away, didn't say a word. I had to stay right where I was, of course. I didn't dare get off the base, because if I did they'd tag me out.

A few seconds later I had my back turned and he comes over again, and this time he grabs my cap right off my head. I was embarrassed and I started to laugh.

"Well," I said, "I got it all shaved off the other day." I wanted to explain to him why there was no hair on my head, you know.

But he didn't wait for me to finish. He reached up and slapped me right on top of my bare head. With my own cap, too!

Boy, that was too much. So I turned around and grabbed my cap, and at the same time gave him a good healthy kick in the shins. We were about to really go to it when the game started again, and I think the inning ended on the next pitch, so that was that. Anyway, as you can see, that horse liniment didn't do a heck of a lot of good.

A funny thing about that Series, playing second base for Detroit was Jimmy Delahanty. We had known each other since we were kids in

The first World Series, the Pirates versus the Red Sox, in 1903: "It was sort of hard to keep the game going sometimes, to say the least"

Cleveland. In fact, it was because of his big brother, Ed, that I had gotten started in baseball in the first place.

I was born in French Creek, New York, but my folks moved to Cleveland in the early 1880's, when I was five years old. We lived in an Irish neighborhood in Cleveland, and the Delahantys lived nearby. There were six brothers, Ed, Tommy, Joe, Jim, Frank, and Willie. All of them except Willie eventually made the Big Leagues.

Of course, Ed was the best ballplayer of them all. He was a terrific hitter. Once he hit four home runs in one game, you know, and twice he got six hits in one game. I always admired Ed. As a matter of fact, I still do.

Well, the Delahantys lived on a street where there was a firehouse, and all us kids used to gather around in front of it every evening to watch the horses come out for what they called the "Eight O'Clock Call." The Delahanty kids used to hang around there a lot.

One day a baseball man came around the neighborhood looking for

Ed. We found out later he was the manager of the Mansfield club in the Ohio State League. Everybody knew Ed, so when this fellow asked where he could find him he was told to try down at the firehouse. And sure enough, that's where Ed was.

This fellow evidently asked Ed if he'd like to join the Mansfield club, and evidently Ed said yes, because that night Ed didn't come home. He left word for his folks where he was going, and what he was going to do, and he just took off. Actually, Mansfield isn't so far from Cleveland, maybe about 75 miles, and Ed was about nineteen years old at the time, so it wasn't as bad as it sounds.

As soon as his mother and father found out what had happened, the first thing they did was to come to my father, wanting to know what they should do. They were pretty shook up, and they thought they should go and bring Ed home right away. For some reason, what they really wanted was for *my* Dad to go and fetch him.

"I want you to go get Ed," Mrs. Delahanty told Dad. "He hasn't any business in Mansfield, and he should be here working."

Dad started to laugh. He said, "Listen, you've got a boy who only wants to play baseball. He tells you he's working, and what's he doing? He's always out playing ball somewhere. Give him a break. Who knows, maybe he can make the grade." And he wouldn't go after Ed.

Well, of course, Ed made good in a big way. One year later he was up there with the Philadelphia Phillies, and from then on that's all us kids around the neighborhood thought of. He was everybody's hero. It got so that's all Dad could talk about: Ed Delahanty, Ed Delahanty, Ed Delahanty. That's all we heard.

I was supposed to be learning the printer's trade. Dad had a job printing shop. He was the outside man soliciting business and then he had a printer, and I was the printer's devil. But I loved to play ball, little as I was, and Dad would always encourage me. "If Ed can do it, so can you," he'd say.

Finally, when I got a chance to go with Hanover in the Cumberland Valley League—that was in 1896, when I was eighteen—my father got all excited. I think they offered me $35 a month and board. "You get out of here and go," he said. "Look where Ed Delahanty is."

So I went. Not that I had any objections, you understand. And a few years later there I was, playing against Ed, who always had been my idol, and later against Tommy, Joe, Jim, and Frank, as well.

When I was about fourteen or fifteen years old, Ed Delahanty was the one everybody in my neighborhood looked up to. Later, after Ed

Tommy Leach in 1902

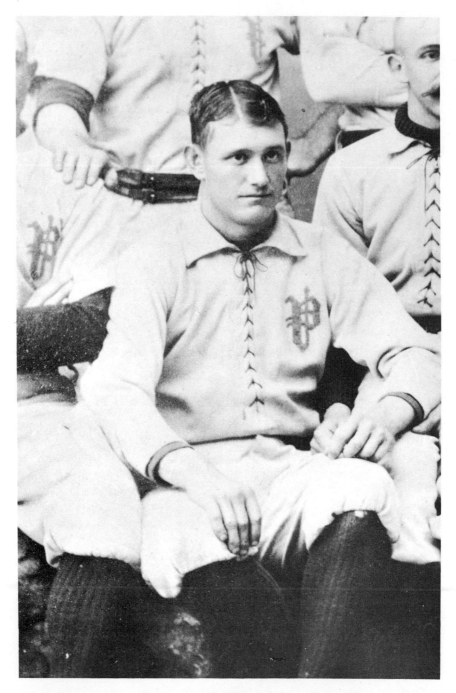

Ed Delahanty, the pride of the Phillies (and of Cleveland)

died in that tragic way at Niagara Falls, the big hero of all the kids in Cleveland became Napoleon Lajoie, the Cleveland second baseman. What a ballplayer that man was! Every play he made was executed so gracefully that it looked like it was the easiest thing in the world. He was a pleasure to play against, too, always laughing and joking. Even when the son of a gun was blocking you off the base, he was smiling and kidding with you. You just *had* to like the guy.

You might think this is all a lot of malarkey, but I really believe baseball was a more exciting game back in those days. It was more rugged, first of all. Take the equipment. We had little gloves that would just fit over your hand. Now they have those big nets, and they catch the ball in the webbing. But we had to catch the ball with our hands.

And the fields. Now the lowest minor leagues have better fields to play on than we had in the major leagues. You never knew how a ball was going to bounce in those days. Lots of times we'd get a rake and go out and rake the ground around our own positions.

The style of play is very different now, too. We used to play a running game, a lot of bunting and base stealing. I stole almost 400 bases in my Big League career, and that wasn't considered much at all. Heck, Fred Clarke stole over 500, and Honus over 700. All of us on one team, mind you. Even the fellows who were considered the power hitters in those days used to run the bases a lot. Like Sam Crawford, the strong boy—he stole about 400 bases, and so did other big guys, like Jake Beckley and Dan Brouthers.

Today they seem to think that the most exciting play in baseball is the home run. But in *my* book the most exciting play in baseball is a three-bagger, or an inside-the-park home run. You used to see a fair number of them in the old days, but now they're the rarest plays in baseball. For sheer excitement, I don't think anything can beat when you see that guy go tearing around the bases and come sliding into third or into the plate, with the ball coming in on a line from the outfield at the same time. Now *that's* something to write home about.

3   *Davy Jones*

Two or three years ago Base Ball critics in the East and West began to agitate the question of signaling by the umpires to announce their decisions.

At first the judges of play did not want to signal. They thought it detracted from their dignity to go through a dumb show resembling the waving of the arms of a semaphore.

That did not deter the Base Ball critics from their stand. With good-natured persistence they urged upon the umpires the necessity of the new idea, and by and by the officials of the league took up the subject and suggested that it would be worth a trial.

It was finally experimented with and has been one of the very best moves in Base Ball as a medium of rendering decisions intelligible, and now there is not an umpire but uses his arms to signal. If he did not, two-thirds of the spectators at the immense crowds, which have been patronizing Base Ball for the last two years, would be wholly at sea as to what was transpiring on the field, except as they might guess successfully.

Even the older umpires, who were more loath to give their consent to the new system on the field, are now frank enough to admit that it has been of invaluable assistance to them in making their decisions understood when the size of the crowd is such that it is impossible to make the human voice carry distinctly to all parts of the field.   *—Spalding's Base Ball Guide,* 1909

O H, THE GAME WAS VERY DIFFERENT in my day from what it's like today. I don't mean just that the fences were further back and the ball was deader and things like that. I mean it was more *fun* to play ball then. The players were more colorful, you know, drawn from every walk of life, and the whole thing was sort of chaotic most of the time, not highly organized in every detail like it is nowadays.

I was playing in the Big Leagues in 1901, when Mr. William McKinley was President, and baseball attracted all sorts of people in those days. We had stupid guys, smart guys, tough guys, mild guys, crazy guys, college men, slickers from the city, and hicks from the country. And back then a country kid was likely to *really* be a country kid. We'd call them hayseeds or rubes. Nowadays I don't think there's much difference between city kids and country kids. Anyway, nothing like there used to be.

Back at the turn of the century, you know, we didn't have the mass communication and mass transportation that exist nowadays. We didn't have as much schooling, either. As a result, people were more unique then, more unusual, more different from each other. Now people are all more or less alike, company men, security minded, conformity—that sort of stuff. In everything, not just baseball.

Talk about colorful guys, take Rube Waddell or Germany Schaefer. I doubt if fellows like that could exist in baseball today. Too rambunctious, you know. They'd upset the applecart.

I played with Germany Schaefer on the Chicago Cubs in 1902, and again on the Detroit Tigers later on. What a man! What stunts he could pull! I used to laugh at that guy till I cried. Far and away the funniest man I ever saw. He beat Charlie Chaplin any day in the week.

One day when I was on the Tigers—I think it was 1906, my first year with Detroit—we were in Chicago, playing the White Sox. Red Donahue was pitching for us and Doc White, that great little left-hander, was pitching for the White Sox. We were behind, 2–1, going into the ninth inning. Then in the ninth we got a man on first base with two out, and the next man up was Donahue, who was easily one of the worst hitters in the league. So Bill Armour, who was managing Detroit then, looked up and down the bench and spotted Germany Schaefer sitting there— talking, as usual, to whoever would listen.

"How would you like to go up there and pinch-hit?" Bill asked him.

"Sure," he says, "I'd love to. I always could hit Doc White."

Meanwhile, Red Donahue is already getting all set in the batter's box. Red was an awful hitter, but there was nothing in the whole world he loved more than digging in at that plate and taking his cuts.

"Hey, Red," yells Schaefer, "the manager wants me to hit for you."

"What?" Red roars. "Who the hell are you to hit for me?" And he slams his bat down and comes back and sits way down at the end of the bench, with his arms folded across his chest. Madder than a wet hen.

Well, Schaefer walked out there and just as he was about to step into the batter's box he stopped, took off his cap, and faced the grandstand.

"Ladies and gentlemen," he announced, "you are now looking at Herman Schaefer, better known as Herman the Great, acknowledged by one and all to be the greatest pinch hitter in the world. I am now going to hit the ball into the left field bleachers. Thank you."

Then he turned around and stepped into the batter's box. Of course, everybody's giving him the old raspberry, because he never hit over two or three home runs in his life. But by golly, on the second ball Doc White pitched he did just exactly what he said he would: he hit it right smack into the left-field bleachers.

Boy oh boy, you should have seen him. He stood at that plate until the ball cleared the fence, and then he jumped straight up in the air, tore down to first base as fast as his legs would carry him, and proceeded to slide headfirst into the bag. After that he jumped up, yelled "Schaefer leads at the Quarter!" and started for second.

He slid into second—yelled "Schaefer leads at the Half!"—and continued the same way into third and then home. After he slid into home he stood up and announced: "Schaefer wins by a nose!" Then he brushed himself off, took off his cap, and walked over to the grandstand again.

"Ladies and gentlemen," he said, "I thank you for your kind attention."

Back on the bench everybody was laughing so hard they were falling all over themselves. Everybody except Red Donahue. He's still sitting there at the end of the bench with his arms folded, like a stone image, without the slightest expression of any kind on his face.

The next day we went back to Detroit to play against Cleveland, and Bill Armour promptly put Germany right into the lineup, at second base. And, of course, everybody at the game had read about what Schaefer had done the day before. So in the first inning, when Schaefer comes up to bat for the first time, the crowd naturally gives him a terrific ovation. "Hurray, Schaefer!" And the stands are buzz, buzz, buzzing about what he'd done the day before.

Unfortunately, the Cleveland pitcher that day was Addie Joss, who Schaefer couldn't hit with a paddle. A corking good pitcher. Three swings, and Schaefer strikes out. Never came close to the ball.

The second time at bat it's still "Hurray, Schaefer!" but not quite as loud as the first time. Well, he strikes out again, just as badly as before. Third time up, no commotion at all. Silence. This time he popped up.

The fourth time it's Schaefer's turn to bat it's the ninth inning, I'm on first, and we're two runs behind. And as he approaches the plate for the last time that day the crowd starts to make just as much noise as they did the first time. Only this time they're all yelling, "Take him out. Take the bum out!"

Ha! That's baseball. A hero one day and a bum the next. But always lots of laughs. I saw all the great ones, you know, in *both* leagues. I was in the American League in 1901 and again from 1906 through 1913.

Germany Schaefer, little Danny Callahan, and Sam Crawford

and in the National League from 1902 through 1904. Actually, I played in *three* major leagues, because I jumped to the Federal League in 1914 and spent two years there. And, of course, I was in three World Series with the Detroit Tigers—1907, '08, and '09. So, all in all, there weren't very many topflight players between 1900 and 1915 who I didn't play either with or against at one time or another.

Funny thing, I never expected to be a ballplayer in the first place. I wanted to be a lawyer. Well, as a matter of fact I *became* a lawyer. I went to law school at Dixon College in Illinois and graduated in 1901, but I got to playing ball and never did go back to the law.

I received an athletic scholarship at Dixon, one that included both baseball and track. Actually, track was my real specialty back then. I was always very fast, fast enough to beat Archie Hahn several times before he won the Olympics in 1904. You probably don't remember Archie Hahn, but he was the fastest man in the world at the turn of the century. Won the 60-meter dash, the 100-meter dash, *and* the 200-meter dash in the 1904 Olympics. Ranks right up there with Jim Thorpe and Jesse Owens as one of the greatest runners who ever lived. Odd, isn't it, that Jim Thorpe and Jesse Owens are still very familiar names, but hardly anybody seems to remember Archie Hahn any more.

I also played baseball at Dixon College, and that led, accidentally, to my becoming a professional. In 1901, in my senior year, the Dixon team went up to Rockford, Illinois, to play an exhibition game with the Rockford Club in the Three-I League. I had a great day both at bat and in the field, and they offered me a contract: $85 a month. Well, I was a very poor boy, and the prospect of $85 a month right away, compared to years as a law clerk before I could start my own practice, made it hard to turn down. So I signed up and joined the Rockford Club right after graduation.

You realize, of course, that baseball wasn't a very respectable occupation back then. I figured I'd stay in it just a few years, and then go back to the law once I got on my feet financially. To give you an idea about its respectability, I was going with a girl at the time and after I became a professional ballplayer her parents refused to let her see me any more. Wouldn't let her have anything more to do with me. In those days a lot of people looked upon ballplayers as bums, too lazy to work for a living. So Margaret—that was her name—and I had to break up.

Later on I met another girl, a rare and lovely woman, and we got married. Married for 52 years before she passed away. I heard that Margaret married a doctor, a man who later became a famous heart specialist at the Mayo Clinic, and that they lived in Rochester, Minnesota.

Well, a few years ago, believe it or not, I ran into Margaret once again, for the first time in nearly 50 years. Turned out that both of us had been very happily married, but were now both widowed. To make a long story short, we found out we still enjoyed each other's company and decided to get married, over half a century since we'd been high-school sweethearts. That was she who opened the door for you when you first got here.

Anyway, I played six weeks in the summer of 1901 with Rockford in the Three-I League, hit .384, fielded like a blue streak, and before the season was over I was sold to the Chicago Cubs. However, the Milwaukee Brewers in the brand-new American League made me a good offer, so instead of reporting to Chicago I jumped to Milwaukee. See, the American League was an outlaw league in 1901, and Milwaukee was one of the eight teams in the league that very first year.

The next year, 1902, the Milwaukee franchise was transferred to St. Louis and we became the original St. Louis Browns. So not only did I play in the American League the very first year of its existence, but I'm also a charter member of *two* of the teams in that league. Neither one of which exists any longer, a fact for which I assure you I can in no way be held responsible.

I'd been with the St. Louis club about two or three weeks in the 1902 season when we went to Chicago to play the White Sox. It was a rainy Saturday, and as we sat on the bench waiting for the game to begin somebody pointed out Mr. Comiskey, the owner of the White Sox. He was out there in the infield, with his pants rolled up, soaking up water with a couple of sponges and wringing them into a pail, trying to get the diamond in shape to play. That was my first sight of Charles A. Comiskey.

After the game that day I got a phone call from James A. Hart, the owner of the Chicago Cubs. He'd been pretty sore ever since I'd jumped from the Cubs to the American League the previous August. Mr. Hart said he'd like me to come over and talk with him at his office the next morning. Well, why not?

"I see you're going pretty good," he said to me, after I got there.

"Yes, that's right," I said. "We've got a good club."

"You know," he said, "I've lost a lot of good ballplayers to the American League, men like Clark Griffith and Jimmy Callahan, not to mention yourself. I'd like to try to get some of you fellows to move the other way. What would you think about jumping back to the Chicago Cubs?"

"Well," I said, "what have you got to offer?"

So he thought a minute, got up, walked into the next room, and sent the clerk for some cash. I guess he thought I'd find green cash more tempting than a check. (He was right.)

Finally he came back. "How about a two-year contract for $3,600 a year, the highest salary on the club, plus a $500 bonus that you can have right now. Here's the $500!"

Well, what could I do? I was playing for $2,400, and here was a 50 per cent raise plus $500 in cold cash stacked up right in front of me. And, after all, I wasn't even twenty-two years old yet. Besides, everybody was jumping all over the lot in those days: Sam Crawford, Larry Lajoie, Clark Griffith, Willie Keeler, Cy Young, Jack Chesbro, Ed Delahanty. You name him, he was jumping from one league to the other.

So I signed.

Mr. Hart immediately called up the ball park and got the manager of the Cubs, Frank Selee, on the phone. "I've just signed a new outfielder," he said. "I won't tell you who he is, but take it from me he's OK. Put him in center field this afternoon."

So Selee went out on the field and one of the players told me later he looked sort of bewildered.

"Mr. Hart just called me," he said. "He says we've got a new outfielder and I should play him today, but he won't tell me who he is. Things are getting funnier and funnier around this place."

For my part, I left Mr. Hart and went for a long walk. I didn't want to go back to my hotel while the Browns were still there, because I wasn't especially anxious to see any of my teammates. My *former* teammates, that is. After I was pretty sure they'd all gone out to the White Sox park, I went up to the room, packed my grip and bat bag—in those days, you know, we carried our own bats in a little bag—and took off for the Cubs' West Side Grounds at Lincoln and Polk Streets.

And that's the last time I jumped a ball club. Well, almost. The last time until 1914, anyway, when I jumped from the White Sox to the Pittsburgh club in the Federal League. But I was about all through by then, so it hardly counts.

I played three years in the Chicago Cubs' outfield, but in 1904 I got hurt and it looked as though I was finished. The next year I found myself back in the minors, with Minneapolis in the American Association. I came back strong, though, hit .346 that year, and at the end of the season I went back up to the Big Leagues with Detroit.

Which was a real break for me, of course, because, as you well know, we won the pennant in 1907, '08, and '09, and for seven years I got to play in the same outfield with two of the greatest ballplayers who ever lived, Ty Cobb and Sam Crawford. Of course, playing by the side of two fellows like that was a good deal like being a member of the chorus in a grand opera where there are two prima donnas.

I always got along with Sam just wonderfully. In a lot of ways we were very much alike. He's still one of my very best friends. Cobb, though—he was a very complex person—never did have many friends. Trouble was he had such a rotten disposition that it was damn hard to be his friend. I was probably the best friend he had on the club. I used to stick up for him, sit and talk with him on the long train trips, try to understand the man. He antagonized so many people that hardly anyone would speak to him, even among his own teammates.

Ty didn't have a sense of humor, see. Especially, he could never laugh at himself. Consequently, he took a lot of things the wrong way. What would usually be an innocent-enough wisecrack would become cause for a fist fight if Ty was involved. It was too bad. He was one of the

Davy Jones in 1901

greatest players who ever lived, and yet he had so few friends. I always felt sorry for him.

In many ways he was resented by a lot of people because he was so doggone good, and that plus being ignored because he had such a nasty disposition meant that the man was very lonely. Of course, he brought a lot of it on himself, no doubt about that. A lot of times it seemed as though he was just asking for trouble.

Like one time in Detroit, when Cobb was in a batting slump. When Cobb got in a slump you just couldn't talk to him. He'd get meaner than the devil himself. Well, we were playing Boston this day, and Ray Collins was pitching against us. Cobb never did hit Collins too well, so the idea of being in a slump and batting against Collins too didn't go down very well with Ty. He'd just as soon sit this one out.

In about the third or fourth inning of this game I got on base and Ty came up to bat. I watched him for the hit-and-run sign, like I always did, but he didn't flash any. Then suddenly, after the first pitch, he stepped out of the box and hollered down at me, "Don't you know what a hit-and-run sign is?" Yelled it right out at me.

Jake Stahl was the Boston first baseman and he said to me, "Boy, any guy would holler down here like that is nothing but a rotten skunk."

But I knew Cobb, so I just ignored him. Those were his ways, that's all. Well, the second pitch came in and curved over for strike two. And was Cobb ever mad then! He went over and sat down on the bench and yelled, "Anybody can't see a hit-and-run sign, by God, I'm not going to play with him." Meaning me.

He just sat there and wouldn't play. They had to put in another batter. All he wanted, of course, was to get out of the game because he couldn't hit that pitcher. That's all it was, and I was the fall guy. He put the blame on me.

Well, the next day he was still sulking. Wouldn't play, he said. Finally Mr. Navin, the president of the club, called him up to the front office and asked him what was going on.

"I won't play with Jones," Cobb said. "That bonehead can't even see the hit-and-run sign."

"Oh," Mr. Navin said, "suppose he did miss the sign, which the other players tell me he didn't. So what? That's no reason for you not to play. You're just making an excuse because you're not hitting."

"Who told you that?" says Cobb. "Just tell me, *who told you that?*"

"Never mind," Navin said, "that's none of your business. Now you're going to play today, and that's all there is to it. Otherwise you'll be suspended without pay. And it's out of the question to take Jones out of the game, so forget it."

Mr. Navin told me all that afterwards. Well, that shows what kind of a person Cobb could be. Picking on me, of all people! Practically his only friend on the club. But with all that, he was really *some* ballplayer. Corking!

I played in the outfield with Cobb and Crawford for seven years, 1906 through 1912, the greatest years in Detroit's baseball history. Three pennants. What a team! I was generally the lead-off man in the batting order, because of my speed. Usually it was Jones leading off, then Germany Schaefer or Donie Bush, Sam Crawford batting third, Cobb fourth, Claude Rossman next, the first baseman, and then George Moriarty, the third baseman. Jimmy Delahanty was in there somewhere, and Charlie Schmidt, the big catcher.

Being the lead-off man, by the way, resulted in my holding the unique distinction of being the first man to ever face Walter Johnson in a major-league game. He broke in late in 1907, in a game against us, and since I led off, naturally I was the first man to face him. And that was the beginning of Walter's long and amazing career. The *very* beginning. Boy, could that guy ever fire that ball! He had those long arms, absolutely the longest arms I ever saw. They were like whips, that's what they were. He'd just *whip* that ball in there.

It was during those years, I think about 1908, that I saw Germany Schaefer steal first base. Yes, *first* base. They say it can't be done, but I saw him do it. In fact, I was standing right on third base, with my eyes popping out, when he did it.

We were playing Cleveland and the score was tied in a late inning. I was on third base, Schaefer on first, and Crawford was at bat. Before the pitcher wound up, Schaefer flashed me the sign for the double steal—meaning he'd take off for second on the next pitch, and when the catcher threw the ball to second I'd take off for home. Well, the pitcher wound up and pitched, and sure enough Schaefer stole second. But I had to stay right where I was, on third, because Nig Clarke, the Cleveland catcher, just held on to the ball. He refused to throw to second, knowing I'd probably make it home if he did.

So now we had men on second and third. Well, on the next pitch Schaefer yelled, "Let's try it again!" And with a blood-curdling shout he took off like a wild Indian *back to first base*, and dove in headfirst in

Walter Johnson: "He had those long arms, absolutely the longest arms I ever saw"

a cloud of dust. He figured the catcher might throw to first—since he evidently wouldn't throw to second—and then I could come home same as before.

But nothing happened. Nothing at all. Everybody just stood there and watched Schaefer, with their mouths open, not knowing what the devil was going on. Me, too. Even if the catcher *had* thrown to first, I was too stunned to move, I'll tell you that. But the catcher didn't throw. He just stared! In fact, George Stovall, the Cleveland first base-man, was playing way back and didn't even come in to cover the bag. He just watched this madman running the wrong way on the base path and didn't know *what* to do.

The umpires were just as confused as everybody else. However, it turned out that at that time there wasn't any rule against a guy going from second back to first, if that's the way he wanted to play baseball, so they had to let it stand.

So there we were, back where we started, with Schaefer on first and me on third. And on the next pitch darned if he didn't let out another war whoop and take off *again* for second base. By this time the Cleve-land catcher evidently had enough, because he finally threw to second to get Schaefer, and when he did I took off for home and *both* of us were safe.

These are fond memories, you know. I haven't thought about these things in years. Yes, those were wonderful days. Of course, one sad thing, a lot of the boys didn't realize how short their baseball life would be, and they didn't prepare themselves for when their playing days would be over. I was very lucky, compared to most, having gone to college and all.

However, I never did return to the law. What happened was that I had a brother who worked in a drugstore back home in Cambria, Wis-consin, and on my baseball money I helped put him through a course in pharmacy at the University of Michigan. After he was through and had his license, we went into partnership and opened up Davy Jones' Drug Store in downtown Detroit. That was in 1910, while I was playing for Detroit, see.

Well, the thing was a huge success. After a home game I'd join him at the drugstore and jerk sodas and talk about the game. The fans loved it. Business was so terrific that after awhile we had *five* stores. I got so I was spending all my free time in the stores, and when we went on the road I took pharmacy textbooks along to study.

After I was through with baseball—that was in 1915, when I was thirty-five—I sublet my home in Detroit and went out to California for a vacation. I bummed around for a month or two, but soon I started to get restless. So I wound up taking a two-year course in pharmacy at the University of Southern California. I got my degree, came back and took my state board exam from the Michigan Board of Pharmacy, and stayed in the drug business until I retired, thirty-five years later.

But getting back to baseball, that story of Germany Schaefer running from second to first reminds me of another incident that happened when I was with the Chicago Cubs in 1902. We had a young pitcher on that club named Jimmy St. Vrain. He was a left-handed pitcher and a right-handed batter. But an absolutely terrible hitter—never even got a loud foul off anybody.

Well, one day we were playing the Pittsburgh Pirates and Jimmy was pitching for us. The first two times he went up to bat that day he looked simply awful. So when he came back after striking out the second time Frank Selee, our manager, said, "Jimmy, you're a left-handed pitcher, why don't you turn around and bat from the left side, too? Why not try it?"

Actually, Frank was half kidding, but Jimmy took him seriously. So the next time he went up he batted left-handed. Turned around and stood on the opposite side of the plate from where he was used to, you know. And darned if he didn't actually hit the ball. He tapped a slow roller down to Honus Wagner at shortstop and took off as fast as he could go . . . but instead of running to first base, he headed for *third!*

Oh, my God! What bedlam! Everybody yelling and screaming at poor Jimmy as he raced to third base, head down, spikes flying, determined to get there ahead of the throw. Later on, Honus told us that as a matter of fact he almost *did* throw the ball to third.

"I'm standing there with the ball in my hand," Honus said, "looking at this guy running from home to third, and for an instant there I swear I didn't know *where* to throw the damn ball. And when I finally did throw to first, I wasn't at all sure it was the right thing to do!"

4   *Sam Crawford*

Samuel Earl Crawford, who prefers to be called Wahoo Sam, played major-league baseball for 19 years, from 1899 through 1917. He was fast: he typically stole 25 to 30 bases a season. He could hit: the record books credit him with 2,964 major-league hits, a figure exceeded by very few men in the history of baseball.* And he could hit with power: he led the National League in home runs in 1901, and the American League in 1908 and 1914.

In combination, these elements resulted in 312 major-league triples, still the most three-baggers ever hit by one man. It is almost inconceivable that this record will ever be broken. Willie Mays, the closest approximation to a modern-day Sam Crawford, accumulated but 140 triples during his 22 seasons in the majors.

Most baseball writers of that period agree that Sam Crawford was the outstanding power hitter of the dead-ball era. H. G. Salsinger, eminent Detroit sports writer who covered the Detroit Tigers throughout the era of Cobb and Crawford, recalls that "I have seen right fielders, playing against the fence, catch five fly balls off Crawford's bat in one game, five fly balls that would have cleared the fence any time after the season of 1920, when the jackrabbit ball was introduced."

I DON'T KNOW how you found me, but since you're here you might as well come in and sit down. I don't have much time, though. Got a lot of things to do. But it's a hot day, so come in and rest awhile.

Yeah, I'm sort of hard to find. Still bounce around a lot, you know. Always on the move. Probably a hangover from all those years in base-

---

* There is still considerable dispute over the total number of hits accumulated by Wahoo Sam. Some insist that the correct total should be 3,051. The case for the latter figure was best stated by H. G. Salsinger (in the Detroit *News* of May 20, 1957) upon the occasion of Sam Crawford's induction into the Baseball Hall of Fame:

"According to the official records, Crawford is credited with a lifetime total of 2,964 hits, but he should rightfully be credited with 3,051. When Crawford began his career, records were kept in a careless and haphazard manner. Crawford made his professional debut with Chatham in the Canadian League in 1899, but after 43 games he advanced to Grand Rapids in the Western League, where he made 87 hits and batted .334.

"Ban Johnson was president of the Western League in 1899. At the same time he was organizing the American League, which he launched in the spring of 1900. The National Commission ruled that any player from the Western League entering either

ball—Boston today, Detroit tomorrow, never long in one place. I do have a house down in Hollywood, but I can't take that town. Too much smog. Too many cars, all fouling up the air. Can hardly breathe down there. Too many people, too. Have to stand in line everywhere you go. Can't even get a loaf of bread without standing in line. Pretty soon they'll be standing in line to get into the john! That's not for me.

No, I don't have a telephone. If I had a lot of money I wouldn't have one. I *never* was for telephones. Just don't like them, that's all. Anybody wants to talk to you, they can come to see you. I do have a television over there—it was a gift—but I never turn it on. I'd rather read a book. Don't even watch the ball games. Oh, maybe the World Series, but that's about it. I like to do what I like to do, that's all. I don't see why I should watch television just because everybody else does. I'd rather read a book, or fix up the garden, or just take a walk with my wife, Mary, and see what's going on, you know.

Heck, I don't even buy a newspaper. Nothing but trouble in it. Just spoils your day. You get up in the morning, feel pretty good, get hold of a paper, and what do you see? Nothing but trouble. Big headlines about bombs and war and misery. It ruins the day. That's the way I look at it, anyway. Maybe I'm wrong, I don't know.

So you're doing a book about baseball in the old days. Why does a young fellow like you want to spend his time on something like that? Do you remember what Robert Ingersoll used to say? "Let the dead past bury its dead." That's what he used to say. Robert Ingersoll, remember him? A great man. I always admired him. He was a very famous lecturer in the late 1800's. Very famous and very controversial. He was supposed to be an atheist, but he wasn't really. More a skeptic, more an agnostic, than an atheist. You should read his *Lectures* some time. Very interesting. Now he's forgotten. Hardly anybody even remembers his name any more. That probably proves something, but I'm not sure what.

Anyway, those days are all back in the past. We're going to spend the rest of our lives in the future, not in the past: "Let the dead past bury its dead." On the other hand, Santayana said: "Those who forget the past are condemned to repeat it." So maybe there are two sides to

---

the old National League or the new American League would be credited with all hits he made in the Western League.

"Crawford joined Cincinnati and was therefore entitled to the 87 hits he made for Grand Rapids. In compiling his lifetime record the statistician overlooked these 87 hits and gave him credit for 2,964 instead of his rightful 3,051."

this matter. But I don't think we'll ever repeat the old days in baseball. They'll never come back. Everything has changed too much.

You know, there were a lot of characters in baseball back then. Real individualists. Not conformists, like most ballplayers—and most people—are today. Rube Waddell, for instance. Boy, there was one of a kind. They never made another like him. I played on the same team with Rube back in 1899, the Grand Rapids club in the old Western League. We were both just starting out, but it wasn't hard to see even then that Rube was going to really be something. He won about 30 games for us that season and hardly lost any.

He used to pour ice water on his pitching arm. Yeah, ice water. We'd kid him, you know, tell him he didn't seem to have much on the ball that day, and ask him why he couldn't get it over the plate.

"Listen," he'd say, "I'll show you guys whether I've got anything or not. Fact is, I've got so much speed today I'll burn up the catcher's glove if I don't let up a bit."

And he'd go over to the water barrel—we had a barrel filled with ice water in the dugout—and dip the dipper in and pour ice water all over his left arm and shoulder.

"That's to slow me down a little," he'd say. And then he'd go out there and more likely than not he'd strike out the side.

Rube was just a big kid, you know. He'd pitch one day and we wouldn't see him for three or four days after. He'd just disappear, go fishing or something, or be off playing ball with a bunch of twelve-year-olds in an empty lot somewhere. You couldn't control him 'cause he was just a big kid himself. Baseball was just a game to Rube.

We'd have a big game scheduled for a Sunday, with posters all over Grand Rapids that the great Rube Waddell was going to pitch that day. Even then he was a big drawing card. Sunday would come and the little park would be packed way before game time, everybody wanting to see Rube pitch. But half the time there'd be no Rube. Nowhere to be found. The manager would be having a fit. And then just a few minutes before game time there'd be a commotion in the grandstand and you'd hear people laughing and yelling: "Here comes Rube, here comes Rube."

And there he'd come, right through the stands. He'd jump down on to the field, cut across the infield to the clubhouse, taking off his shirt as he went. In about three minutes—he never wore any underwear—he'd run back out in uniform and yell, "All right, let's get 'em!"

By the end of that season—1899—we were both in the Big Leagues, Rube with Louisville and me with Cincinnati. I should say Big *League*, because there was only one major league then, the National League. The American League didn't start until a couple of years later, and it was a few years after that before the National League recognized it. It was sort of like the way it is now in professional football.

By 1903, though, we were both in the American League. I jumped to the Detroit Tigers and Rube went with Connie Mack's Philadelphia Athletics. We had some great battles after that, the Tigers and the A's, some great fights for the pennant. From 1905 through 1914, you know, either the Tigers or the A's won the pennant every year but two. The White Sox won it in 1906 and the Red Sox in 1912. But except for those two years, we won it in 1907, '08, and '09, and Connie won it the others.

Rube was at his peak those years he was with Connie. He was amazing. Way over 20 wins every season, and always leading the league in

Rube Waddell:
"They never made
another like him"

strikeouts. How good he'd have been if he'd taken baseball seriously is hard to imagine. Like I say, it was always just a game with Rube. He played 'cause he had fun playing, but as far as he was concerned it was all the same whether he was playing in the Big Leagues or with a bunch of kids on a sandlot.

The main thing you had to watch out for was not to get him mad. If things were going smoothly and everyone was happy, Rube would be happy too, and he'd just go along, sort of half pitching. Just fooling around, lackadaisical, you know. But if you got him mad he'd really bear down, and then you wouldn't have a chance. Not a chance.

Hughie Jennings, our manager at Detroit, used to go to the dime store and buy little toys, like rubber snakes or a jack-in-the-box. He'd get in the first-base coach's box and set them down on the grass and yell, "Hey, Rube, look." Rube would look over at the jack-in-the-box popping up and down and kind of grin, real slow-like, you know. Yeah, we'd do everything to get him in a good mood, and to distract him from his pitching.

When you think about people like Rube Waddell, and there were lots of other off-beat characters around then, also, you start to get some idea of how different it all used to be. Baseball players weren't too much accepted in those days, either, you know. We were considered pretty crude. Couldn't get into the best hotels and all that. And when we did get into a good hotel, they wouldn't boast about having us. Like, if we went into the hotel dining room—in a good hotel, that is—they'd quick shove us way back in the corner at the very end of the dining room so we wouldn't be too conspicuous. "Here come the ballplayers!" you know, and back in the corner we'd go.

I remember once—I think it was in 1903—I was with the Detroit club, and we all went into the dining room in this hotel, I believe in St. Louis. Well, this dining room had a tile floor, made out of little square tiles. We sat there—way down at the end, as usual—for about 20 minutes and couldn't get any waiters. They wouldn't pay any attention to us at all. Remember Kid Elberfeld? He was playing shortstop for us then, a tough little guy. Later he played for many years with the Yankees, up on the hilltop. Anyway, Kid Elberfeld says, "I'll get you some waiters, fellows."

Darned if he didn't take one of the plates and sail it way up in the air, and when it came down on that tile floor it smashed into a million pieces. In that quiet, refined dining room it sounded like The

Charge of the Light Brigade. Sure enough, we had four or five waiters around there in no time.

Yeah, Kid Elberfeld, what a character he was. Kid Gleason was on the Detroit club about then, too. Another rugged little guy. Do you know that those guys actually *tried* to get hit with the ball when they were up at bat? They didn't care. They had it down to a fine art, you know. They'd look like they were trying to get out of the way, but they'd manage to let the ball just nick them. Anything to get on base. That was all part of the game then.

Kid Gleason used to be on that old Baltimore Oriole team in the 1890's. You know, with Willie Keeler and McGraw and Dan Brouthers and Hughie Jennings, who later became our manager at Detroit. That whole crew moved over to Brooklyn later. I played against those guys when I came up with Cincinnati, in 1899, and let me tell you, after you'd made a trip around the bases against them you knew you'd been somewhere. They'd trip you, give you the hip, and who knows what else. Boy, it was rough. There was only one umpire in those days, see, and he couldn't be everywhere at once.

Ned Hanlon used to manage that Baltimore club, but those old veterans didn't pay any attention to him. Heck, they all knew baseball inside out. You know, ballplayers were tough in those days, but they were real smart, too. Plenty smart. There's no doubt at all in my mind that the old-time ballplayer was smarter than the modern player. No doubt at all. That's what baseball was all about then, a game of strategy and tactics, and if you played in the Big Leagues you had to know how to think, and think quick, or you'd be back in the minors before you knew what in the world hit you.

Now the game is all different. All power and lively balls and short fences and home runs. But not in the old days. I led the National League in home runs in 1901, and do you know how many I hit? Sixteen. That was a helluva lot for those days. Tommy Leach led the league the next year—with six! In 1908 I led the American League with only seven. Do you know the most home runs Home Run Baker ever hit in one year? It was twelve. That was his best year. In 1914 Baker and I tied for the lead with the grand total of eight each. Now, little Albie Pearson will hit that many accidentally. So you see, the game is altogether different from what it was. Then it was strategy and quick thinking, and if you didn't play with your old noodle you didn't play at all.

Like I said, those old Baltimore Orioles didn't pay any more attention to Ned Hanlon, their manager, than they did to the batboy. When I came into the league, that whole bunch had moved over to Brooklyn, and Hanlon was managing them there, too. He was a bench manager in civilian clothes. When things would get a little tough in a game, Hanlon would sit there on the bench and wring his hands and start telling some of those old-timers what to do. They'd look at him and say, "For Christ's sake, just keep quiet and leave us alone. We'll win this ball game if you only shut up."

They would win it, too. If there was any way to win, they'd find it. Like Wee Willie Keeler. He was really something. That little guy couldn't have been over five feet four, and he only weighed about 140 pounds. But he played in the Big Leagues for 20 years and had a lifetime batting average of close to .350. Think of that! Just a little tiny guy.

"Hit 'em where they ain't," he used to say. And could he ever! He choked up on the bat so far he only used about half of it, and then he'd just peck at the ball. Just a little snap swing, and he'd punch the ball over the infield. You couldn't strike him out. He'd always hit the ball somewhere. And could he fly down to first! Willie was really fast. A real nice little guy too, very friendly, always laughing and kidding.

You know, there were a lot of little guys in baseball then. McGraw was a fine ballplayer and he couldn't have been over five feet six or seven. And Tommy Leach, with Pittsburgh—he was only five feet six and he couldn't have weighed over 140. He was a beautiful ballplayer to watch. And Bobby Lowe, who was the first player to ever hit four home runs in one game. He did that in 1894. That was something, with that old dead ball. Bobby and I played together for three or four years in Detroit, around 1905 or so.

Dummy Hoy was even smaller, about five-five. You remember him, don't you? He died in Cincinnati only a few years ago, at the age of ninety-nine. Quite a ballplayer. In my opinion Dummy Hoy and Tommy Leach should both be in the Hall of Fame.

Do you know how many bases Dummy Hoy stole in his major-league career? Over 600! That *alone* should be enough to put him in the Hall of Fame. We played alongside each other in the outfield with the Cincinnati club in 1902. He had started in the Big Leagues way back in the 1880's, you know, so he was on his way out then, and I had been up just a few years, but even that late in his career he was a fine outfielder. A *great* one.

I'd be in right field and he'd be in center, and I'd have to listen real

*Wee Willie Keeler hitting 'em where
they ain't*

careful to know whether or not he'd take a fly ball. He couldn't hear, you know, so there wasn't any sense in me yelling for it. He couldn't talk either, of course, but he'd make a kind of throaty noise, kind of a little squawk, and when a fly ball came out and I heard this little noise I knew he was going to take it. We never had any trouble about who was to take the ball.

Did you know that he was the one responsible for the umpire giving hand signals for a ball or a strike? Raising his right hand for a strike, you know, and stuff like that. He'd be up at bat and he couldn't hear and he couldn't talk, so he'd look around at the umpire to see what the pitch was, a ball or a strike. That's where the hand signs for the umpires calling balls and strikes began. That's a fact. Very few people know that.

Another interesting thing about Dummy Hoy was the unique doorbell arrangement he had in his house. He had a wife who was a deaf mute too, and they lived in Cincinnati. Instead of a bell on the door, they had a little knob. When you pulled this knob it released a lead ball which rolled down a wooden chute and then fell off onto the floor with a thud. When it hit the floor they felt the vibrations, through their feet, and they knew somebody was at the door. I thought that was quite odd and interesting, don't you?

It's funny how little things like that come back to you, after all these years. That was over 60 years ago when we played together. He was a little fellow, like I said, only five feet five. But he had real large, strong hands. He used to wear a diamond ring—we all did in those days—but his knuckles were so big that he had a ring with a hinge on it. A real hinge. He couldn't get a ring that would go over his big knuckles and still fit right, so he had one made with a hinge so that he could put it on and then close it and it would lock in place. Did you know that he once threw three men out at home plate in one game? From the outfield, I mean. That was in 1889. And still they don't give him a tumble for the Hall of Fame. It's not right.

In those days, believe it or not, it was tougher to throw a guy out at home than it is today. That might sound sort of silly, but it's true. One reason is that the ball was often lopsided. No kidding. We'd play a whole game with one ball, if it stayed in the park. Another reason is that when I broke in the Big Leagues we only had one umpire in a game, not four like they have today. And you *know* that one umpire just can't see everything at once. He'd stand behind the catcher until a man got on base, and then he'd move out and call balls and strikes from behind the pitcher. He'd be out there behind the pitcher with, say, a man on second base, and the batter would get a hit out to right field. Well, the umpire would be watching the ball and the batter rounding first and trying for second. Meanwhile, the guy who was on second would cut third base wide by fifteen feet on his way home. Never came anywhere close to third base, you know. We'd run with one eye on the ball and the other on the umpire!

Did you ever hear of Tim Hurst? He was a very famous umpire back then. A real tough character. He was wise to this deal, of course, where the runner doesn't come anywhere close to touching third base. Well, Jake Beckley was playing first base for us—with the Cincinnati club in 1899 or 1900 or so—and he came sliding into home one day. A real big slide, plenty of dust and all, even though no one was even trying to tag him out. Tim had been watching a play at second all the while.

"You're out!" yells Tim.

Jake screamed to high heaven. "What do you mean, I'm out?" he roared. "They didn't even make a play on me."

"You big S.O.B.," Tim said, "you got here *too* quick!"

Yeah, old Tim knew what was going on. I was an umpire too, for awhile, you know—in the Pacific Coast League from 1935 to 1938—long after I finished playing. Umpiring is a lonesome life. Thankless job. Thankless. You haven't got a friend in the place. Only your partner, that's all. He's the only man in the whole place who is for you. Everybody else is just waiting for you to make a mistake. There's a bench over here, and a bench over there, and thousands of people in the stands, and every eye in the whole damn place is watching like a hawk trying to get something on you.

I had a good partner, too. I booked in with a fellow named Jack Powell, a wonderful umpire and a wonderful person as well. He'd tell me not to fraternize with the players. I felt that I could kid around with them a little, you know. What the heck, I'd been a ballplayer myself. But he said, "Don't do it, don't fool with the players, don't have anything to do with them. If you do, sooner or later they'll put you on the spot."

And that's the way it turned out. He was right. It's a thankless and a lonely way to live, so I quit it.

But even then, in the thirties, the game was a lot different from the way it had been when I played. The lively ball and the home run were well entrenched by the thirties. Heck, like I said, we'd play a whole game with one ball, if it stayed in the park. Lopsided, and black, and full of tobacco juice and licorice stains. The pitchers used to have it all their way back then. Spitballs and emery balls and whatnot. But there were some great pitchers in those days: Jack Chesbro and Cy Young and Ed Walsh.

Ed Walsh, seemed like I was batting against that guy every other day. Great big, strong, good-looking fellow. He threw a spitball—I think that ball disintegrated on the way to the plate and the catcher put it back together again. I swear, when it went past the plate it was just the spit went by.

Of course, the greatest of them all was Walter Johnson. Boy, what a pitcher Walter was! He was the best I ever faced, without a doubt. Did you know that I was playing with Detroit the day Walter Johnson pitched his first major-league game? His very first. In fact, I beat him. I'm not being egotistical, you know, but it's a fact. I hit a home run off him and we beat him—I believe the score was 3–2.

I think that was late in 1907. We were after the pennant that year, our first pennant, and we needed that game badly. Big Joe Cantillon was managing Washington at the time. You know Joe? You know *of* him. He was a nice guy, Joe was, always kidding. Anyway, before the game Joe came over to the Detroit bench and said, "Well boys, I've got a great big apple-knocker I'm going to pitch against you guys today. Better watch out, he's plenty fast. He's got a swift."

He told us that, you know. And here comes Walter, just a string of a kid, only about eighteen or nineteen years old. Tall, lanky, from Idaho or somewhere. Didn't even have a curve. Just that fast ball. That's all he pitched, just fast balls. He didn't *need* any curve. We had a terrible time beating him. Late in the game I hit one—I can remember it as though it were yesterday—it went zooming out over the shortstop's head, and before they could get the ball back in I'd legged it all the way around. In those days the grounds were very big, you know, and if you hit one between the outfielders you could often make it all the way around the bases. Nowadays you very seldom see an inside-the-park home run, they've pulled those fences in so. But in those days most home runs were like that.

Yes, Joe Cantillon was a kidder, but he wasn't kidding that day. That Walter was fast! I batted against him hundreds of times after that, of course, and he never lost that speed. He was the fastest I ever saw, by far.

Did you ever see those pitching machines they have? That's what Walter Johnson always reminded me of, one of those compressed-air pitching machines. It's a peculiar thing, a lot of batters are afraid of those machines, because they can gear them up so that ball comes in there just like a bullet. It comes in so fast that when it goes by it *swooshes*. You hardly see the ball at all. But you *hear* it. *Swoosh,* and it smacks into the catcher's mitt. Well, that was the kind of ball Walter Johnson pitched. He had such an easy motion it looked like he was just playing catch. That's what threw you off. He threw so nice and easy—and then *swoosh,* and it was by you!

Walter was a wonderful person, too, you know. He was always afraid he might hit somebody with that fast ball. A wonderful man, in every way. Warm, and friendly, and wouldn't hurt a soul. Easily the greatest pitcher I ever saw. Of course, I never saw Grover Cleveland Alexander very much, or Christy Mathewson. They were in the National League, and from 1903 on I was with Detroit in the American League.

I must say, though, that the greatest all-around ballplayer I ever saw was in the National League. I played against him for four years, from 1899 through 1902, when I was with Cincinnati and he was first with Louisville and then with Pittsburgh. People always ask me about Ty

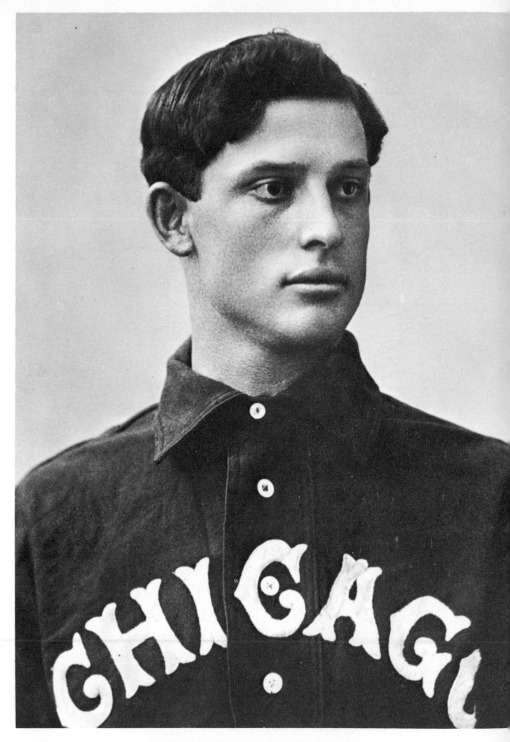

Ed Walsh: "Great big, strong, good-looking fellow"

Cobb, you know: "You played in the outfield next to Cobb for all those years. Don't you agree that he was the greatest player who ever lived?"

Cobb was great, there's no doubt about that; *one* of the greatest. But not *the* greatest. In my opinion, *the* greatest all-around player who ever lived was Honus Wagner.

Cobb could only play the outfield, and even there his arm wasn't anything extra special. But Honus Wagner could play any position. He could do everything. In fact, when I first played against him he was an outfielder, and then he became a third baseman, and later the greatest shortstop of them all. Honus could play any position except pitcher and be easily the best in the league at it. He was a wonderful fielder, terrific arm, very quick, all over the place grabbing sure hits and turning them into outs. And, of course, you know he led the league in batting eight times.

You'd never think it to look at him, of course. He looked so awkward, bowlegged, barrel-chested, about 200 pounds, a big man. And yet he could run like a scared rabbit. He had enormous hands, and when he scooped up the ball at shortstop he'd grab half the infield with it. But boy, Honus made those plays! He looked awkward doing it, not graceful like Larry Lajoie, but he could make every play Lajoie could make and more. Talk about speed. That bowlegged guy stole over 700 bases in the 21 years he played in the Big Leagues. A good team man, too, and the sweetest disposition in the world. The greatest ballplayer who ever lived, in my book.

Cobb and Wagner met head on in the 1909 World Series, you know, Detroit against Pittsburgh. We lost in seven games, the first time the Series went the full seven games. Wagner stole six bases in that Series, as many as our whole team, and Cobb stole only two. Honus was one of those natural ballplayers, you know what I mean? Like Babe Ruth and Willie Mays. Those fellows do everything by pure instinct. Mays is one of the few modern players who are just as good as the best of the old-timers. Although I guess the best center fielder of them all was Tris Speaker. He played in real close and could go back and get those balls better than anyone I ever saw.

Don't get me wrong. I'm not running Cobb down. He was terrific, no doubt about it. After all, he stole almost 900 bases and had a batting average of .367 over 24 years in the Big Leagues. You can't knock that. I remember one year I hit .378—in 1911, I think it was—and I didn't come anywhere close to leading the league: Joe Jackson hit .408 and Cobb hit .420. I mean, that's mighty rugged competition!

I played in the same outfield with Cobb for 13 years, from 1905 through 1917. I was usually in right, Cobb in center, and Davy Jones and then Bobby Veach in left. Davy Jones, he was the best lead-off man in the league. I've seen a lot of lead-off men, but I never saw one who came close to being Davy's equal. The lineup usually was Davy Jones, Donie Bush, Cobb, and Crawford, although sometimes I batted third and Cobb fourth. That Donie Bush was a superb shortstop, absolutely superb. I think he still holds a lot of records for assists and putouts.

They always talk about Cobb playing dirty, trying to spike guys and all. Cobb never tried to spike anybody. The base line belongs to the runner. If the infielders get in the way, that's their lookout. Infielders are supposed to watch out and take care of themselves. In those days, if they got in the way and got nicked they'd never say anything. They'd just take a chew of tobacco out of their mouth, slap it on the spike wound, wrap a handkerchief around it, and go right on playing. Never thought any more about it.

We had a trainer, but all he ever did was give you a rubdown with something we called "Go Fast." He'd take a jar of Vaseline and a bottle of Tabasco sauce—you know how hot that is—mix them together, and rub you down with that. Boy, it made you feel like you were on fire! That would *really* start you sweating. Now they have medical doctors and whirlpool baths and who knows what else.

But Ty was dynamite on the base paths. He really was. Talk about strategy and playing with your head, that was Cobb all the way. It wasn't that he was so fast on his feet, although he was fast enough. There were others who were faster, though, like Clyde Milan, for instance. It was that Cobb was so fast in his *thinking*. He didn't outhit the opposition and he didn't outrun them. He outthought them!

A lot of times Cobb would be on third base and I'd draw a base on balls, and as I started to go down to first I'd sort of half glance at Cobb, at third. He'd make a slight move that told me he wanted me to keep going—not to stop at first, but to keep on going to second. Well, I'd trot two-thirds of the way to first and then suddenly, without warning, I'd speed up and go across first as fast as I could and tear out for second. He's on third, see. They're watching him, and suddenly there I go, and they don't know what the devil to do.

If they try to stop me, Cobb'll take off for home. Sometimes they'd catch him, and sometimes they'd catch me, and sometimes they wouldn't get either of us. But most of the time they were too paralyzed to do anything, and I'd wind up at second on a base on balls. Boy, did that ever create excitement. For the crowd, you know; the fans were always wondering what might happen next.

Cobb was a great ballplayer, no doubt about it. But he sure wasn't easy to get along with. He wasn't a friendly, good-natured guy, like Wagner was, or Walter Johnson, or Babe Ruth. Did you ever read Cobb's book? He wrote an autobiography, you know, and he spends a

Ty Cobb: "He was dynamite on the base paths"

lot of time in there telling how terrible he was treated when he first came up to Detroit, as a rookie, in 1905. About how we weren't fair to him, and how we tried to "get" him.

But you have to look at the other side, too. We weren't cannibals or heathens. We were all ballplayers together, trying to get along. Every rookie gets a little hazing, but most of them just take it and laugh. Cobb took it the wrong way. He came up with an antagonistic attitude, which in his mind turned any little razzing into a life-or-death struggle. He always figured everybody was ganging up against him. He came up from the South, you know, and he was still fighting the Civil War. As far as he was concerned, we were all damn Yankees before he even met us. Well, who knows, maybe if he hadn't had that persecution complex he never would have been the great ballplayer he was. He was always trying to prove he was the best, on the field and off. And maybe he was, at that.

One thing that really used to get Ty's goat was when I'd have a good day and he didn't. Oh, would he ever moan then. Walter Johnson and I were very good friends, and once in a while Walter would sort of "give" me a hit or two, just for old-time's sake. But when Ty came up there, Walter always bore down all the harder. There was nothing he enjoyed more than fanning Ty Cobb.

You see, Walter always liked my model bat. Somehow he got the idea that my bats were lucky for him. So very often when the Senators came to Detroit Walter would come into our clubhouse and quietly ask me if I could spare a bat for him.

"Sure, Walter," I'd say, "go take any one you want."

He'd go over to my locker, look them over, pick one out, and quietly leave. Well, whenever the occasion arose when it wouldn't affect a game, Walter would let up a bit on me and I'd have a picnic at the plate—like, if Washington had a good lead and it was late in the game. I'd come up to bat and Gabby Street, Walter's catcher, would whisper, "Walter likes you today, Sam."

That was the cue that the next pitch would be a nice half-speed fast ball. So I'd dig in and belt it. Of course, if it was a close game all that was out the window. The friendship deal was off then. Cobb never did figure out why I did so well against Walter, while he couldn't hit him with a ten-foot pole.

Well, this is more than I've talked in years, and it's good. I don't see many people, and even when I do I don't talk about baseball too much.

I read a lot. My favorite writer is Balzac. A wonderful writer. But I rarely talk about baseball. There are very few people around, you know, who remember those old days. Once in a while I meet some elderly man who says, "I can remember seeing you play. My father took me to see you when I was a kid." But very seldom.

It's like when I got elected to the Hall of Fame, back in 1957. I was living in a little cabin at the edge of the Mojave Desert, near a little town called Pearblossom. Nobody around there even knew I'd been a ball player. I never talked about it. So there I was, sitting there in that cabin, with snow all around—it was February—and all of a sudden the place is surrounded with photographers and newspapermen and radio-TV reporters and all. I didn't know what in the world was going on.

"You've just been elected to the Hall of Fame," one of them said to me.

The people living around there—what few of them there were—were all excited. They couldn't figure out what was happening. And when they found out what it was all about, they couldn't believe it. "Gee, you mean old Sam? He used to be a ballplayer? We didn't even know it. Gee!"

From then on, of course, I've gotten thousands of letters. I still get a lot. Mostly from kids, wanting autographs. Sometimes they send a stamped envelope, and sometimes they don't. But I've answered every one by hand. In 1957, when I was elected to the Hall, I also went back to Detroit. It was the fiftieth anniversary of all the players who were still alive who had been on that 1907 pennant-winning team. I enjoyed that, but I wouldn't put on a uniform. I went out in civilian clothes and waved to the fans, but I refused to put on a uniform. I want to be remembered the way I used to be. When they think of Sam Crawford in a Detroit uniform I want them to think of me the way I was way back then, and no other way.

Yes, those were days I'll never forget. There were always a lot of laughs playing ball back then. I guess it must still be that way today. A lot of sadness and disappointment, too, like losing three straight World Series and never winning a pennant after 1909. But always a lot of laughs. Like ballplayers and their superstitions. I'm only a little superstitious. I won't walk under a ladder, that's all. But a lot of them were obsessed with that stuff. For instance, butterflies flying across the field. A white butterfly meant something, and a red one meant something else. Paticularly those big red ones—monarchs, they called them—they really meant

Walter Johnson and teammate Clyde Milan

something special. The manager would look out and say, "Boy, oh boy, oh boy, there goes a red one." They really believed that stuff, you know.

Before Hughie Jennings became the manager at Detroit—that was in 1907—Bill Armour was our manager. He had managed Cleveland before that, and in 1905 he became the Detroit manager. He'd go nuts if he saw a cross-eyed bat boy. Bill would take one look at him and get an expression on his face like he was about to die.

"Get rid of him, get rid of him," he'd yell. "Or leave him stay, but get him out of my sight. I don't want to see him."

Naturally, we spent half our time searching for cross-eyed kids, so we could sneak them in as bat boys!

Everything wasn't gay and carefree, of course. In lots of ways it wasn't the easiest life in the world. We had to travel a lot, you know, and travel conditions were pretty rugged then. We had sleeper trains in the Big Leagues in 1899 and 1900, when I broke in, but the sleepers had gaslights in them, not electric lights. They used to go around and light them up at night. We spent a lot of our lives living out of our grips, on trains and in hotels. The hotels weren't the best in the world, and the trains had coal-burning engines. So you'd wake up in the morning covered with cinders. They had fine little screens on the train windows, but the cinders would still come through.

And there were tragedies, you know, like the death of Big Ed Delahanty in the middle of the 1903 season. Ed was only in his mid-thirties and was still going strong as an outfielder with Washington when he died. I think Ed was the best right-handed hitter I ever saw, really a great hitter. It's hard to choose between him and Honus. He was the second man in history to hit four home runs in a game. Bobby Lowe did it in 1894, and Ed a couple of years later, and then nobody did it again for 40 or 50 years. Twice he got six hits in one game. Quite a hitter. I think his lifetime batting average was close to .350.

Ed was born and raised in Cleveland, the oldest of six brothers. And five of them became Big League ballplayers. We had one of them with the Tigers—Jimmy, a second baseman. Ed's death was tragic. The Washington club was coming back from somewhere—I don't remember where—and their train had come to the suspension bridge there at Niagara Falls. It stopped before it went across, and Ed got off for a minute. But the train started up without him, and Ed began to walk across the bridge. The watchman, the guard at the bridge, tried to stop him, and they had a fight or something. Nobody knows just what happened. Anyway, Ed fell off the bridge and was killed. They found his body a couple of miles below the Falls. It was too bad. He was a nice guy.

How did I get started in baseball? Well, I played ball all the time as a kid, you know. I always loved it. I grew up in Wahoo, Nebraska.

"Wahoo Sam." I insisted they put that on my plaque at the Hall of Fame. That's my home town, and I'm proud of it. Darryl Zanuck came from Wahoo, did you know that? Also Howard Hanson, of the Eastman Conservatory of Music. I remember when Darryl Zanuck was a little towheaded kid running around the streets. His mother and father owned the hotel there in Wahoo. That was a long time ago. My dad ran a general store, just a little country store where they sold everything.

In those days baseball was a big thing in those little towns. The kids would be playing ball all the time. Nowadays basketball and football seem to be as popular among kids as baseball, maybe more so, but not then. And we didn't have radio, you know, or television, or automobiles. I guess, when you come to think of it, we spent most of our childhood playing ball.

Heck, we used to make our own baseballs. All the kids would gather string and yarn and we'd get hold of a little rubber ball for the center. Then we'd get our mothers to sew a cover on the ball to hold it all together. We didn't use tape to tape up the outside, like kids did 10 or 20 years later. We didn't see much tape in those days, about 1890 or so. Of course, they had tape then, electrical tape, but not much.

I can remember very well the first electric lights in Wahoo, on the street corner. Just one loop of wire, kind of reddish. We used to go down to the corner and watch this light go on. That was a big deal. Then we'd go over to the powerhouse, where the dynamos were, and see where they made the electricity. After that came the arc lights, with two carbons coming together. That was the next step. But the first ones were just one loop of wire in the bulb, and they gave kind of a reddish glow.

Of course, there were regular baseballs made back then. We'd call them league balls. But we couldn't afford to buy them, not us kids. That was for the men to play with. For bats we'd find some broken bat and nail it up, or sometimes even make our own.

Every town had its own town team in those days. I remember when I made my first baseball trip. A bunch of us from around Wahoo, all between sixteen and eighteen years old, made a trip overland in a wagon drawn by a team of horses. One of the boys got his father to let us take the wagon. It was a lumber wagon, with four wheels, the kind they used to haul the grain to the elevator, and was pulled by a team of two horses. It had room to seat all of us—I think there were 11 or 12 of us—

and we just started out and went from town to town, playing their teams.

One of the boys was a cornet player, and when we'd come to a town he'd whip out that cornet and sound off. People would all come out to see what was going on, and we'd announce that we were the Wahoo team and were ready for a ball game. Every little town out there on the prairie had its own ball team and ball grounds, and we challenged them all. We didn't have any uniforms or anything, just baseball shoes maybe, but we had a manager. I pitched and played the outfield both.

It wasn't easy to win those games, as you can imagine. Each of those towns had its own umpire, so you really had to go some to win. We played Freemont, and Dodge, and West Point, and lots of others in and around Nebraska. Challenged them all. Did pretty well, too.

We were gone three or four weeks. Lived on bread and beefsteak the whole time. We'd take up a collection at the games—pass the hat, you know—and that paid our expenses. Or some of them, anyway. One of the boys was the cook, but all he could cook was round steak. We'd get 12 pounds for a dollar and have a feast. We'd drive along the country roads, and if we came to a stream, we'd go swimming; if we came to an apple orchard, we'd fill up on apples. We'd sleep anywhere. Sometimes in a tent, lots of times on the ground, out in the open. If we were near some fairgrounds, we'd slip in there. If we were near a barn, well . . . .

That tour led to my getting started in professional baseball. We beat the West Point team, and after the tour was over I got a letter from the manager at West Point, Nebraska, asking if I wanted to play with them. He said they'd pay me, or at least get me a job. I was apprenticing to be a barber at the time. So I went up there, and there I met a fellow from Omaha who had been with Chatham in the Canadian League. His name was Johnny McElvaine. He was going back the next season and wanted me to go along with him. So Johnny wrote the manager of the Chatham team and told him about me, and they sent back transportation money for both of us. That was in 1899. I was only nineteen at the time.

Yeah, I was going to be a barber. But then baseball came along, and I never went back to barbering. I was learning the trade the hard way, there in Wahoo. And I do mean the hard way. Cleaning cuspidors, and washing windows, and mopping the floor. Then sometimes they'd let me

lather somebody and get them ready for the real barber. And sometimes
a tramp would come through and want a haircut, and I could practice
on him. That's the way we learned in those days.

That was a tough way to make a living. Stand on your feet from
seven in the morning to ten or eleven o'clock on a Saturday night.
Saturday was the big haircutting day. All the farmers would come
in then, hay in their hair and all. We used to give a haircut and a
shave and a shampoo for thirty-five cents. Ten cents for a shave, twenty-
five for a haircut, and they'd throw in the shampoo. Now a haircut alone
costs two dollars. Looks like the same old quarter haircut to me.

So when I got this chance to play professional ball, I didn't think
twice about it. At Chatham I got $65 a month, plus board. That was
pretty good. A dollar was a dollar in those days, you know. That
Canadian League was just a little six-club league. Folded up about July.
From there I was sold to Grand Rapids in the Western League, where

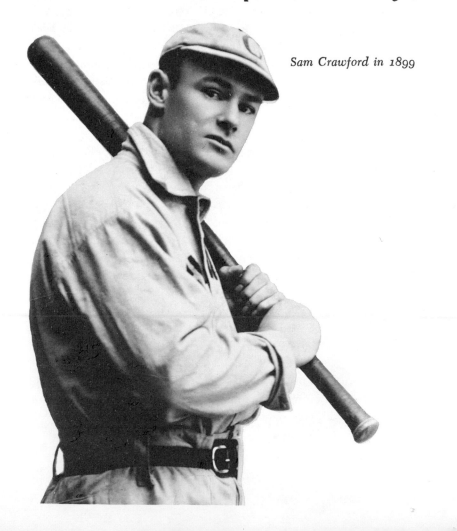

Sam Crawford in 1899

I played with Rube Waddell, and in September they sold me to Cincinnati in the National League. All three leagues in one year, and I hit over .300 in all of them. So there I was, in 1898 touring Nebraska with the Wahoo team in a wagon, and in 1899 playing in the Big Leagues with the Cincinnati Reds.

All that was pretty exciting for a nineteen-year-old kid. I'd never been anywhere before that. At Cincinnati I made about $150 a month, which was a lot of money in those days, especially for me. There were a lot of old-timers on that Cincinnati club in 1899: Buck Ewing, who was managing, Biddy McPhee, Tommy Corcoran, Harry Steinfeldt, Al Selbach, Jake Beckley, Noodles Hahn—lots of them. Biddy McPhee played second base for 18 years in Cincinnati, one position. From 1882 to 1899. And Noodles Hahn, you never hear his name anymore. He was a first-rate left-hander. Talk about starting and finishing games, that guy pitched 41 complete games in 1901. Between 1899 and 1904 he started something like 225 games and completed about 210 of them.

Well, then the American League started up, about 1900 or so, and the players started jumping back and forth, from one league to the other. Larry Lajoie and Elmer Flick jumped from the Phillies to Cleveland, Ed Delahanty from the Phillies to Washington, Jack Chesbro from the Pirates to the Yankees—they were the Highlanders then—and Willie Keeler from Brooklyn to the Yankees. I left Cincinnati and went over to Detroit in 1903, and stayed there for 15 years.

Boy, here I am still talking. Hard to believe. I hope I haven't said anything I shouldn't. There are a lot of the old-timers still left, you know, and they're liable to say, "That fathead, who the hell does he think he is, anyway, popping off like that!"

I wouldn't want them to say that. Because I'd rather they remember me as a pretty straight sort of a guy, you know. So that when I kick off they'll say, "Well, good old Sam, he wasn't such a bad guy, after all. Everything considered, he was pretty fair and square. We'll miss him."

That's the way I'd like it to be.

5 *George Gibson*

The number of times a catcher is injured in a season is surprising. At one time in 1909, for example, George Gibson of the Pittsburgh Pirates had black and blue marks imprinted by nineteen foul tips upon his body, a damaged hand, a bruise on his hip six inches square where a thrown bat had struck, and three spike cuts. Yet he had not missed a game and was congratulating himself on his "luck."
—JOHNNY EVERS and HUGH FULLERTON, *Touching Second*, 1910

L OTS OF PEOPLE think that baseball is strictly an American game, but it was popular here in Canada, too, as far back as the 1890's. I know, because that's when I started playing ball around here. Dad had his own construction business, but he was also a great baseball fan and always encouraged me to play. We had four pretty good teams in a municipal weekend league—London North, South, East, and West. I began as a catcher for London West in 1898, when I was eighteen years old, and took to it like a duck takes to water. Lots of times I didn't even wear a catcher's mask in those days; I couldn't see clearly enough through it, so I'd take it off. And of course many's the day I'd come home with a black eye or a bloody nose.

In a few years I was behind the plate for Montreal, which was then in the Eastern League. I didn't get paid much, but it sure beat hauling bricks! See, it was a choice between working all day long on one of Dad's construction jobs or having every day a holiday—playing ball. So my brothers helped Dad with the business and I played ball.

In the middle of the 1905 season, Montreal sold me to the Pittsburgh Pirates. There was an ex-Big Leaguer on the Montreal club by the name of Candy LaChance who'd been around and knew the ropes. He said to me, "Listen, Gibby, they sold you. It wasn't a trade, it was a sale. Pittsburgh probably paid anywhere from $4,000 to $5,000 for your contract and you should be able to get at least a thousand of that."

So when I got to Exposition Park in Pittsburgh, I asked Mr. Barney Dreyfuss, the Pittsburgh owner, for $1,000. Mr. Dreyfuss looked at me in a strange sort of way and said, "I don't know what you're talking about, son. I *paid* $4,000 for you, I didn't *get* $4,000. If you want some of that

70

money—which, by the way, you are not entitled to—you'd better take it up with Mr. Hagen, the Montreal owner, not me."

Well, it was too late for that, so all I did was make a mental note to think ahead from then on and get what was coming to me when the time was right. Besides, this was my chance in the Big Leagues and I sure didn't want to go back to the minors even if it was with a Canadian team.

Pittsburgh had a pretty fair country catcher when I got there in 1905 named Heinie Peitz. He'd been in the Big Leagues a long time, so long that his arm was almost gone. He used to throw the ball like a rainbow down to second base.

The first time I got in a game, a few weeks after I arrived, was in Redland Field in Cincinnati. Later it was called Crosley Field. They had a spitball pitcher going against us and I didn't get any hits that day. But the first time one of the Cincinnati players got on first base, he tried to steal

George Gibson around 1910

second. I rocked back on my heels and threw a bullet, knee high, right over the base. Both the shortstop and second baseman—Honus Wagner and Claude Ritchey—ran to cover second base, but the ball went flying into center field before either of them got near it.

I was burning up, and when the inning ended I almost ran to the bench determined to give them a piece of my mind. See, I figured they were trying to make me look bad, letting the throw go by, because I was a rookie. Trying to protect Heinie Peitz's job is what I figured.

But Wagner came in, threw his arms around me, and said, "Just keep throwing that way, kid. It was our fault, not yours." What had happened was that they had gotten so used to Heinie Peitz's rainbows that any throw on a straight line caught them by surprise.

I don't know why, but I was never a very good hitter. Lots of years I had trouble hitting my weight and my lifetime batting average is only .236. Never could figure it out. It wasn't for lack of trying, because I always got out to the park early to practice. But it didn't seem to do much good.

Here I was a teammate of Honus Wagner, one of the best hitters in baseball, and I had trouble getting a loud foul. Once I said to him, "Honus, I can't seem to get the hang of it. I *try* hard enough, but it doesn't seem to do any good. What am I doing wrong?"

He said, "Look, the secret is to follow the ball from the time it leaves the pitcher's hand until it gets to the plate."

I liked Honus so I didn't say anything to him, but that didn't sound like much of a secret to me. Heck, I could do *that*. After all, I was a *catcher*: that's all I did all day long—watch the ball from the time it left the pitcher's hand until it got to the plate. Big deal! It's clear to me that it must have been something *else* that Honus did and he didn't even know what it was himself.

Since I was such a lousy hitter, I had to be a pretty good catcher to stay in the Big Leagues from 1905 to 1918. Most of the time I'd throw to the bases right off my heels. I'd never get up. Just sit there on my heels and fire the ball.

Actually, though, I always figured that *thinking* was my real specialty. A lot of a catcher's job is mental, you know. The pitcher shouldn't have to think about what kind of pitch he should throw. That's the catcher's responsibility. The catcher should learn the strengths and weaknesses of the opposing batters and the abilities of his own pitchers and then decide what pitch is best in each situation. The pitcher's job is to do what his catcher tells him to do!

Catching's a pretty rough deal and you better love it or do something else for a living. Every finger on my right hand has been broken at least twice. I have two sons, George and Bill, both of whom are medical doctors in Pittsburgh, and one of them once X-rayed that hand. He couldn't believe the number of times each finger had been broken.

I used to put on some adhesive tape and keep on playing. Just tape two fingers together and make the good one work the bad one.

Roger Bresnahan of the New York Giants was the first catcher to wear shin guards, must have been around 1908 or so. His were long and high with a big knee flap. Practically came up to your thigh. When we first saw Bresnahan and his new shin guards, I laughed but Fred Clarke, our manager, says to me, "Gibby, that's something I want you to get."

Clarke told our trainer to find out where Bresnahan got them and order a pair for me. When they came, boy! They were as big as chest protectors. The first time I put them on in a game, I got tangled up in them running after a foul ball and fell down. I just sat there, unbuckled them, threw them away, and never wore them again.

That was a real fine Pittsburgh ball club I joined in 1905. Fred Clarke, one of the nicest men I ever met, was our manager and left fielder, Honus was at shortstop, Tommy Leach on third, and Sam Leever and Deacon Phillippe were two of the best pitchers in the league. Both of them won 20 games that year. We finished among the top three in the National League every single year from then through 1912, including winning the pennant and the World Series in 1909.

We faced the Detroit Tigers in that World Series and of course they had Ty Cobb. So I knew I had my work cut out for me. We beat them in seven games, I caught every single inning, and Cobb stole only two bases. The whole Detroit team stole only six bases while we stole eighteen. Heck, Honus alone stole six for us.

Right after the Series was over, the next day, Barney Dreyfuss called me into his office. He was sitting behind his big desk with a blank contract in front of him, and he said, "Gibby, what do you want to sign for next year?"

"I don't want to sign now," I told him. "You know that I never sign before February."

"Well," he said, "you had a fine year and a great Series and I'd just as soon get this settled for next year."

"I don't want to do that, Mr. Dreyfuss," I said. "If I sign now and you trade me over the winter, then I've got to go for whatever's in that contract. But if I don't sign and you trade me, it gives me an opening to go to

Manager Fred Clarke, Tommy Leach, and Honus Wagner

the new club and negotiate terms with them. That's why I'd rather wait."

"Listen," he said, "nobody's going to trade you and you know it. You caught 150 games this year and seven more in the World Series, so how could we get along without you?"

And with that he picked up the blank contract, turned it around to face me, and said, "Here, make it out yourself. Put your own figure in there."

"All right," I said, "I'll sign for $12,000. But I want one thing in that contract. You've got to promise me that when you think I'm through, and can't do the job anymore, you'll give me my unconditional release. I don't know whether it'll be one year or ten years from now, but when that time comes I don't want you to sell my worn-out carcass for a lousy $1,800 after you've gotten all the good out of it." See, $1,800 was the waiver price then. They'd put a guy on the waiver list, and if any other club claimed him they could have him for the $1,800 waiver price. I didn't mind if I was traded or sold for a decent amount, but to be sold for the waiver price was demeaning!

"Gibby, I'll write it right in the contract," he said.

"No," I said, "you've always been a man of your word with me. When the time comes when I'm through, whenever that is, just tell me and release me. That's all."

"It's a promise," Mr. Dreyfuss said.

Well, that was 1909. One day in early August, 1916, I pick up the newspaper and read that Barney Dreyfuss asked waivers on me, and John McGraw claimed me for the New York Giants for $1,800.

I was furious. I went straight to the front office. "Mr. Dreyfuss," I said, "you broke your promise. You want to make $1,800 on my broken-down carcass after you've gotten all the good out of it. Well, you're not going to do it. You may drive me out of baseball, but you're not going to make a *dime* on my carcass."

He tried to offer some lame excuse, but I was out of the door before he could finish. Then I phoned John McGraw. "Mac," I said, "get your money back, because I'm not reporting to the Giants. I'm going home."

Which is just what I did. I came right back here to this very house in London, Ontario, Canada. I built this place in 1912. Wanted a place to go to in the off-season that was out of earshot of a train whistle. Heard enough of them from April to September.

That winter, 1916, the telephone rang. The very phone you see right here. I wouldn't have a new one put in for anything. See, you take the receiver off the hook and then you push this little button on the side. That rings the operator on the party line. There's about 25 of us on the party line. I've been here since 1912 and that's how old that phone is.

Anyway, it was John McGraw calling. He wanted me to join the Giants next year as a part-time player and coach. "Mac," I said, "I don't want Barney Dreyfuss to make a dime on me. I gave him a hundred cents on the dollar for twelve years. Now he wants to get a lousy $1,800 on my burnt-out carcass and I won't let him do it."

"I understand," McGraw said. "I think you're absolutely right. But, on the other hand, I need you here next year. I need a good pitching coach and you're the man I want. I'll tell you what I'll do. I'll give you $1,800, too, the same as I pay Dreyfuss, and I'll even give you your salary for last August and September. How about it?"

Well, what could I do? So the next March I reported to Marlin Springs, Texas, for spring training with the Giants. McGraw wanted me to help get the pitchers in shape. One of the trainers had heard about these new calisthenics, so McGraw asked me, "Gibby, what do you think about calisthenics for the pitchers, like some of the other clubs are using?"

"No," I said, "*absolutely not*. That's not for ballplayers, Mac. For yourself, fine. If you want to reduce, fine. But not in spring training. Baseball is different, Mac. We're not a bunch of ballet dancers. We don't need calisthenics."

"Won't it help get my pitchers in shape?" he asked me.

"I'll get your pitchers in shape, Mac," I said, "and I'll do it without any of those new-fangled calisthenics."

What I did was what we'd always done. I hit fly balls and had the pitchers chase them. I took the pitchers down to a corner of the field and hit one fly ball after another, *just* out of their reach. If they caught the ball, they'd get a quarter. They'd run and run, trying to catch it, but I was pretty good at hitting it just beyond their range. After so long, they'd lunge for the ball, miss it, and just lie there, too pooped to get up.

"Okay," I'd yell. "Next!" Beats calisthenics any day.

I stayed with McGraw for two years, managed Toronto in the International League for a year, and then in the fall of 1919, that same phone rang again. Of all the people in the world, it was Barney Dreyfuss. "What are you going to do next year, Gibby?" he asked me.

"I'm not sure," I answered. "Probably manage Toronto again, although we haven't signed a contract yet."

"Well, how would you like to manage the Pittsburgh Pirates instead?"

Just like that. It took me a few minutes to recover from the shock. "I don't know, Barney," I said. "Seems to me we have a couple of things to settle between us before I could even consider it."

"Like what?" he asked.

Barney Dreyfuss, owner of the Pittsburgh Pirates from 1900 until his death in 1932

"Like in the first place," I said, "you broke your promise and got $1,800 for my worn-out carcass three years ago. Second, you didn't pay me my salary for August and September that year. I know I went home in August, but that's on account of you didn't keep your word."

"All right," he says, "I'll give you that $1,800 I got from McGraw and pay you your salary for August and September, too. What do you say?"

Well, naturally, I said yes. As you know, I'd already gotten both the $1,800 and the back pay from John McGraw. But Barney Dreyfuss didn't know that, and as far as I was concerned he owed it to me anyway for breaking his promise.

So I became the first Canadian-born Big League manager. Still the only one, I think, to this day. I managed the Pirates on and off for about 15 years, and then retired and came back home. Didn't win any pennants but we came close a few times. Always seemed to fade in the stretch. I have a sneaking suspicion we'd have won those pennants if I only could have gotten my pitchers into a little better shape.

⑥ *Jimmy Austin*

The ball once struck off,
Away flies the boy
To the next destined post,
And then home with joy.
—*Anonymous, 1774*

I GUESS MOST PEOPLE must have thought I was crazy. Twenty-four years old and leaving a good job to go off and play a boys' game. After just finishing four years of apprenticeship, too, and finally getting to be a full-fledged machinist.

In a way, I guess it did look like I was off my rocker. But it all depends on how you look at it. Me, I was always crazy about baseball. See, I was born in Swansea, Wales, and I didn't come to this country until I was eight years old. So I had to make up for a lot of baseball I'd missed up to then. I never could get enough of it. Even now, eighty-five years old, my Christmas present from my wife is always *The Sporting News,* and I still read that thing from beginning to end the same day it gets here.

So *I* knew it was the right thing to do. It's true that I didn't get to the Big Leagues until I was almost thirty. But I was still playing regular when I was past forty, and then I stayed on another 20 years as a coach. Golly, if I had it to do all over the only thing I'd do different would be to start sooner and stop later. It was great.

Heck, I even played in a Big League game when I was fifty years old. It was near the end of the 1929 season, and I was coaching for the old St. Louis Browns. Dan Howley was the manager that year. It was late in the game and we were way ahead, and some of the fellows were kidding me about how good a player I'd been. Well, darned if Dan didn't haul off and put me right in there at third base. Fifty years old I was. I had two chances and handled them both clean, and got up to bat once. Boy, I wish I'd gotten a hit.

My Dad was a shipbuilder in Wales. He came over here in 1885 and

78

settled in Cleveland, where he went to work doing the same sort of thing. A couple of years later he brought the rest of the family over. After I finished school I went to work at Westinghouse, where I wound up becoming a machinist-apprentice. Well, a month after my four years of apprenticeship had ended—that would be 1903—the union went out on strike, and of course I had to go out with the rest of the boys.

I was puttering around the house one day, when a fellow came to the front door. My mother had died, and my sister—I was the oldest of eight children—was keeping house. I was in the back yard doing something, and she came back and said, "Jim, you're wanted. Some gentleman would like to see you."

I went out front, and it was a guy from Warren, Ohio. He says, "You're Jim Austin? I've heard of you. You play ball around here with the Franklin Athletic Club, don't you?"

"Yes I do," I said.

"Well," he says, "how would you like to come to Warren and play independent ball? We have a pretty good little league, all factory teams, and we can pay you $40 a month plus a job."

"All right," I said. It didn't take me long to make up my mind. Hell, I'd always wanted to be a ballplayer. Ed Delahanty and Bill Bradley and Tommy Leach had all come from Cleveland and made it. Why not me? Besides, we were out on strike, so I didn't have any money coming in, anyway.

"That's fine," he says. "Now do you know where I might be able to get a good outfielder?"

"Why sure," I said. "I can get you the best outfielder in town." So I went to Dode Paskert's house and told him about it, and he went with me to Warren.

Well, we played in that little independent league that summer, and then I went back to work at Westinghouse in the fall. The next spring, though, I got a letter from the Dayton club in the Central League. That was in organized ball. Somebody had recommended both Dode and me to Dayton, and they made offers to both of us. So off we went to Dayton.

We played together there for three years, and then in 1907 they sold Dode to Atlanta in the Southern League and me to Omaha in the Western League. I stole 97 bases with Omaha in 1908, and at the end of the season I was sold to the New York Yankees. I played for 14 years

The Dayton club in the Central League in 1904. Jimmy Austin is on the far right in and Dode Paskert is on the far right, top row.

in the American League. Dode wound up with Cincinnati and played for 15 years in the National League. So I guess you might say we both made good.

Of course, they weren't called the Yankees then. We were called the New York Highlanders, because we played in a little park—it only seated about 15,000—located at 168th Street and Broadway, which was on pretty high ground. You could look from the stands and see all the way down the Hudson River. Sometimes we were called the Hilltoppers.

The Highlanders had a pretty good team when I joined them in 1909. We ended fifth in 1909, and second behind the Athletics in 1910. Three real old-timers were on that club when I got there: Willie Keeler, Kid Elberfeld, and Jack Chesbro. Gee, they were great fellows. They were all close to forty by then, and they didn't play much longer, but I got a thrill just being on the same team with them.

You know, you hear all that stuff about the old-timers being so rough on rookies in those days. Well, you can't prove it by me. Those guys were swell to me.

Wee Willie Keeler was still a pretty good ballplayer, even then. He could loop 'em over the infield better than anybody I ever saw. Wonderful fellow. I was too shy to say anything to him, but he came to me one day and said, "Jim, you've got a great career ahead of you. If I can help you in any way, you just say the word." How about that?

And Kid Elberfeld. Golly, I was out after the Kid's third-base job, but he always treated me fine. One day the Kid got in a hassle with Tim Hurst, the tough old umpire, and got suspended for five days and was fined 50 bucks. The Kid slid into second base, safe on a double, sure as could be, and Tim, who was umpiring behind the plate, called it a foul ball. Well, the Kid started arguing with Tim, and while he's talking he's all the while jabbing Tim in the belly with his finger. Finally, Tim took his mask off and whammo! He whacked it right across the Kid's nose. After they separated them, they were both suspended.

Anyway, the point of all this is that George Stallings, who was our manager then, put me in at third base while the Kid was out. And do you know that Elberfeld insisted on me sleeping in a lower berth on the train. The lower berths were for the regulars. Us second-stringers slept in the uppers. I was climbing into my upper one night, after I'd been in there at third base a few days, and the Kid saw me. He grabbed me by the ankles and said, "Where do you think you're going?"

"This is my berth," I said.

"The hell it is," he said.

"The hell it ain't," I said. "I've had it ever since I've been with the club."

"Well, you're not going to have it anymore," he says. He marched me over to the club secretary and says, "Put the youngster down in a lower berth. Take mine if you have to. He's playing every day, hustling like the devil out there, and he needs his rest." That's the way the old-timers treated a rookie in those days. At least that's the way they treated me.

Stallings was a fine manager. One of the best. Like I said, we finished in second place in 1910, and you've got to say he deserved a lot of the credit for that. Talk about cussing! Golly, he had 'em all beat. He cussed something awful. Once, in a game, he gave me a real going over. Later that night he called me in and said, "Jim, I'm sorry about this afternoon. Don't pay any attention to me when I say those things. Just forget it. It's only because I get so excited and want to win so bad."

Late in the 1910 season we had just finished a series in Cleveland and were on the boat going over to play Detroit. Nobody could find Hal Chase. Hal had been the Highlanders' first baseman for years. Well, he'd just disappeared. The next day we found out what had happened. When we had gotten on the boat for Detroit, he had taken the train to New York. He'd gone to Mr. Farrell, the president of the club, and complained about Stallings and a lot of other things. Mr. Farrell supported Chase, so Stallings quit, and Chase was made the new manager. God, what a way to run a ball club!

Well, you know how good a manager Hal Chase was: so good that he took over a club that finished second in 1910 and took them straight to sixth place in 1911. And the year after that they wound up last. And you know what Stallings did a few years later with the Boston Braves: he managed them from last place on the fourth of July to win the pennant, and then beat the Athletics in the World Series.

Anyway, one of the first things Chase did after he was made manager was trade me and Frank LaPorte to the St. Louis Browns. Stallings always liked Frank and me. He liked us because we hustled. "The Pepper Kid," Stallings always used to call me. And because Stallings liked us, Hal traded us. Boy, that Chase was something. He finally left baseball when he got mixed up in gambling and that sort of stuff. He was always like that.

I remember in 1910 we had a utility infielder on the Highlanders by the name of Jack Knight. Somebody gave Jack a new bat, and it just suited him. Boy, he hit like a fool with it. Hal Chase had a thousand bats himself, but he always wanted the other guy's, especially if it was somebody's who was hitting good. So Hal says, "You don't mind if I use your bat, do you Jack?"

"I'd rather you didn't," Jack said, "because it's the only one I've got."

Well, by gosh, Chase got so mad that he took Jack's bat and slammed it up against the dugout wall as hard as he could. That's the kind of guy he was. So they made him the manager!

It turned out, though, that it was a big break for me, him trading me to the Browns like that. Because I stayed there for over 20 years, as a player until 1922 and as a coach for 10 more years after that. When I went to St. Louis in 1911 the Browns were *the* team in that town, you know. It wasn't until the late twenties and the thirties that the Cardinals became the big team in St. Louis.

When I got to St. Louis, Bobby Wallace was the manager. One of the greatest fielding shortstops who ever lived, you know. It was a delight to play third base next to that fellow. Bobby played most of his career with the Browns. He was their regular shortstop from 1902 to about 1914 or so. Anyway, they made Bobby a playing manager in 1911, but he wasn't very happy as a manager, and in the middle of the 1912 season they got George Stovall to replace him. Bobby stayed at shortstop, though, for a few more years. George was a playing manager, too. He managed and played first base.

However, George spit himself out of a job the next year. Yeah, that's right, he expectorated himself right out of a job. He got into an argument with an umpire by the name of Charlie Ferguson. It was an awful rumpus. They were hollering at each other and one thing and another, and finally Ferguson threw George out of the game.

Well, before he left, George had to go back to first base to get his glove. Our dugout was on the third-base side. So Stovall walked, as slow as he could, all the way around behind the umpire and to first base, picked up his glove, and then started back the same way, maybe even slower. Well, the longer he walked the madder he got. And the longer he took, the madder the umpire got.

As George came around behind Ferguson on the way back to our dugout, the umpire told George to hurry it up. I guess that was the straw that broke the camel's back, because George let fly with a big glob of tobacco juice—p–tooey!—that just spattered all over Ferguson's

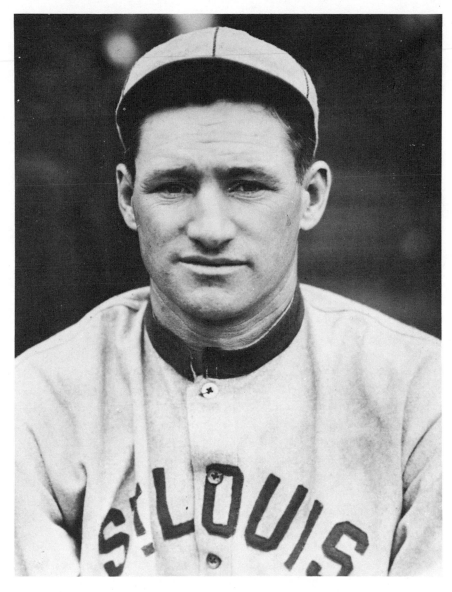

Jimmy Austin

face and coat and everywhere else. Ugh, it was an awful mess. It was terrible. George always did chew an uncommonly large wad, you know.

Well, they suspended George for that. In fact, they went and threw him clear out of the League. I don't believe he ever played another game in the American League, although I think that George did manage the Kansas City club in the Federal League later on.

So there we were in the middle of the season—that was 1913—without a manager. So who did Mr. Hedges, the president of the club, ask to be temporary manager until they got a new one? Of all people, *me*.

Mr. Hedges called me in after Stovall was suspended and said, "Jim, will you come out to my apartment tonight?"

"Sure," I said. "Where is it?" How was I supposed to know where the devil he lived?

He told me, so I went out there, and when I got there here's this Branch Rickey fellow. He'd been a second-string catcher years before with St. Louis, but since then he'd become a lawyer and was at the University of Michigan as a teacher or a baseball coach or something.

"Jim, I want you to meet Mr. Rickey," said Mr. Hedges. "Mr. Rickey is going to be the manager next year, but we'd like you to finish out as manager for the rest of this season." Which, of course, I did.

So that's how I met Branch Rickey. A year or two later Branch brought George Sisler to the Browns. Branch had been his coach at the University of Michigan. And you know the tremendous ballplayer Sis became. One of the very greatest who ever lived. Golly, he hit like blazes: .407 one year and .420 another. He was unbelievable with that bat. Really, you had to see it to believe it.

You know what happened last December? The phone rang and some guy with a real rough voice says, "Are you going to be home tomorrow?"

"Yeah, I'll be home tomorrow," I said.

"Well, I expect to be there about lunchtime."

"Who the hell is this?" I said.

"It's Branch Rickey," he says.

So old Branch showed up and we spent hours talking about old friends and replaying old ball games. It was great.

I was Branch's Sunday manager, you know. He'd promised his mother and father he'd never go near a ballpark on Sunday, so I managed the team for him every Sunday all the time he was with the Browns.

Just think of me, a third baseman, playing most of my years throwing over to either Hal Chase or George Sisler at first base. Why, that's *heaven* for a third baseman. There's no doubt that they were the two greatest-fielding first basemen who ever lived, and that's in *anybody's* book.

Of the two, I guess I'd have to say that Chase was the better fielder. In a way I hate to say that, but you have to give the devil his due. Sis was a better all-around ballplayer. He started with us as a pitcher, you know. I was at third base one day in 1915 when he outpitched Walter Johnson and beat him, 2–1. And, of course, Sis was a better hitter, one of the best of all time. But just on fielding alone, I'm afraid I'd have to pick Chase.

And pitchers—boy, did we ever have 'em. Lefty Grove was fast, and Sandy Koufax is, too. But you should have seen Walter Johnson. On a cloudy day you couldn't see the ball half the time, it came in so fast. That's the honest-to-goodness truth. But I'd rather bat against Walter than some of those other fast-ball pitchers, because Walter was so damned careful. He was too good a guy, scared stiff he'd hit somebody. A lot of the others didn't care—the hell with you, you know.

I remember one day Walter had us beat, 10–2 or something like that, and he yells in to me, "Here's one right in there. Let's see you hit it."

Well, he threw a medium fast one in, letter-high, and I hit it clear over the right-field fence. Laugh? I don't know which one of us was laughing harder as I was going around the bases. But of course that was the exception. Usually I couldn't come close to hitting Walter, and neither could anyone else. I was playing against him that day in 1913 when he pitched his 54th consecutive scoreless inning, to beat Jack Coombs' record of 53 in a row. He reached 56 straight scoreless innings of pitching before we finally got a run off of him. I guess that record still stands even today, over half a century later.

And old Rube Waddell. What a card that big guy was. You know, when I first came to the Big Leagues they didn't have clubhouses in most parks, especially not for the visiting team. We'd get into uniform at the hotel and ride out to the ball park in a bus drawn by four horses. They used to call it a tally-ho in those days. We'd sit on seats along the sides and ride, in uniform, to the ballpark and back.

That ride was always a lot of fun. Kids running alongside as we went past, and rotten tomatoes once in a while. Always lots of excitement when the ball club rode by, you know, with plenty of yelling back and forth, as you can well imagine.

But what I started to tell you about was Rube Waddell. When I was with the Highlanders, Rube was with the St. Louis Browns. He'd left Connie Mack by then and was near the end of his career. This day I'm thinking about we were riding to the ball park in the tally-ho to play the Browns, knowing Rube was going to pitch against us. As we got near the park somebody yelled "Hey look, there's Rube."

Lajoie says—

"I drink Coca-Cola regularly and have been doing so for several years. It is the most refreshing beverage an athlete can drink, and after a hard game I make my way to a Soda Fountain and get a glass. I can make $10,000 a year playing baseball, while I couldn't make more than 50 cents a day at anything else, and I am taking care of myself so that I may be in the game for several years yet to come."

A glass for you will cure that headache, run down and exhausted feeling. Brightens you up, refreshes and exhilerates you. Step into the first Soda Fountain and prove it for yourself.

Coca-Cola

is the best beverage for quenching the thirst. Refreshing and invigorating when one is in training and has none of the "let down" qualities of alcoholic beverages. A few bottles on the bench will quiet the nerves when the game is close

5c. Everywhere.

Waddell says—

More than once a bottle of your Coca-Cola has pulled me through a tight game. There is nothing better for pitchers in hot weather. I find Coca-Cola stimulating both to body and mind. and is the only beverage of the kind that does not leave an after effect. In every game I work, I keep a bottle or two on the bench for an emergency, and I can say that Coca-Cola has never yet failed me.

(Signed) G. E. (Rube) Waddell.

A 1906 advertisement

And darned if it wasn't. He was scheduled to pitch that day, but there he was, standing out in front of the swinging doors of a saloon with a mug of beer that big. He's waving and yelling to us, and while we're yelling and laughing back and forth he holds up the beer, like as to say "Skoal," and downs the whole thing, chug-a-lug, right like that. And as the tally-ho continued on, we saw Rube go back into the saloon.

Doggone it, though, when game time came, darned if Rube wasn't out there ready to pitch. I'll never forget it as long as I live. He went along all right for three innings, but in the fourth we got two men on base and then Rube grooved one to me, which I promptly hit over the fence. As I'm trotting around the bases Rube is watching me all the way, and as he kept turning around on top of the mound he got dizzy, and by golly he fell over right on his rear end. Fell over right flat on his can!

Oh, that started everybody to laughing so hard we could hardly play. Some guys laughed so much they practically had a fit. All except the St. Louis manager, Jack O'Connor. He came running out and yelled, "Come on out of there. You didn't want to pitch anyhow." Somehow that made everybody laugh all the more. Good old Rube. In his life he gave a lot of people a lot of enjoyment.

So did Babe Ruth, too. The Babe was always friendly, a real nice guy who'd go out of his way any time to do you a favor. I guess when you talk about the greatest baseball player who ever lived it has to be either the Babe, Ty Cobb, or Honus Wagner. I didn't see much of Wagner, 'cause he was in the National League, but I played for years against both Cobb and Ruth, and I'd hate to have to choose between them. Golly, both of those guys could beat you in so many ways it wasn't funny.

Ty could get real nasty on the field, you know. Off the field, though, he was a pretty good guy. See that picture? It's a famous picture. It's Cobb sliding into third, and the other guy is me, being knocked sprawling. He took my left foot with his shoulder as he came in, and down I went. See the ball near my right knee? Look at Cobb's face. That guy wanted to win in the worst way.

Ty was fair enough on the bases, though, He nicked me a couple of times, but it was my fault. I don't blame him. I remember one day Ty was on first base and Sam Crawford hit a single out to right field, on which Ty comes all the way around to third. I just stood there, nonchalant, as though nothing's happening. At the last minute here comes the ball as Ty is sliding in, and I grabbed it real quick and in the same motion pushed his foot off the bag as I tagged him.

"It's Ty Cobb sliding in to third, and the other guy is me"

Well, the umpire called Ty out. Ty didn't move a muscle. Just lay there on the ground. Then he looked up at me, and in that Southern brogue of his he said, very slowly, "Mister, don't you ever *dare* do that no more."

When Cobb was out there on that ball field, look out. He wasn't anybody's friend then. He was out to win, regardless. But I got along with him all right off the field. He was a better guy off the field than he was on.

Now Babe Ruth, he was different. What a warmhearted, generous soul he was. Always friendly, always time for a laugh or a wisecrack. The Babe always had a twinkle in his eye, and when he'd hit a homer against us he'd never trot past third without giving me a wink.

The Babe would give you the shirt off his back. All you had to do was ask him. The big fellow wasn't perfect. Everybody knows that. But that guy had a heart. He really did. A heart as big as a watermelon, and made out of pure gold.

7 *Fred Snodgrass*

Often I have been asked to tell what I did to Fred Snodgrass after he dropped that fly ball in the World Series of 1912, eleven years ago. Well, I will tell you exactly what I did: I raised his salary $1,000.
                    —JOHN J. McGRAW, *My Thirty Years in Baseball*

I LOOK BACK at my years in baseball with a tremendous amount of pleasure. Yes, I'd love to do it all over again, and that in spite of the fact that I had what might be called a rather stormy career in baseball.

For over half a century I've had to live with the fact that I dropped a ball in a World Series—"Oh yes, you're the guy that dropped that fly ball, aren't you?"—and for years and years, whenever I'd be introduced to somebody, they'd start to say something and then stop, you know, afraid of hurting my feelings. But nevertheless, those were wonderful years, and if I had the chance I'd gladly do it all over again, every bit of it.

Of course, playing baseball was more than just fun. For a youngster, it was quite an education, too. Especially it was an education to play under John J. McGraw. He was a great man, really a wonderful fellow, and a great manager to play for.

Naturally, McGraw and I didn't always see things alike. I was a head-strong, quick-tempered, twenty-year-old kid when I joined the Giants in 1908. And sometimes Mr. McGraw would bawl the dickens out of me, as he did everybody else. Any *mental* error, any failure to think, and McGraw would be all over you. And I do believe he had the most vicious tongue of any man who ever lived. Absolutely! Sometimes that wasn't very easy to take, you know.

However, he'd never get on you for a mechanical mistake, a fielding error or failure to get a hit. He was a very fair man, and it was only when you really had it coming to you that you got it. And once he'd bawled you out good and proper, and I do mean proper, then he'd forget it. He wouldn't ever mention it again, and in public he would

91

always stand up for his players. It was really a lot of fun to play for McGraw.

As a matter of fact, it was because Mr. McGraw's favorite form of relaxation was watching the ponies that I became a professional ball-player in the first place. He loved to follow the horses, you know, and in February of 1908 he came out here to Los Angeles to attend the races. He didn't bring his team, he was out here by himself. While he was here, he'd put on a uniform and work out to get himself in shape before spring training began, so he could sort of get the jump on all those old-timers who were on the Giants then.

At the time, the only contact I had with baseball was playing Sundays on a semipro team called the Hoegee Flags. (We were sponsored by a sporting-goods house, and on our backs we had flags of all nations.) We played teams all over southern California, and I still remember the one that was toughest. It was a team down by Santa Ana, for which Walter Johnson pitched. If people think Walter was fast later on, they should have seen him then. Whew! Most of the time you couldn't even see the ball!

Anyway, one of my friends was helping Mr. McGraw work out at the ball park, shagging flies for him and things like that. McGraw asked a question about me, remembering I guess that the year before the Giants had played three exhibition games against St. Vincent's College in Los Angeles and that as a student there I had caught for St. Vincent's. Mr. McGraw had been the umpire, and we had argued and quarreled constantly all through those three games.

"Oh, Snodgrass is the best catcher in semipro around here," my friend said.

"Well," McGraw said, "if you see him, tell him I would like to talk to him."

Word got to me, and I discussed it with my parents. There didn't seem to be any harm in talking to him, so I called him up at his hotel. He asked me to meet him in the lobby the next day, which I did.

"Are you thinking about playing baseball?" McGraw asked me.

"A little bit," I said, "but not too seriously. Although I did have an offer from Peoria in the Three-I League."

He reached into his pocket and said, "Here's a contract. Take it home and talk it over with your father and mother. If they think you ought to try baseball, our train leaves for spring training in four days. Let me know what you decide, will you?"

Well, as you can well imagine, I was on that train four days later, going to Marlin, Texas. That's the way I got started in baseball. Of course, my contract only called for $150 a month. And, to tell the truth, at the time I couldn't even name all the clubs in the two Big Leagues. But suddenly there I was, at spring training with the New York Giants.

You see, in those days they didn't have an army of coaches and scouts and things of that kind. The way they got young players was by direct observation themselves. Or some friend of the club would tip off John

The Giants at Marlin, Texas, in the spring of 1913: ". . . every day, twice a day . . . we walked from the hotel to the ball park along some railroad tracks that ran close by." This picture was taken by Christy Mathewson.

McGraw, or other managers, that here was a likely kid, and they would bring him up and look him over.

The Giants had bought a piece of property in Marlin, Texas, a town of about 4,000 or 5,000 people, and had constructed a ball park there for spring-training purposes. They thought that in a little town like that they could keep the fellows under control better. The ball park was about two miles from our hotel, and every day twice a day, morning and afternoon, we walked from the hotel to the ball park along some railroad tracks that ran close by. We trained there every spring I was with the Giants, which was until 1915.

Of course, spring training was very different in those days, compared to today. It was simpler, and it was tougher. Today you have specialized teachers and coaches and schools and blackboards, and all that sort of thing. You have mass calisthenics and mechanical pitchers and moving pictures to look at to see what you're doing wrong, and a host of other things. Maybe it's helpful and maybe it isn't. I guess it must be.

But we didn't have any of those things. We didn't have ten coaches, each a professional teacher in some aspect of baseball. We had one old-timer, Arlie Latham, who had been a first-rate ballplayer and who was a fine fellow, but who was probably the worst third-base coach who ever lived. They didn't make a specialty of such things then. In those days, you see, it was strictly up to the individual to improve himself and to get himself into condition. If he was intelligent, and if he was a man who wanted to make that team and become a first-class baseball player, he himself had to have it in his heart to work at it. He wasn't made to do things. In fact, he wasn't even encouraged very much.

Of course, we trotted to and from the park every day, and McGraw insisted that we run so many times around the park, and naturally we'd have batting and fielding practice. However, it was practically impossible for a youngster, a rookie, to get up to the plate in batting practice. A youngster was an outsider, and those old veterans weren't about to make it easy for him to take away one of their jobs. The Giants then had mostly rough and tough old characters, men who had been around quite a while—men like Mike Donlin, Joe McGinnity, Cy Seymour, Spike Shannon, and a lot of others. When I came up in 1908 it was mostly a team of veterans, a lot of them nearing the end of their base-ball careers. But that didn't mean they accepted that fact.

And yet, when I look back, I realize that I owe a great deal to one of those veterans. I was assigned to room with Spike Shannon. He was about thirty years old and had been an outfielder in the Big Leagues for about five years. He took me under his wing, helped me, encouraged me, and told me what to do and what not to do. I doubt if I'd have made the club that year if it hadn't been for Shannon.

But I did make it. I was the third-string catcher in 1908, behind Roger Bresnahan and Tom Needham. I sat on the bench all through that season. That was the year of the famous Merkle incident, when we should have won the pennant but didn't. In 1909 I was still the third-string catcher until the last month of the season, when McGraw put me in the outfield for about 20 games. In 1910 I was a catcher again in spring training, and when the season opened I was once more spending most of my time sitting on the bench. By then Bresnahan had left and Chief Meyers was doing most of the catching.

Then on the first road trip of the 1910 season McGraw came to me in the hotel in Cincinnati.

"Snow," he said, "how would you like to play center field?"

Well, I had been very unhappy sitting on the bench, and I immediately thought he was going to send me out to some minor league club. So I said, "With what club?"

"Why, *this* club, of course."

"You mean you're going to take Cy Seymour out of center field?"

"Yes," he said, "would you like to try it?'

So from then on I was the regular center fielder for the Giants. I never went back to catching. I was also the substitute first baseman for Fred Merkle whenever something happened and Merkle couldn't play. As a matter of fact, I preferred playing first base. I didn't particularly like the outfield. You can be out there all day without a chance, or maybe just backing up some play. I like to be in the middle of things and fight a little bit.

That was quite a team we had in those days, you know. We won the pennant in '11, '12, and '13. Fred Merkle was at first base, Larry Doyle at second, Al Bridwell and then Art Fletcher at short, and Art Devlin or Buck Herzog at third. In the outfield Red Murray was on one side of me, and Josh Devore or George Burns on the other. The battery was Chief Meyers behind the plate and Mathewson, Rube Marquard, Jeff Tesreau, Leon Ames, Hooks Wiltse, Otis Crandall, or Bugs Raymond pitching. What a club that was!

Marquard! What a great record Rube had. In 1912 he won 19 straight games, almost every one a complete game. And I still remember that wonderful 21-inning game he pitched against Pittsburgh—I think it was in 1914. We won that game, 3–1, in 21 innings, and Rube pitched the whole game. As a matter of fact, I think Babe Adams pitched all 21 innings for Pittsburgh, too. You know, in those days pitchers were *expected* to pitch the whole game. Today it's entirely different. Five or six pitchers a game isn't at all unusual now. But then it was a disgrace if a pitcher didn't finish what he started.

And Mathewson! The great pitcher that he was! He pitched a complete game almost every time he went out there. Matty was the greatest pitcher who ever lived, in my opinion. He was a wonderful, wonderful man, too, a reserved sort of fellow, a little hard to get close to. But once you got to know him, he was a truly good friend.

Matty could do *everything* well. He was checker champion of half a dozen states—he'd play several opponents simultaneously and beat them all—a good billiard player, a pretty fair golfer, and a terrific poker player. He made a good part of his expenses every year playing poker. He was a good bridge player, too.

And did you know that he never pitched on Sunday, or even dressed in uniform? Of course, in those days we never played Sunday ball in the East—in New York, Philadelphia, Boston, or Pittsburgh—although we did in Chicago, St. Louis, and Cincinnati. But Matty never would. I'm not saying that he was a very religious man, but he got started that way, I guess because of some belief he had, and he continued it throughout his career.

For contrast, we also had Bugs Raymond. Bugs drank too much and came to an early tragic end, but when he was sober, and sometimes when he wasn't, he was one of the greatest spitball pitchers who ever lived. McGraw tried to help him, but he didn't succeed. He tried fining him when he'd break training, but fining Bugs didn't have any effect. Bugs would go into any bar, pull a baseball out of his pocket and autograph it, and he'd get all the free drinks he wanted. Actually, McGraw didn't keep the fines; he would send the money to Bugs' wife, although he never let Bugs know this.

Even when he wasn't drinking, Bugs did the strangest things. I remember once, in spring training, we all went to a fish fry on the final day before leaving camp. Somebody brought along a couple of target guns, and we were all shooting at targets. Bugs said, "Here, hit this." And he took out his pocket watch, a very good watch that had been given to him in the minor leagues. I remember Al Bridwell was shooting at the time. Bugs threw the watch up in the air, and Al put a bullet right through the middle of it!

On the way back to New York that same spring, we stopped for three days at the Belvedere Hotel in Baltimore. The Belvedere was one of the finest hotels in the East, and they just about tripled our eating allowance there, because it was so expensive. Bugs was never seen by anybody all three days we were there. On the morning we were to leave for New York we were all down in the lobby, reading the newspapers and waiting to go, when somebody saw two waiters and two bus boys going into the elevators, all with loaded trays. It turned out to be Bugs Raymond's breakfast. Bugs hadn't eaten at the hotel for the three days, and sure enough he had taken the menu and figured out exactly the amount that he could spend, item by item. He spent the whole three days' meal allowance for that breakfast. And, of course, he was too much under the weather to eat any part of it!

Bugs had a good sense of humor and was a lot of fun. But he couldn't stay away from drinking, and as a result you never could be sure he'd show up. McGraw tried bringing his wife and children along with the team, both at home and on the road, so they could be with him all the time. It worked pretty well for a while, but then that flew all to pieces, too. Bugs and McGraw finally had it out one night on the train, and Bugs was told that the next time he didn't show up would mean the end of his career.

The next day we were playing in St. Louis. We were supposed to be at the park at noon, and by two o'clock Bugs still hadn't shown up. Finally, we saw Bugs, in civilian clothes, walking across the field toward the clubhouse out beyond center field. McGraw met him at the door.

"Bugs," he said, "you're through in baseball. Here's your uniform [that was the year we had to buy our own uniforms]. See Mr. Foster, and he'll give you a ticket back to New York. You're through with the Giants."

When we finally got back to New York ourselves, hanging in the window of the nearest saloon to the Polo Grounds was Bugs Raymond's uniform, with a sign on it that said "Bugs Raymond Tending Bar Here."

That was in 1911, and Bugs never pitched another game in professional baseball. He was an outcast, and the next year, at the age of thirty, he died.

But when I think of my teammates on the Giants, other than Bugs

Bugs Raymond

Raymond, I can't name a single player that I ever saw under the influence of liquor. A lot of those boys were rough and tough, but they weren't heavy drinkers. A few beers now and then, that was about it.

I will tell you something about those players, though, that I think is usually overlooked. They were rough and tough, all right, but they were good thinkers, too. Players in my day played baseball with their brains as much as their brawn. They were intelligent, smart ball-players. Why, you *had* to be! You didn't stay in the Big Leagues very long in those days unless you used your head every second of every game.

You see, it was a different game then compared to today. Now they're all trying to hit the ball over the fence. It's mostly brute strength. They're always trying to get a flock of runs at once. But in my day a home run was a rarity. You *couldn't* hit balls over the fence in most parks in those days, because the ball was too dead! So we were always playing for small scores, for one run or two.

As a result, there was a premium on intelligence in those days, on the ability to outwit and outthink the other team. And on speed and strategy. We used heavier, thicker bats and choked up on them so we could bunt more effectively and place our hits. Very few held the bat all the way down at the end, the way they do today. The only one I can remember was Frank Schulte, with the Cubs in the famous days of Tinker to Evers to Chance. Schulte held the bat down at the end. But most of us were choke hitters who punched at the ball trying to get singles and doubles, not home runs.

For example, take a simple thing like the art of getting hit with the ball when you're at bat. To get up there and deliberately *attempt* to get hit by a pitched ball. It's a lost art today; just not done anymore. I used to lead the league in that. I had baggy uniforms, a baggy shirt, baggy pants—any ball thrown close inside, why I turned with it and half the time I wasn't really hit, just my uniform was nicked. Or the ball might hit your bat close to your hands and you'd fall down on your belly, and while you were down you'd try to make a red spot by squeezing your hand or something. If you had a good red spot there, the umpire might believe it hit you rather than the bat. And off you'd go to first base.

Of course, in those days baseball was a pitcher's game much more than it is today. Not only did we have a dead ball, but pitchers were allowed to use such deliveries as the spitball, the emery ball, and what have you. And we hardly ever saw a new baseball, a clean one. If the ball went into the stands and the ushers couldn't get it back from the spectators, only then would the umpire throw out a new one.

He'd throw the ball out to the pitcher, who would promptly sidestep it. It would go around the infield once or twice and come back to the pitcher as black as the ace of spades. All the infielders were chewing tobacco or licorice, and spitting into their gloves, and they'd give that ball a good going over before it ever got to the pitcher. Believe me, that dark ball was hard to see coming out of the shadows of the stands.

Also, there were a lot of pitchers in those days who were quick-delivery artists. You didn't dare step into the batter's box without being ready, because somebody with a quick delivery would have that ball by you before you knew what happened. That was part of the game. The instant you stepped into that batter's box you had to be ready. If you were looking at your feet or something, the way they do today to get just the right position and all, well, by that time the ball would already be in the catcher's mitt. Particularly I remember Pat Flaherty, of the Boston Braves, and Joe McGinnity of the Giants was another—both quick-return artists. The catcher would throw them the ball and bang, right back it would come!

But to get back to this matter of intelligence and thinking in baseball. You know, a lot of what I read in newspapers and books about baseball in the old days is absolutely 100 per cent wrong. For instance, they seem to think that John McGraw directed every move we made on the field, that he was an absolute dictator who told us when to do this and when to do that, down to the last detail. Well, that's just not so, and it wasn't so for most other managers, either.

The fact of the matter is that thinking and alertness were crucial aspects of baseball then. Most of the time we were on our own. We used our own judgment. Nowadays they look at the manager or the coach for directions on almost everything. They aren't permitted to use their own judgment. They are told what to do on every darn pitch. But in our time we were supposed to *know* how to play baseball, and were expected to do the right thing at the right time.

McGraw allowed initiative to his men. We stole when we thought we had the jump and when the situation demanded it. We played hit-and-run when we felt that was what was called for. We bunted when we thought it was appropriate. Every player on the team was expected to know how to play baseball, and that was the kind of a game baseball was in those days. How many games do you see lost today just because they don't know how to bunt? That's a lost art, too. There was a lot of strategy in baseball then, and there isn't very much today. We played a game in which the two key words were "think" and "anticipate."

Of course, McGraw took charge sometimes. At certain points in a game he'd give instructions. But most of the time, as I say, the initiative was ours. The player of my day was allowed to think for himself, instead of having somebody do his thinking for him.

Why, do you know that we hardly ever had a pregame meeting on the Giants the whole eight years I was there? Hardly ever! Today they always have a meeting before the game to discuss what they're going to do. We didn't *need* any meetings. Most of us spent all our waking hours talking baseball anyway, so it would have been silly to have a meeting. Just about the only meetings we ever had on the Giants while I was there were to divide up the World Series money.

And signs! McGraw hardly ever used signs. The belief that he signaled what was to be done on every play is ridiculous. We were supposed to do things on our own. For instance, we had a base-running club. In 1911, '12, and '13 we had six or seven men who would each average 40 or so stolen bases a season. In 1911 we stole 347 bases. Just the New York Giants—347 stolen bases in one season! Look it up, if you don't believe it. And most of the time we ran on our own. We had signs among ourselves, so we could tell each other what we were planning to do. Signs between the batter and a man on base, for instance. But those were *our* signs, not McGraw's.

On rare occasions, McGraw would indeed tell us to steal. Do you know how he'd do it? On his fingers, with the deaf-and-dumb sign language. A deaf mute, Dummy Taylor, was a pitcher on the club, so all of us knew the sign language. McGraw would sit there on the bench and spell out S-T-E-A-L so plain that anyone in the park who could read deaf-and-dumb language would know what was happening. We had no complicated signals. A nod of the head, or something in sign language; he might just as well have said "go on," like that, and off you'd go.

We could all read and speak the deaf-and-dumb sign language, because Dummy Taylor took it as an affront if you didn't learn to converse with him. He wanted to be one of us, to be a full-fledged member of the team. If we went to the vaudeville show, he wanted to know what the joke was, and somebody had to tell him. So we all learned. We practiced all the time. We'd go by elevated train from the hotel to the Polo Grounds, and all during the ride we'd be spelling out the advertising signs. Not talking to one another, but sitting there spelling out the advertising messages. Even today, when I pass a billboard I find myself doing it.

Intelligent as they were, most ballplayers were also superstitious in those days. Just as they are today, for that matter. There's an interesting true story about that. Hard to believe, but true. Early in the 1911 season we were playing in St. Louis, and in those days neither team had a dugout in that park. We had a bench under an awning, about halfway between the grandstand and the foul line. We—the Giants—were having batting practice, when out of the grandstand walked a tall, lanky individual in a dark suit, wearing a black derby hat. He walked across

Manager John J. McGraw on the third base coaching lines (about 1908)

the grass from the grandstand to the bench, and said he wanted to talk to Mr. McGraw. So some of us pointed McGraw out, and he went over to him.

"Mr. McGraw," he said, "my name is Charles Victory Faust. I live over in Kansas, and a few weeks ago I went to a fortune-teller who told me that if I would join the New York Giants and pitch for them that they would win the pennant."

McGraw looked at him, being superstitious, as most ballplayers were —and are. "Well, that's interesting," he said. "Take off your hat and coat, and here's a glove. I'll get a catcher's mitt and warm you up, and we'll see what you have."

They got up in front of the bench and tossed a few balls back and forth. "I'd better give you my signals," Charles Victory Faust said. So they got their heads together, and he gave McGraw five or six signals. Mr. McGraw would give him a signal, and he would proceed to wind up. His windup was like a windmill. Both arms went around in circles for quite a little while, before Charlie finally let go of the ball. Well, regardless of the sign that McGraw would give, the ball would come up just the same. There was no difference in his pitches whatsoever. And there was no speed—probably enough to break a pane of glass, but that was about all. So McGraw finally threw his glove away and caught him bare-handed, thinking to himself that this guy must be a nut and he'd have a little fun with him.

"How's your hitting?" McGraw asked him.

"Oh," he said, "pretty good."

"Well," McGraw said, "we're having batting practice now, so get a bat and go up there. I want to see you run, too, so run it out and see if you can score."

Word was quickly passed around to the fellows who were shagging balls in the infield. Charlie Faust dribbled one down to the shortstop, who juggled it a minute as Charlie was turning first, and then they deliberately slid him into second, slid him into third, and slid him into home, all in his best Sunday suit—to the obvious enjoyment of everyone.

Well, that night we left for Chicago, and when we got down to the train and into our private Pullman car, who was there but Charles Victory Faust. Everybody looked at him in amazement.

"We're taking Charlie along to help us win the pennant," the superstitious Mr. McGraw announced.

So, believe it or not, every day from that day on, Charles Victory Faust was in uniform and he warmed up sincerely to pitch that game. He thought he was going to pitch that *particular* game. Every day this happened. To make a long story shorter, this was 1911, and although Charlie Faust warmed up every day to pitch, he never pitched a game.

He wasn't signed to a contract, but John J. McGraw gave him all the money that was necessary. He went to the barbershop almost every day for a massage and a haircut, he had plenty of money to tip the waiters— in the small amounts that we tipped in those days—and we *did* win the pennant.

Charles Victory Faust: "His windup was like a windmill."
Notice that Charlie does not have a baseball.

Spring came around the next year and Charles Victory Faust appeared in the training camp. He warmed up every day in 1912, and *again* we won the pennant.

In 1913 he was again in the spring-training camp, and during the season he continued to warm up every day to pitch. By that time he had become a tremendous drawing card with the fans, who would clamor for McGraw to actually put him in to pitch. Finally, one day against Cincinnati they clamored so hard and so loud for McGraw to put him in to pitch that in a late inning McGraw *did* send him to the mound. He pitched one full inning, without being under contract to the Giants, and he didn't have enough stuff to hit. They didn't score on him. One of those nothing-ball pitchers, you know.

Well, it was Charlie Faust's turn to come to bat when three outs were made, but the Cincinnati team stayed in the field for the *fourth* out to let Charlie come to bat. And the same thing happened then that happened the very first time that Charlie ever came on the field in St.

Louis in his Sunday clothes: they slid him into second, third, and home.

He was such a drawing card at this point that a theatrical firm gave him a contract on Broadway in one of those six-a-day shows, starting in the afternoon and running through the evening, and he got four hundred dollars a week for it. He dressed in a baseball uniform and imitated Ty Cobb, Christy Mathewson, and Honus Wagner. In a very ridiculous way, of course, but *seriously* as far as Charlie was concerned. And the fans loved it and went to see Charlie on the stage. He was gone four days, and we lost four ball games!

The fifth day Charlie showed up in the dressing room at the Polo Grounds, and we all said to him, "Charlie, what are you doing here? What about your theatrical contract?"

"Oh," he said, "I've got to pitch today. You fellows need me."

So he went out there and warmed up, with that windmill warm-up he had that just tickled the fans so, and we won the game. And in 1913 we won the pennant *again*.

That fall I joined a group of Big Leaguers and we made a barnstorming trip, starting in Chicago and going through the Northwest and down the Coast and over to Honolulu. In Seattle, who came down to the hotel to see me but Charlie Faust.

"Snow," he said to me, "I'm not very well. But I think if you could prevail on Mr. McGraw to send me to Hot Springs a month before spring training, I could get into shape and help the Giants win another pennant."

But, unfortunately, that never came to pass. Because Charlie Faust died that winter, and we did not win the pennant the next year. Believe it or not, that's the way it happened. It's a true story, from beginning to end.

Which reminds me of that other pennant we did not win, which as I said before we should have won. That was in 1908, the year of the famous Merkle incident. For almost 60 years poor Fred Merkle has been unfairly blamed for losing the pennant for us in 1908. What actually happened was quite understandable, and anyone who puts all the blame on Merkle has to be blind to a lot of other things that happened that season, things which contributed just as much, if not more, to our losing the pennant.

Fred Merkle had joined the Giants in the fall of 1907, at the age of eighteen, before I joined the following spring. So in 1908, when I met him, and when the so-called Merkle "bonehead" occurred, he was a kid only nineteen years old. As a result of what happened he took more abuse and vituperation than any other nineteen-year-old I've ever heard of.

There were six of us youngsters who made the club that year: Fred Merkle, Larry Doyle, Art Fletcher, Buck Herzog, Otis Crandall, and me. Mostly we were bench warmers. I was a substitute catcher behind the great Roger Bresnahan, so you know I didn't play much. And Fred Merkle was the substitute first baseman behind Fred Tenney. He was nineteen and I was twenty, and we were both amazed that we were even on the Giants. I doubt if either of us got to play in as many as 25 games that season.

Anyway, as soon as a game was over at the Polo Grounds, any game, all of us fellows who were sitting on the bench were in the habit, when the last out was made, of jumping up and running like the dickens for our clubhouse, which was out beyond right center field. We wanted to get there before the crowd could get on the field.

In those days, as soon as a game ended at the Polo Grounds the ushers would open the gates from the stands to the field, and the people would all pour out and rush at you. Of course, all they wanted to do was touch you, or congratulate you, or maybe cuss you out a bit. But, because of that, as soon as a game was over we bench warmers all made it a practice to sprint from the bench to the clubhouse as fast as we could. And that was precisely the reason why Fred Merkle got into that awful jam. He was so used to sitting on the bench all during the game, and then at the end of the game jumping up with the rest of us and taking off as fast as he could for the clubhouse, that on this particular day he did it by force of habit and never gave it a second thought.

The famous game in which it all happened took place in New York in late September of 1908. The Giants were playing the Chicago Cubs and we were both about tied for the league lead, with only a week or two of the season remaining. Merkle was playing first base for us. I think Fred Tenney, the regular first baseman, was injured or something, and that this was the very first game Merkle had been put in the starting lineup all season.

Mathewson was pitching for us, against Jack Pfiester for the Cubs. The game went down to the last half of the ninth inning, with the score tied 1–1. And then, in the last of the ninth, with two out and Moose McCormick on first, Merkle hit a long single to right and McCormick went to third. Men were on first and third, with two out. The next man up was Al Bridwell, our shortstop. Al hit a line single into center field. McCormick, of course, scored easily from third—he could have walked in—with what appeared to be the winning run.

Merkle started for second base, naturally. But the minute he saw the ball was a safe hit, rolling toward the fence out in right center, with McCormick across the plate and the game presumably over and won, he turned and lit out for the clubhouse, exactly as he had been doing all season long. And that was Merkle's downfall. Because technically the rules of baseball are that to formally complete the play he had to touch second base, since Bridwell now occupied first.

As soon as McCormick crossed the plate, *everyone* thought the game was over. Everyone except Johnny Evers, anyway. The crowd began to come on the field, we bench sitters sprinted out through right center field for our clubhouse, as usual, along with Merkle and everybody else, and the two umpires walked toward their dressing room, which was behind the press box in back of home plate. So neither of the umpires saw what happened after that, because they were both going directly opposite from where the ball went.

Well, of course, what happened was that the great infield of Steinfeldt, Tinker, Evers, and Chance were playing for Chicago, and Johnny Evers, an old-timer at the game, saw that Merkle hadn't touched second base. Evers began to call to the Cub's center fielder, Artie Hofman, to go and get the ball. Hofman hadn't even chased it, because the game was over as far as he was concerned. But Evers made so much noise about getting the ball and throwing it in to second base, that Hofman finally retrieved it and threw it in.

However, Joe McGinnity, another old-timer, was coaching at third base for us, and he sensed what was going on. He ran out, intercepted the ball, and threw it up into the left field bleachers. He threw it clear out of the park. They say Evers got another ball from somewhere else and touched second with it, but I don't think so. I never saw that.

By this time, of course, there were thousands of people milling around on the infield, absolute bedlam around there. Frank Chance, the Chicago manager, went into the umpires' dressing room and insisted that the two umpires—Hank O'Day and Bob Emslie—come out and see what was going on. Chance claimed Evers had gotten the ball and touched second base with it, so that Merkle was out and the game should continue, still a 1–1 tie. And since the field was now total chaos, that the game should be forfeited to Chicago both because of McGinnity's interference and because the Giants couldn't clear their own field. So Chance dragged the umpires out there and said, "Look at this." They saw these thousands of fans on the field, arguing, milling around, not knowing what was going on, complete pandemonium. Everything was in an uproar.

Finally, Hank O'Day, who was the senior umpire, ruled that Merkle was indeed out, the third out, that therefore McCormick's run didn't count, and that the game had ended in a tie, 1–1. It was appealed to the highest league levels, but after three days of deliberations they finally upheld the umpires and ruled that it was a tie game and would have to be replayed as a play-off game after the season, if necessary. Well, it was necessary. We ended the season tied for first place with the Cubs, and the game had to be played over to decide the pennant race. As you know, the Cubs beat us in that play-off game, so we didn't win the pennant in 1908.

In that famous play-off game, by the way, we tried to get Frank Chance thrown out of the game, but didn't succeed. Before the game we talked over in the clubhouse how in the world we could get Chance out of there. Matty was to pitch for us, and Frank always hit Matty pretty well. We felt if we could get him out, in some way, that we had a better chance of winning the play-off game and the pennant. Besides, we thought the pennant was ours by right, anyway. We thought the call on Merkle was a raw deal, and any means of redressing the grievance was legitimate.

So it was cooked up that Joe McGinnity was to pick a fight with Chance early in the game. They were to have a knockdown, drag-out fight, Chance and McGinnity, and both would get thrown out of the game. Of course, we didn't need McGinnity, but they needed Chance. McGinnity did just as he was supposed to. He called Chance names on some pretext or other, stepped on his toes, pushed him, actually spit on him. But Frank wouldn't fight. He was too smart. And they beat us, with Chance getting a key hit and Three-Fingered Brown beating Christy Mathewson. I believe that was the year Brown won 29 games and Matty won 37.

It is very unfair to put all the blame on Merkle for our losing the pennant in 1908. McGraw never did, and neither did the rest of us. It was mostly the newspapers. They were the ones who invented the term "bonehead."

How could you blame Merkle, when we lost the play-off game, and besides that we lost five other games *after* the Merkle incident? If we had won any one of those five games we would have won the pennant in the regular season, and we wouldn't even have had to play a play-off game. We lost a double-header to Cincinnati, and then we played the Philadelphia Phillies and Harry Coveleski pitched against us three times in one week. He pitched against us on Tuesday, Thursday, and Saturday, and beat us all three times. That's when he acquired the nickname "Giant Killer." Coveleski beating us three times in one week surely wasn't Merkle's fault.

And do you know that we ran Harry Coveleski clear out of the league the next season. It was the craziest, most foolish thing that ever happened. McGraw was told by a friend of his who had managed Coveleski in the minor leagues, before he came up to Philadelphia, that Coveleski always carried some bologna in his back pocket and chewed on that bologna throughout the game—and that he did this more or less secretly, maybe somewhat ashamed of his habit. It was sort of an obsession with him.

So this manager told McGraw, and McGraw saw to it that some of us players would always meet Coveleski as he was going to and from the pitcher's box whenever he pitched against us. We'd stop him and say, "Hey, give us a chew of that bologna, will you?" Well, this so upset this fellow that he couldn't pitch against us to save his life. He never beat us again, word got around the league and the other clubs started doing the same thing, and it chased him right back to the minors—or at least that's what we Giants always claimed.

Often when the Merkle "bonehead" is recalled, in the next breath they talk about Snodgrass' "$30,000 muff." I've had to live with it for years— "Oh yes, you're the guy that dropped the fly ball in the World Series, aren't you?"

I never lost that World Series. I never took the blame for losing any World Series. I was terribly incensed a few years ago when a book on baseball facts and history came out. A friend of mine said to me, "Have you seen the book?" I said that I hadn't.

"Well," he said, "you'd better get a copy. They have a section in there on World Series Heroes and Goats, and you're listed as the Goat in the 1912 World Series."

So I got hold of a copy and read it. It said that in the 1912 World Series, the Red Sox versus the Giants, in the 10th inning of the last game Fred Snodgrass, the center fielder for the Giants, dropped an easy fly ball and let the tying and winning runs score. And thereby lost the Series for the Giants.

I did drop a fly ball. There's no doubt about that. But I didn't let the tying and winning runs score; I couldn't very well, because it happened with the *first* man up in the bottom of the 10th inning. It was the eighth and last game of the Series (one game had ended in a tie) and the score was tied, 1–1, at the end of the regulation 9 innings. In the top of the 10th we scored a run—on a hit by Fred Merkle, by the way—and went into the bottom of the 10th with Matty pitching and a one-run lead. If we could have held that one-run lead, we would have won the World Series.

The first man up for Boston in the bottom of the 10th was Clyde Engle, who was pinch-hitting for Smoky Joe Wood. He hit a great big, lazy, high, fly ball halfway between Red Murray in left field and me. Murray called for it first, but as center fielder I had preference over left and right, so there'd never be a collision. I yelled that I'd take it and waved Murray off, and—well—I dropped the darn thing. It was so high that Engle was sitting on second base before I could get it back to the infield.

Well, Harry Hooper was the next batter. And in the 10th inning of a tie game, the last game of a World Series, we were just certain that he would bunt to move the man over to third. So my position in center field was fairly close in behind second. Matty was holding Engle close to second, so that we could get him at third on the bunt, and I was in pretty close, figuring that if Matty threw to second and the ball got by second in any way I could still keep Engle from going to third.

But instead of bunting, Hooper cracked a drive way over my head. I made one of the greatest plays of my life on it, catching the ball over my shoulder while on the dead run out in deep left center. They always forget about that play when they write about that inning. In fact, I almost doubled up Engle at second base. He was turning third when I caught the ball. He thought it was gone, you know, and the play at second was very close.

So that's one out. Then Matty walked Steve Yerkes, unfortunately, with what proved to be the winning run. Two men on and only one out. And up comes Tris Speaker, one of the greatest hitters in the game. The crowd was making so much noise it was deafening.

What does Speaker do but take a swing at the ball and hit a nice easy pop-up, a foul ball, over near first base. Suddenly the crowd was so quiet you could have heard a pin drop. And that ball was never touched. Merkle didn't have to go thirty feet to get it, it was almost in the first-base coaching box. Chief Meyers, our catcher, tried to catch it, but couldn't quite get there. It was too far from home plate. Matty could have put it in his hind pocket himself. But no one ever touched it.

Well, given that reprieve, Speaker hit a clean line drive over the first baseman's head that scored the man I put on and put Yerkes on third base. Another long fly to right by Larry Gardner and Yerkes scored after the catch. The game is over and, according to the newspapers, Fred Snodgrass lost the World Series. I did drop that fly ball, and that did put what turned out to be the tying run on base, but that's a long way from "losing a World Series." However, the facts don't seem to matter.

Oh, those were stormy days. I always seemed to be getting involved in hassles of one sort or another. Like the time when they claimed I spiked Home Run Baker. That was in the 1911 World Series, when we were playing Connie Mack's Philadelphia Athletics. In fact, that was the Series in which Frank Baker acquired his famous nickname of Home Run Baker. He hit two home runs against us in that World Series, and in those days that was an extraordinary performance.

Before the Series began, we had been told by friends that Baker was spike-shy, that he'd get out of your way at third base if the occasion arose. But to start at the beginning: in the 1905 World Series, six years before, the Giants had beaten the Athletics four games to one. That was the Series in which Matty had shut out the A's three times and Joe McGinnity had shut them out once. In that Series the Giants had been dressed in black broadcloth uniforms.

So superstitious McGraw, and he *was* superstitious, he ordered new black broadcloth uniforms for the 1911 Series. We went out on the field first, all dressed in black, and as we sat on the bench waiting for the Athletics to walk past us to get to the visiting team's bench, we all had a shoe off in one hand and a file in the other, and we were all busily sharpening our spikes. We figured that might have some effect on them, because we were a base-running club and we wanted them to get the idea that they'd better get out of our way. As I said, we stole 347 bases that season.

Well, I happened to be the first man in the game to get to second base who had occasion to try to go to third. Chief Bender was pitching

Part of the crowd at Shibe Park in Philadelphia awaiting the start of the 1911 World and the crowded rooftops across the street.

Series. Although it hardly looks it, 20th Street runs between the right-field wall

for the A's, and throwing his beautiful curve in the dirt, and the catcher was having trouble digging it out. One pitch got away from the catcher and I lit out for third base.

But Baker knew that we had been told that he was spike-shy, and he just had guts enough to try to block me off that base. So he was down on one knee in front of the bag, with the ball, waiting for me to slide. Well, I couldn't hook the bag, in or out, because he'd ride me right off, so all I could do was go hard into him and try to upset him, which I did, and I was safe. In doing so I cut his pants, from his knee clear to his hip. They went and got another pair of pants and a blanket, put the new pants on him right at third base, and the game proceeded.

This same play happened again a few days later. I'm on second, a passed ball, and I take off for third. This time I was out, but I ripped his pants again, plus a little abrasion on his leg. Not a cut, no blood, nothing like that. Oh, I was the dirtiest player in baseball! Newspaper stories told how I'd jumped at Baker waist high, which wasn't true at all, and how I'd deliberately spiked him. Was I ever roasted! They built it up until Baker's bone showed from the knee to the hip.

In fact, a news report went out that some fanatic had shot Snodgrass in the hotel, and it was reported that I had been taken to the hospital in critical condition. They didn't have radio then, and that story went out over the wires. My parents out here in California heard that I had been killed, and it was several hours before a retraction came out and they found out I was all right.

And then there was that crazy incident in Boston, when Mayor Curley tried to have me thrown out of a game. That was in 1914, the year of the Boston Braves "Miracle Team," which came from last place on July 4th to beat us out for the pennant. We had been leading the league all season. But the Braves made this wonderful climb up the ladder from last place until by Labor Day, playing against the Giants, they had a chance to pass us and go into first place.

The crowd that wanted to get into the ball park in Boston that day was far greater than the seating capacity, so they started putting specta-tors in the outfield. In fact, the Boston Braves borrowed Fenway Park from the Red Sox that day, because the Braves' own park was too small to hold the crowd. They put ropes up in the outfield and thousands of people were sitting and standing behind the ropes, right on the playing field. They were standing right behind my back in center field.

We had a big inning in about the sixth or seventh inning and scored four runs to go well ahead of Boston. I came up to bat after we'd scored all those runs, with nobody on base and two men out. George Tyler, who was pitching for the Braves, was pretty disgusted by then, and he took it out on me by aiming four shots straight at my head. I

Fred Snodgrass

hit the dirt four times, and the fourth one hit the button on my cap. So on my way to first base I went by way of the pitcher's box. I stood in front of that guy and called him everything I could think of. He never said a word. Finally, when I ran out of adjectives, I went over to first base. Meanwhile, that huge crowd was hooting and hissing and booing me, and making a terrific din. They knew they weren't going to get into first place that day, and they were pretty sore about it.

When I got to first base, Tyler looked over at me and tossed the ball into the air and dropped it, a pantomime of the fact that two years before I'd dropped that fly ball in the World Series. Well, the crowd just loved that, and the hooting and booing got even louder, if that was possible. The next man made the third out, and I started out for my position in center field. And as I approached the crowd behind the ropes out there, booing and yelling at me, I just thumbed my nose at the whole bunch of them. Just an old-fashioned nose-thumbing, to let them know what I thought of them.

Well, that *really* set them off. It was the signal for all the pop bottles and trash of any kind that people had to come flying out on the field, in my general direction. The place was in an uproar.

And just then a fellow jumped out of his box seat near the home dugout, and marched onto the field, accompanied by a couple of high-helmeted policemen. He had on a long-tailed coat, spats, and a top hat, and he paraded over to the umpires. It was the Honorable James M. Curley, the Mayor of Boston. He said I had insulted the good citizens of Boston and demanded that I be removed from the field immediately. It was just before election time, and he was making what you might call a grandstand play for votes.

After a big argument, Bill Klem, who was umpiring, chased him off the field, and the game was finally finished without further trouble. But you can bet I didn't play a very deep center field the rest of that game, and they tell me that after the last out was made in the ninth inning I ran in from center field so fast that I was easily the first one into our dugout.

Well, life has been good to me since I left baseball. My lovely wife, Josephine, and I have enjoyed success and things have gone well, very well, through these many years. In contrast, my years in baseball had their ups and downs, their strife and their torment. But the years I look back at most fondly, and those I'd like most to live over, are the years when I was playing center field for the New York Giants.

⑧ *Stanley Coveleski*

Stanislaus Kowalewski was born in 1890. Thirty years later, as Stanley Coveleski, he became one of the few pitchers in the history of baseball to pitch three
winning games in a single World Series. Pitching for Cleveland in the 1920
World Series, he hurled three complete games, permitted Brooklyn but five hits
in each, and triumphed over the likes of Rube Marquard, Leon Cadore, and
Burleigh Grimes.

Coveleski played in the major leagues from 1916 through 1928, winning 214
games over that 13-year period, mostly for the Cleveland Indians. In five of
those seasons he won 20 or more games, and in all but four he won 15 or more.

Older brother Harry gained early fame with the Philadelphia Phillies, later
won over 20 games three years in a row with the Detroit Tigers. The two
together won far more major league games (297) than any other pitching
brothers. Jesse and Virgil Barnes won 213, Dizzy and Paul Dean 200, in both
cases less than the number won by Stanley alone.*

HAD FOUR BROTHERS, all ballplayers. Oldest was Jacob, a pitcher.
Killed in the Spanish-American War in 1898. They say he could
throw a ball fast as you could hit one. Next was Frank. Got the
rheumatism. Played with an outlaw league in Philadelphia. The rheumatism ended that. John, he tried out with the A's. Eddie Collins beat him
out. Then Harry and me. Five of us. I'm the youngest.

Harry and me, we both made it to the Big Leagues. Harry was a lefty
and I was a righty. Harry started first. He was four years older than
me. He signed with the Phillies in 1905 and they optioned him to Lancaster in the Tri-State League. That's where he was when the Phillies
recalled him in September of 1908. Harry came up and beat the Giants
three times in one week, and knocked them right out of the pennant.

Most people think it was Merkle lost the 1908 pennant for the Giants.
Well, they're wrong. It was Harry Coveleski. He was just a rookie, but
he beat the Giants three times in the last week of the season. Pitched

---

* Since this book was originally published, in 1966, both the Perry brothers (Gaylord and
Jim) and the Niekro brothers (Phil and Joe) have outdistanced the Coveleski brothers in
number of games won.

every other day for a week, and beat them three in a row. That was *after* the Merkle business and *that's* what lost the pennant for McGraw that year. The Giants would have won the championship if they'd beat Harry even one of those three games.

"Giant Killer" Coveleski they called him after that. They say McGraw never forgave Harry for that. A lot of nonsense. They also say that the Giants ran him out of the league next season. Something about harmonicas or bologna or something. Supposed to have gotten Harry's goat. What a lot of bull that story is.

Nobody ever ran Harry out of any league. What happened is that he got hurt the next season. Went back down to the minors for a few years. But his arm came back later, and he came back up with Detroit and did fine. He was with Detroit when I was with Cleveland. They always wanted us to pitch against each other, but we refused. Wouldn't do it. And they never forced it. Hard to say what would have happened if they had.

Actually, Harry beating the Giants three times in 1908 probably changed *my* life more than it did his. See, I never played much baseball when I was a kid. How could I? When I was twelve years old I went to work in the coal mines.

I was born in 1890 in Shamokin, Pennsylvania. That's anthracite country, about halfway between Scranton and Harrisburg. When I was twelve years old I was working in the mines from seven in the morning to seven at night, six days a week. Which means a 72-hour week, if you care to figure it up. For those 72 hours I got $3.75. About 5¢ an hour. There was nothing strange in those days about a twelve-year-old Polish kid in the mines for 72 hours a week at a nickel an hour.

What *was* strange was that I ever got out of there. Like I said, I never played much baseball in those days. I couldn't. Never saw the sunlight. Most of the year I went to work in the dark and came home in the dark. I would have been a natural for night baseball. Never knew the sun came up any day but Sunday.

But every evening after I got home I'd throw stones at tin cans. I don't know why. Just for something to do, I guess. Heck, we didn't have any television then, or radio, or automobiles, or even a telephone or electric lights. Had to do *something*. So I threw stones. I'd put a tin can on a log, or tie it to a tree, and stand maybe 40 or 50 feet away and throw stones at it. Did that every night till it was time to go to bed. I did that for so many years I could hit one of those things blindfolded.

Harry Coveleski, the Phillies'
"Giant Killer," in 1908

"He was with Detroit
when I was with Cleveland.
They always wanted us
to pitch against each
other, but we refused."

Connie Mack and family before the opening of the 1911 World Series

Well, the semipro team in town heard about me being so good throwing stones at tin cans and they asked me if I'd like to pitch for them. That was in 1908, when I was eighteen. Of course, maybe being Harry's kid brother had something to do with it, too. Then, before I knew what hit me, I was signed to a contract with Lancaster, and I was out of those damn mines for good.

Never forget leaving home for the first time to go play with Lancaster. It was the first time I ever rode on a train. Had to get a new suit of clothes to go off to the big city, but was too bashful to buy it. So Mom and Dad went to town, picked one out, and brought it home to fit it on me. Then when I got to Lancaster I was too shy to eat in the hotel with the rest of the team. I'd go to a hot-dog stand and eat by myself instead. Pay for it out of my own pocket. After a couple of weeks some of the players got suspicious, never seeing me around. So one day they followed me and caught me eating my hot dogs. After that they made me go to the hotel dining room with them. I'm glad they did.

I pitched for Lancaster for a few years, then went up for a trial with the Athletics late in 1912. With Connie Mack. Connie was a good manager. He was a very considerate man. If you did something wrong, he'd never bawl you out on the bench, or in the clubhouse. In the evening he'd ask you to take a walk with him, and on the way he'd tell you what you'd done wrong.

One day Connie called me in and told me I was to start that day. My first Big League game. I was a little nervous, but not too much. Hell, I'd been around by then. Four years in the Tri-State League. I figured I could do the job. Ben Egan caught me. Remember Big Benny?

"All you have to do is throw it right to me," Ben said. "I'll give you a good target. Just aim for my glove."

So that's what I did. Pitched a three-hitter. I aimed at Big Benny's glove, and it was just like throwing stones at tin cans. I didn't know the batters. Hadn't been there long enough to learn their weaknesses. All I knew was to aim at his glove. But that was enough. I *always* had good control. From throwing those stones. You know, once—with Cleveland, later on—I pitched seven full innings without throwing a single ball. Every pitch I threw was either a strike or was hit by the batter. Not one pitch in seven innings that wasn't over the plate.

I did OK in that trial with the Athletics—won two and lost one. But I couldn't break into that pitching staff Connie had then. Chief Bender, Eddie Plank, Jack Coombs, Herb Pennock. Don't know who

Stanley Coveleski

could have beat them out. So Connie sent me back to the minors, out to the Coast.

I put in two years with Spokane, and then one with Portland in the Pacific Coast League, and I guess that year with Portland—1915—was the turning point. I was twenty-five years old, was in my seventh year in the minors, and was starting to wonder if I'd *ever* make it to the Big Leagues. I had good control, a good curve, a good fast ball, and a good slow ball. But evidently that wasn't enough.

One day I was watching one of the Portland pitchers throwing spitballs. "By Gosh," I said to myself, "I'm going to try to throw that."

I started working on the spitter, and before long I had that thing down pat. Had never thrown it before in my life. But before that season was over it was my main pitch, and the next year I was up with the Cleveland Indians. That pitch—the spitball—kept me up there for 13 years and won me over 200 games.

I got so I had as good control over the spitball as I did over my other pitches. I could make it break any of three ways: down, out, or down and out. And I always knew which way it would break. Depended on my wrist action. For the spitball, what you do is wet these first two fingers. I used alum, had it in my mouth. Sometimes it would pucker your mouth some, get gummy. I'd go to my mouth on *every* pitch. Not every pitch would be a spitball. Sometimes I'd go maybe two or three innings without throwing one. But I'd always have them looking for it.

They outlawed the spitter in December, 1920. Said only certain established spitballers could continue to throw it after that. Me and sixteen others was all. Maybe the great year I had in 1920 had something to do with it. I don't know. They wanted to shift the odds more in favor of the batter.

Well, that's the way it is in baseball. I enjoyed playing ball. But it's a tough racket. There's always someone sitting on the bench just itching to get in there in your place. Thinks he can do better. Wants your job in the worst way: back to the coal mines for you, pal!

The pressure never lets up. Doesn't matter what you did yesterday. That's history. It's tomorrow that counts. So you worry all the time. It never ends. Lord, baseball is a worrying thing.

9   *Al Bridwell*

Time is of the essence. The rhythms break,
More varied and subtle than any kind of dance;
Movement speeds up or lags. The ball goes out
In sharp and angular drives, or long, slow arcs,
Comes in again controlled and under aim;
The players wheel or spurt, race, stoop, slide, halt,
Shift imperceptibly to new positions,
Watching the signs according to the batter,
The score, the inning. Time is of the essence.

. . . .

Remember Bridwell, Tenney, Merkle, Youngs,
Chief Meyers, Big Jeff Tesreau, Shufflin' Phil?
Remember Mathewson, and Ames, and Donlin,
Buck Ewing, Rusie, Smiling Mickey Welch?
Remember a left-handed catcher named Jack Humphries,
Who sometimes played the outfield, in '83?

Time is of the essence. The shadow moves
From the plate to the box, from the box to second base,
From second to the outfield, to the bleachers.

Time is of the essence. The crowd and players
Are the same age always, but the man in the crowd
Is older every season. Come on, play ball!
                —ROLFE HUMPHRIES, "Polo Grounds"

THERE WERE A LOT of great ballplayers in my day, no doubt about it. But there are a lot of great ballplayers *today*, too. No doubt about that, either. Take Willie Mays. I've seen Speaker, Cobb, Hooper —oh, all the great outfielders—but I've never seen anyone who was any better than Willie Mays. Maybe just as good, but not better.

Mays can throw, field, hit, run, anything. He can work a pitcher into losing a ball game any time he gets on base. Of course, Cobb was a better hitter. But Mays—I don't know, there's just something about him.

A lot of people will tell you that the modern player can't compare to the old timer. Not even in the same league, they say. Well, maybe they're right, but I don't think so. I don't think there's ever been a better outfielder than Mays, or a better left-handed pitcher than Sandy Koufax, or a better third baseman than Brooks Robinson, just to name three that are playing today.

Fellows like Honus Wagner and Three-Fingered Brown were great, and they'd be just as great if they were playing today. I'm not saying the old-timers weren't good. Sure they were. But the modern players are good, too. In other sports, like basketball and football, everyone admits the modern player is *better* than the old-timer. And in track it's obvious. The records prove it. How many four-minute miles were run before 1915? Before 1950, for that matter?

But in baseball a lot of people seem to think that there hasn't been a first-rate player since the days of Cobb and Ruth. It just doesn't stand to reason, does it? I'm not saying they're all better players today than they used to be. But doesn't it stand to reason that at least some of them are just as good? That's the least you can say. After all, Maury Wills *did* break Cobb's record, didn't he?

The modern player has it pretty tough in a lot of ways. Of course the gloves are better now, and the fields are smoother, but on the other hand we used to travel by train and make only three trips around the circuit a season. Now they hop all over the place in planes, and I think that's a lot rougher. Also, now they play at night a lot. Their eating and sleeping habits are always being disrupted, which is something we didn't have to worry about.

Actually, I don't think the greatest man in baseball was Cobb or Ruth or Wagner. I think it was Branch Rickey. I think he's done more for baseball than any man who ever lived. Fact is, Branch Rickey has been my hero ever since back in the late 1890's.

See, he was born in Lucasville, Ohio, just north of Portsmouth here. I was born up in the hills near Friendship, Ohio, which is only a few miles west of Portsmouth. There were twelve in our family, three brothers and seven sisters, and we lived up there in a little hollow. Dad worked in the lumber camps.

We moved here to Portsmouth when I was a kid, in 1888, and of course I played ball every chance I got. When I was about twelve we had a neighborhood team, and we'd play teams from other parts of town. At that time the Negro kids weren't allowed to go above 9th Street, or across Chillicothe Street. That's the way it was. If we'd catch one of them in our territory, or they'd catch one of us in theirs, it'd be just too bad.

But all the kids in the different parts of town had ball teams and we got together and formed a sort of league. About four or five teams, each from a different section of town. Well, the colored teams and white teams started to challenge each other, and before you know it we were playing each other all the time and not thinking a thing about it. Did away with all that trouble we'd had before, and brought us all together. Before long any kid could go anywhere in town he wanted. I'm not saying baseball did it all. But it helped.

About 1899, when I was fifteen, I joined an amateur team here called the Victors. We played once a week or so. That's how I first met Branch Rickey. He was playing with the Lucasville team and they came down here to play us. He was a catcher, and a good one. They beat us, and after the game Branch wanted to wrestle all comers. He got three or four challengers, and had them all in the dust. All in good fun, you know. And from that time on, he was a kind of hero of mine.

Later on, I played with a semipro team in town, the Navies. Portsmouth's a big port city, you know. Played shortstop for them for three years. In the fall of 1902 we played an exhibition game with the Columbus club of the American Association, and after the game Bobby Quinn, who was business manager for Columbus, asked me if I would stop by and see him that evening at the hotel where he was staying.

I hurried home and ate supper, put on my Sunday suit, and rushed down to the hotel. When I got there he asked me straight out, "How would you like to play for the Columbus team?"

Well, I was flabbergasted. I didn't know what to say. It was so out of my reach. On the Navies we'd each get maybe $5 a game, sometimes $10 if the crowd was good.

"How much would I get?" I asked him. I was hoping maybe he'd say $75 a month.

"How about $150 a month?" he said.

I almost jumped out of my chair. "I can't think of anything I'd like better!"

"OK," he said, "here's a contract. You'll report next spring."

See, $150 a month was an awful lot of money to me. It meant $900 a year—we only got paid for the season, which was about six months—and at the time I was making something like $150 a year. Yeah, that's right, $150 a year.

Al Bridwell
in 1908

When I was thirteen years old I quit school and went to work in a shoe factory. Ten hours a day, six days a week, and I got $1.25 a week. I took that envelope home to my mother. By 1902, when I was eighteen, I was up to $3 a week. That's about $150 a year. Even that looked big to me, because the family was having kind of a hard time getting along. That's why I went to work in the first place. I started off for school one morning and wound up over at the shoe factory. So $150 *a month* to play baseball looked like a fortune to me.

I did pretty well with Columbus, but nothing remarkable. One day, about two years later, Garry Herrmann came up from Cincinnati to watch us play. He was the owner of the Cincinnati Reds and was interested in buying our third baseman, Bill Friel. As it happened, that day Bill didn't have a very good day, but I had a crackerjack of one. So instead of buying him, he bought me. And that's how I got to the Big Leagues.

You see, the way it was then it was pretty much of an accident whether you got into professional ball at all, and if you did, there was still a lot of luck involved in getting up to the Big Leagues. Now they have scouts who watch a man for weeks to see what he can really do, but then there were no scouts or anything like that. It was just my good luck that the one day Bobby Quinn saw me I had a good day, and the same for when Garry Herrmann saw me. They both made snap judgments and took a chance on me.

So I joined the Cincinnati Reds in the spring of 1905, right after my twenty-first birthday. I signed for $2,100, with the understanding that if I made good it would be $2,400 the next year. Joe Kelley was the manager of the Reds at that time, the old Baltimore Oriole outfielder and first baseman. Miller Huggins was the second baseman and Harry Steinfeldt the third baseman. I was the utility man that season, both infield and outfield.

The veterans didn't exactly fall all over themselves helping me in spring training. After I'd made the club, though, after the season started, they started to get more friendly. Of course, every once in a while you had to kind of assert yourself a little and let them know you had some guts. They'd try to keep you away from the plate during your turn in batting practice, and sometimes you had to pick up a bat and drive them away. But once the season started it was mostly one big happy family.

A funny thing happened near the end of that season. We had about a month left to play when Harry Steinfeldt—who was a good friend—came over to me one day and said, "Kid, you're going to be the regular third baseman pretty soon, maybe starting today."

"What do you mean?" I asked him. I knew that some other club in the league was after him, and although I didn't know which one, I thought it was one of the contenders. The Reds were a second-division ball club at that time.

"Wait and see," he says, "something might happen. You never can tell in this game."

Well, about the second or third inning that day a foul ball went up off third base, near the railing, and Steiney ran over to catch it. As he did, he tumbled over the railing and hurt himself and had to leave the game. So they sent me out to play third in his place, and I finished the season at that position.

That winter Steiney was traded to the Chicago Cubs for Hans Lobert, and he became the third baseman in the famous Tinker-Evers-Chance infield. So you can figure what you want to out of that.

By the way, you know they say that Joe Tinker at shortstop and Johnny Evers at second base played alongside each other for years and never spoke to each other off the field. Didn't get along. They say the same was true of Ty Cobb and Sam Crawford at Detroit. I don't know if it's so, but that's what they say.

That winter Garry Herrmann sent me another $2,100 contract. Same as I'd gotten in 1905. I sent it back, reminding him that I'd understood it would be for $2,400 if I made good, which it seemed to me I had. We wrote back and forth, and finally I got mad and wrote him that I absolutely would not sign for $2,100 again. I'd rather go back to semipro ball. So it wound up that they traded me to the Boston Braves for Jim Delahanty, and in the spring of 1906 I reported to the Boston Braves instead of the Cincinnati Reds. They weren't called the Braves then. I think they were called the Nationals at that time.

I was the regular shortstop for Boston for the next two years. Fred Tenney was the manager and also played first base. He'd been Boston's regular first baseman since about 1895 and was very popular there. I think he came from somewhere in Massachusetts, too. He'd graduated from Brown University. Very nice guy. Later Fred Tenney also figured in an indirect way in the Merkle incident. I'll get to that in a minute.

Anyway, we didn't have a very good team in Boston when I was there. It was tough, playing shortstop there, too. They had four spitball

"I was the regular shortstop for Boston for the next two years"
—Al Bridwell in 1906

pitchers on that club, and I had a devil of a time throwing the ball on a straight line from short to first base. The darn thing was always loaded! So I was tickled pink when they traded both me and Fred to the Giants at the start of the 1908 season. That's right, they traded their manager away. I think Tenney was glad to leave, too, because Boston wasn't going anywhere and we knew we'd be right up there with the Giants.

And, of course, we were both excited about playing for McGraw. At least I was, having heard so much about him. And it proved out, too. He was a wonderful man, a real fighter, that's what he was. He'd argue with the umpires, the opposing players, the people in the stands. Anybody wanted to argue, he was ready. I got along with him fine. He only suspended me once, for two weeks. It was on account of I socked him.

Well, I didn't really sock him. It was more of a push. I pushed him, sort of, and he fell down the dugout steps. Well, maybe it was a sock at that. I'm not sure now. After all, it took place about 60 years ago.

What happened was that I missed a sign. It wasn't my fault, it really wasn't. When I got back to the dugout he called me a lot of names and so I hit him. He suspended me for two weeks without pay, but once it was over he forgot about it completely. Never mentioned it again. He was a fighter, but he was also the kindest, best-hearted fellow you ever saw. I liked him and I liked playing for him.

The reason McGraw was a great manager—and he was the greatest —was because he knew how to handle men. Some players he rode, and others he didn't. He got the most out of each man. It wasn't so much knowing baseball. All of them know that. One manager knows about as much about the fundamentals of baseball as another. What makes the difference is knowing each player and how to handle him. And at that sort of thing nobody came anywhere close to McGraw.

I played shortstop four years with the Giants, then back to the Boston Braves for a couple of years, and over to the Cubs in 1913. I replaced Joe Tinker at shortstop there. He went to Cincinnati, where he became the manager. It wasn't easy following Tinker, as you can imagine. Joe had been the Cubs' shortstop since 1902. By the way, Jimmy Archer was still catching for the Cubs in 1913, when I was there. Best arm of any catcher I ever saw. He'd zip it down there to second like a flash. Perfect accuracy, and under a six-foot bar all the way down.

Then I wound up my Big League career with two years in the Federal League. I jumped from the Cubs to the St. Louis club in the Federal League in 1914, when Three-Fingered Brown—who was their manager —offered me $6,500 to sign with him. I'd been making $4,000 with the Cubs, and a 50 per cent raise looked too good to turn down.

Three-Fingered Brown, gee, he was one of the wonders of baseball. What a tremendous pitcher he was. Just as good as Matty, in my book. Better, maybe. The two of them used to hook up all the time, and I think over the years Brown beat Matty way over half the time. I saw Cy Young, too. I guess he must have been the best of all, to win 511 Big League games. But I only saw him near the end of his career, because he had been in the American League. I was playing shortstop behind him, though, when he won his 511th game. We were both with the Boston Braves then—I guess it must have been late in the 1911 season. Both of us went to the Braves near the end of that season, him from Cleveland and me from the Giants. Cy was at least forty-five by then. After that he retired.

You know, as I look back at it all, I've got regrets about certain things since I left baseball. If I'd have done this, or that, I'd be better off. But in baseball—I don't know—I don't really think I'd change a thing. Not a thing. It was fun all the way through. A privilege, that's what it was, a privilege, to have been there.

But let me get back to the Merkle "boner." I guess there's no doubt it's still the most famous play in the history of baseball. For Fred's sake, I wish it had never happened, it caused him so much grief. Let me amend what I said a minute ago: there's *one* thing that happened in baseball I *would* change if I could do it all over again. I wish I'd never gotten that hit that set off the whole Merkle incident. I wish I'd struck out instead. If I'd have done that, then it would have spared Fred a lot of unfair humiliation. Yes, I wish I'd struck out. It would have been better all around.

It all happened on Wednesday, September 23, 1908. Tough pennant race between the Cubs and the Giants, last of the ninth inning, score tied 1–1. It was getting dark and it looked as though the game would be called on account of darkness as soon as we—the Giants, that is—finished our turn at bat in the last half of the ninth.

Then, with two outs and Moose McCormick on first base, Fred Merkle slammed a long single just fair down the right field foul line. Actually, Fred shouldn't even have been playing. He was a substitute first baseman and was only in there because Fred Tenney was hurt. So all of a sudden it's my turn at bat, with the score tied, two outs, and Merkle on first and McCormick on third. It was all up to me.

I stepped in the batter's box—I was a left-handed hitter—and as I was getting set I saw Merkle edging pretty far off first base, almost as though he was going to try to steal. That didn't make any sense, so I stepped out of the box and looked at him and he went back and stood on the bag.

I often think that maybe if I hadn't done that everything would have turned out all right.

Anyway, he went back to first and I stepped back into the box. Jack Pfiester was pitching for the Cubs, a left-hander. We didn't platoon in those days. The fact that Pfiester was a lefty and I was too didn't bother anybody. I was supposed to be able to hit left-handed pitching just as well as right-handed. Well, the first pitch came in to me—a fast ball, waist high, right over the center of the plate—and I promptly drilled a line drive past Johnny Evers and out into right center field. Bob Emslie was umpiring on the bases and he fell on his can to avoid being hit by the ball. I really socked that one on the nose. A clean single.

Three-Fingered Brown:
"Gee, he was one of the
wonders of baseball"

The Polo Grounds after the game: "By this time thousands of people were milling

around the field"

Naturally, I ran to first base and McCormick raced home. McCormick could have walked in, the ball went so far into center field. But Merkle didn't go all the way to second base. Instead, he went halfway down and then cut off and started running for the clubhouse, which was out in right center. Well, all the people were jumping over the railings and running onto the field and yelling, everybody thinking the game was over; so it was a natural reaction, him heading for the clubhouse to get away from the crowd.

Meanwhile, Johnny Evers was standing on second base yelling for Artie Hofman, the Chicago center fielder, to throw him the ball so that he could tag second base. Just like on an ordinary double play, if Evers touched second while in possession of the ball before Merkle got there, Merkle would be out, a force out. And if Merkle was out at second, that would make the third out of the inning, and McCormick's run wouldn't count.

I slowed down after I passed first and was just trotting out to the clubhouse, when all of a sudden somebody gives me a boot in the rear end. It's Moose McCormick. After crossing home plate he noticed all the excitement and figured it was because *I* had failed to touch *first* base.

"What's the matter?" he says. "Don't you know where first base is?"

Well, I sort of got confused myself. I thought I'd touched first, but maybe I hadn't. So we forced our way back through the crowd—by this time thousands of people were milling around the field—and I touched first base again. Then we started working our way in toward home plate, and soon we saw Frank Chance arguing with Hank O'Day, who was umpiring behind the plate and was the umpire in charge. But we didn't really find out what it was all about until we got into the clubhouse and somebody told us. Johnny Evers claimed he had gotten the ball and touched second base, so that Merkle was out. Actually, I never did see any ball get to Evers at second base.

Anyway, you know what happened. Merkle was called out for failing to touch second, the game was ruled to have ended in a 1–1 tie, and eventually we lost the pennant in a play-off game with the Cubs. Three-Fingered Brown beat Matty in the play-off, 4–2.

I think that under the circumstances any ballplayer on any ball club would have done the same thing Merkle did. They did it all the time in those days. In fact, just a few weeks before, in Pittsburgh, the *exact* same thing had happened against the Cubs, with Hank O'Day umpiring, and that time O'Day had refused to allow Johnny Evers' claim that the man should be called out. In any case, I often think if I hadn't held Merkle close to first he'd probably have been all the way down to second before the crowd started onto the field. As it was, being held close to the bag, the crowd rushing on him before he'd made it to second, seeing the winning run already cross the plate, why I think anyone would have done the same thing that Fred Merkle did.

Anyway, he's gone now. The newspapers crucified him. The fans ragged him unmercifully all the rest of his life. But now his worries are over. Only thing I lost out of it was a base hit. Didn't get credit for that base hit. They decided it was a force out at second, instead of a single. Well, what can you do? Those things happen.

Harry Hooper in 1909

1⓪ *Harry Hooper*

For years Harry Hooper has been considered one of the greatest outfielders that ever lived. He is also one of the most dangerous hitters in a pinch that the game has ever known. If I were an American League manager I don't know where I could find a better outfield than Tris Speaker, Ty Cobb, and Harry Hooper. —JOHN J. McGRAW, *My Thirty Years in Baseball*

SURE, I still follow baseball. *Of course* I do. What a question to ask! Those darn Giants . . . sometimes I can't sleep for worrying over them. It didn't used to be so bad. But now that they're only about 75 miles away and I can hear all the games the situation has gotten impossible.

That Willie Mays, he's one of the greatest center fielders who ever lived. You can go back as far as you want and name all the great ones— Tris Speaker, Eddie Roush, Max Carey, Earle Combs, Joe DiMaggio. I don't care *who* you name, Mays is just as good, maybe better. He's a throwback to the old days. A guy who can do everything, and plays like he loves it. And that Koufax. You name a better left-hander in the history of baseball and I'll eat my hat.

I played my first professional baseball right here, in the California State League, in 1907. Actually, I never had any intention of taking up baseball as a career. I expected to be an engineer. Went to St. Mary's College and got my degree in Civil Engineering in 1907. After graduation, I played with the Sacramento club, mainly because they promised to get me a surveying job.

And they did. When I wasn't playing ball I worked as a surveyor for the Western Pacific Railroad. I got $85 a month for playing ball, and $75 a month as a surveyor. I guess you might say that was my bonus, a surveying job.

Actually, my "bonus" was $12.50. Before I graduated I played a few games in that same league, the California State League, with Alameda. That was right near school. This fellow who owned the Alameda club —Mr. McMinnamen—asked me if I'd play on the team the last few months of my senior year, and I agreed, with the understanding that he'd give me my release as soon as I got out of college.

Well, just about the time college was letting out we played a game at Sacramento, and I did pretty well. Charlie Graham was managing Sacramento at the time and he went to Mr. McMinnamen and wanted to buy me, not knowing, of course, that I was due to get my release any day.

So Mr. McMinnamen came to me and said, "Look, I've got a chance to sell you to Sacramento. If you don't say anything about this agreement we have to release you, I'll give you half of whatever we can get."

"OK," I said, "but you better warn them that I'm going to stop playing as soon as I get the right kind of an engineering job. I'll probably quit at the end of the summer."

"All right," he said, "I'll do that. But don't you mention anything about your release."

Later, Charlie Graham told me how the conversation went. First of all, the Alameda owner did tell him about my being an engineer.

"OK," Charlie said, "I understand that. I think we can get him an engineering job he can work at and play ball both. How much do you want for him?"

"Oh, about $200."

"How about $10," Charlie countered.

"Make it $50."

"I'll make it $20."

And they settled on $25. I was sold for $25 lousy dollars. Talk about deflating a guy's ego! So my "bonus" was half of the sale price, namely $12.50.

Later, Charlie told me he smelled a rat the minute the guy asked for $200 when he should have asked for $500. "So I went as low as I could," he said, "just to test the situation out a little more, and it worked."

I had two pretty good years with Sacramento, surveying all the while, when one day near the end of the 1908 season Charlie Graham came to me in the hotel lobby.

"Well," he says, "how would you like to take a look at the Big Indian?"

"Huh?" I didn't know what he was talking about.

"The Big Indian! Boston! How would you like to play with the Boston Red Sox?" he says. "John I. Taylor, the owner of the Red Sox, is coming to town next week and I think he's interested in you."

"Well, I don't know," I said. "I'm not a ballplayer. I'm an engineer.

I'm doing real well at the Western Pacific Railroad and I like my job."

You see, *he* figured I was a ballplayer who did "this other stuff" on the side. But *I* figured I was an engineer who played ball on the side.

"Why not give it a whirl?" he said. "What have you got to lose? You're only twenty-one, and even if you played ball another two years you could still take up 'this other stuff' at the age of twenty-three."

"Well, it would be a nice trip, Boston and all. Get to see some of the country," I thought. "OK, I'll do it. I'll talk to the guy. How much salary do you think I ought to ask for?"

"How much do you think you should get?"

"I have no idea," I said. "Would $2,500 be about right?"

"I think it would," Charlie said. "But that means you should ask for $3,000. Then maybe he'll give you the $2,500."

The California State League, see, was an outlaw league, not in organized baseball. So the Red Sox couldn't just buy my contract. They had to negotiate with me as though I was a free agent. (That didn't hold for the deal where I was sold by Alameda to Sacramento, because they respected each other's contracts within the league. As an outlaw league, they didn't steal players from each other, just from everybody else!)

So one warm August day in 1908 I met Mr. John I. Taylor, owner of the Boston Red Sox, at the corner of 8th and J Streets in Sacramento. We went into a bar and had a glass of beer.

"I hear you're an engineer," he says.

"Yes, I am," I said.

"Well, that's very interesting," he says. "It so happens that we are thinking of building a new ball park in the not too distant future, and we may be looking for someone just like you. Your experience with the Western Pacific will no doubt prove invaluable. By the way, I also hear you are a baseball player."

"Yes, I am," I said.

"I was just wondering," he said, "given your qualifications in both lines of endeavor, how would you like to migrate to Boston."

"I wouldn't mind," I said.

"Well, we'd like to have you," he said. "At the moment, however, we are not in immediate need of engineering assistance. Considering that for the time being at least we would only require your services as a ballplayer, I was also wondering how much money you might want."

"How about $3,000?"

"I'll tell you," he said, "fact is, I was thinking of something in the neighborhood of $2,500. What do you say we compromise at $2,800."

"That seems very equitable to me," I said.

So I finished out the season with Sacramento, said good-bye to Charlie Graham—and told him that from then on he was my unofficial business advisor—resigned my job with the Western Pacific, and started on what I figured would be just a couple of years of playing baseball. And that was the last job I ever had that was connected with engineering.

Fenway Park was built in Boston, and Shibe Park in Philadelphia, and Yankee Stadium in New York, and all the while I was nowhere near a drafting board. I was out there in right field the whole time, drawing a line on a baseball instead of a chart. And, in case you're wondering, I have no regrets.

I joined the Red Sox for spring training in 1909, at Hot Springs, Arkansas. After a week or so I started to get a pretty good idea of my competition. Tris Speaker was there—he'd come up at the end of the previous season—and it looked like he had a stranglehold on the center-field job. There were three other outfielders there also, besides myself, and it looked to me like I belonged on that team: I thought I was as good or better than any of them. But everybody didn't seem to see things my way, because after about three weeks they decided who would be the regulars, and I wasn't among them.

We'd get the Boston papers and I read that ". . . this Hooper appears to be a good prospect, but he needs several years seasoning in the minors before he'll be ready." That made my blood boil. I *knew* I was good enough to make that team.

However, once they'd picked the regulars, us youngsters didn't get much chance to show what we could do. We never really got a proper opportunity during all of spring training. The old-timers kind of had the thing by the horns, you know. Wouldn't even let us have batting practice. A few of us wound up taking our bats into the outfield and having our own batting practice. Spring *training*. Training for what?

Well, we opened up in Philadelphia on April 12, 1909. Played three games there, in brand-new Shibe Park, and I sat on the bench the whole series. I didn't even have a road uniform, and I heard rumors that they were getting ready to ship me to the minors, to St. Paul in the American Association. I was getting hot under the collar, because I knew if they gave me a chance I could do the job.

From Philadelphia we went to Washington. I climbed up to the top

Tris Speaker takes batting practice: "It looked like he had a stranglehold on the center-field job"

of the Washington Monument the first morning there (had to get *some* exercise), and then went out to the ball park, expecting to sit on the bench through another game. But I'd hardly gotten into the clubhouse before the manager—Fred Lake—comes over to me. "Here's a uniform," he says. "You're going to play today."

A lucky combination of circumstances. One of the outfielders was hurt, and another had to go in and play first base because the first baseman was sick. They *had* to play me because they didn't have anybody else. Well, if I'd been ballyhooed as a wonder or something, I'd probably have been a little shaky. But the way it was, nobody expected anything of me, and I went out there determined to show them.

The first time it was my turn at bat we had a chance to score a run.

Man on second and two out. On the bench I could hear everyone saying, "Who's up? Who's up?"

And then, "Oh, it's Hooper—well, too bad."

But I went up there and drove in that run. I got another hit that day, and would have had a third if the pitcher hadn't stabbed a liner headed right for his forehead. One of those instinctive grabs, you know. And in the field I handled myself OK. In other words, everything went just fine. Before the day was over, John I. Taylor was going around shaking everyone's hand, saying, "That's the boy I signed up in California."

And that's how come I never went to St. Paul. I had a good start and a little bit of luck when I needed it. You have to have a little luck, you know. That year and the next we started to form the nucleus of what was to become a great, great Red Sox ball club. We won the American League pennant in 1912, '15, '16, and '18, and in between we finished second twice. From 1912 to 1918 we won four pennants *and* four World Series.

They never did beat us in a World Series. Never. We played four different National League teams in four different World Series and only one of them even came close. That was the Giants, in 1912. We beat them four games to three. We beat Grover Cleveland Alexander and the Phillies four games to one in 1915, the Dodgers four games to one in 1916, and the Cubs four to two in 1918. The best team in all of baseball for close to a decade!

There really were *two* teams, the 1912 team and the 1915 one. The outfield was the same on both—Tris Speaker, Duffy Lewis, and myself— I think acknowledged by most as easily the greatest defensive outfield ever. Larry Gardner was at third base on both teams, and Bill Carrigan and Forrest Cady caught that whole time. But at first base it was first Jake Stahl and then Doc Hoblitzel; at second Steve Yerkes was eventually replaced by Jack Barry; and at short it was first Heinie Wagner and then Everett Scott. And, of course, the whole pitching staff turned over —from Smoky Joe Wood, Hugh Bedient, Charlie Hall, and Buck O'Brien in 1912, it became Ernie Shore, Dutch Leonard, Carl Mays, George Foster, Joe Bush, Sam Jones, and Babe Ruth in 1915 or so.

Babe Ruth joined us in the middle of 1914, a nineteen-year-old kid. He was a left-handed pitcher then, and a good one. He had never been any-where, didn't know anything about manners or how to behave among people—just a big overgrown green pea. You probably remember him with that big belly he got later on. But that wasn't there in 1914. George was six foot two and weighed 198 pounds, all of it muscle. He had a slim waist, huge biceps, no self-discipline, and not much education—not so very different from a lot of other nineteen-year-old would-be ballplayers. Except for two things: he could eat more than anyone else, and he could hit a baseball further.

Lord, he ate too much. He'd stop along the road when we were traveling and order half a dozen hot dogs and as many bottles of soda pop, stuff them in, one after the other, give a few big belches, and then roar, "OK, boys, let's go." That would hold Babe for a couple of hours, and then he'd be at it again. A nineteen-year-old youngster, mind you!

He was such a rube that he got more than his share of teasing, some of it not too pleasant. "The Big Baboon" some of them used to call him behind his back, and then a few got up enough nerve to ridicule him to his face. This started to get under his skin, and when they didn't let up he finally challenged the whole ball club. Nobody was so dumb as to take him up on it, so that put an end to that.

You know, I saw it all happen, from beginning to end. But sometimes I still can't believe what I saw: this nineteen-year-old kid, crude, poorly educated, only lightly brushed by the social veneer we call civilization, gradually transformed into the idol of American youth and the symbol of baseball the world over—a man loved by more people and with an intensity of feeling that perhaps has never been equaled before or since. I saw a man transformed from a human being into something pretty close to a god. If somebody had predicted that back on the Boston Red Sox in 1914, he would have been thrown into a lunatic asylum.

I still remember when the Babe was switched from pitching to become an outfielder. I finally convinced Ed Barrow to play him out there to get his bat in the lineup every day. That was in 1919, and I was the team captain by then. Barrow technically was the manager, but I ran the team on the field, and I finally talked Ed into converting Ruth from a pitcher into an outfielder. Well, Ruth might have been a natural as a pitcher and as a hitter, but he sure wasn't a born outfielder.

I was playing center field myself, so I put the Babe in right field. On the other side of me was a fellow named Braggo Roth, another wild man. Sakes alive, I'd be playing out there in the middle between those two fellows, and I began to fear for my life. Both of them were galloping around that outfield without regard for life or limb, hollering all

Babe Ruth, a left-handed pitcher ("and a good one"), in 1915

the time, running like maniacs after every ball! A week of that was enough for me. I shifted the Babe to center and I moved to right, so I could keep clear of those two.

Sheer self-preservation on my part, pure and simple. I'm still amazed that playing side by side those two never plowed into each other with the impact of two runaway freight trains. If they had, the crash would have shaken the Boston Commons.

Of all the pennants and World Series we won, I guess 1912 was the most exciting. That was the first year the Lewis-Speaker-Hooper outfield really became famous, that was the year Smoky Joe Wood won 16 straight games, the year Snodgrass muffed that fly ball in the last game of the Series—well, all in all, so many things happened that season that it's hard to find another that can compare with it.

I think the thing I remember best about 1912, though, is the pitching of Smoky Joe Wood. Was he ever something! I've seen a lot of great pitching in my lifetime, but never anything to compare with him in 1912. In 1917, for instance, I was in right field for the Red Sox when Ernie Shore pitched his perfect game (against the Senators, I think it was). And in 1922 I was in right field for the White Sox when Charlie Robertson pitched *his* perfect game (against Detroit). I guess there haven't been more than about half a dozen *perfect* games pitched in the history of baseball, and I was the right fielder in two of them. On two different teams, too.

So you might say I've seen some pretty good pitching. But I've never seen anything like Smoky Joe Wood in 1912. He won 34 games that year, 10 of them shutouts, and 16 of those wins were in a row. It so happened that that was the same year Walter Johnson *also* won 16 in a row. (That's *still* the record in the American League, by the way.) And the fact that both of those fellows were so unbeatable that year gave rise to one of the greatest games in the history of baseball.

You see, Walter Johnson set his record first. Walter finally lost a game in August, ending his streak at 16. But Walter hardly had time to accept congratulations, before up loomed Joe Wood, who looked as though he'd take the record right away from Walter before that very season had come to an end.

When Walter's streak ended at 16 in August, Joe Wood had won about 9 or 10 in a row. But then Joe kept adding to it . . . 11 straight . . . 12 straight . . . 13 straight. In early September we were scheduled to play Washington, and the public started to clamor for Walter Johnson himself to be allowed to pitch for Washington when Joe Wood went for us.

"Let Walter defend his record!" That was the cry.

Well, the owners were no fools. So when the Senators came to Boston for this series it was arranged that Walter Johnson and Joe Wood would oppose each other in one of the games. The crowd that jammed Fenway Park that day poured out onto the field, and the team benches were moved out along the foul lines so the fans could be packed in behind them. People were also standing all around on the outfield grass, held back by ropes.

By then Joe had won 13 straight, and Walter really *was* defending

Smoky Joe Wood in 1912:
"Was he ever something!"

A 1912 advertisement

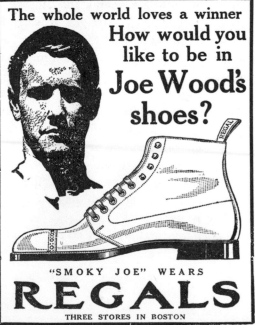

The whole world loves a winner
How would you
like to be in
Joe Wood's
shoes?

"SMOKY JOE" WEARS
REGALS
THREE STORES IN BOSTON

his new record. Well, to make a long story short, Joe Wood beat Walter Johnson that day, and the score was exactly what you'd expect—one to nothing. In the sixth inning Tris Speaker hit one into the crowd standing in left field for a ground-rule double, he scored on a double by Duffy Lewis, and that was the whole story. Not another runner crossed home plate all day. That was probably the most exciting game I ever played in or saw.

After that, Joe won two more games to tie Johnson's record at 16, and then he lost the next time out on an error that let a couple of unearned runs score in the eight or ninth inning. So now they both hold the record. Funny thing, that's also the same year Marquard won 19 straight in the National League.

The tension on Joe was just terrific all that season. First the 16 straight, and then the World Series. I still remember talking to him before one of the Series games and suddenly realizing that he couldn't speak. Couldn't say a word. The strain had started to get too much for him. Well, what can you expect? I think he was only about twenty-two when all this was happening. Mighty young to be under such pressure for so many months.

But he still won three games in that 1912 World Series. The last inning of the last game of that Series was quite a doozy. That's one they'll never forget. The Giants took a 2–1 lead in the top of the tenth, and the first man up for us in the bottom of the tenth was Clyde Engle, pinch-hitting for Joe Wood. He hit the fly ball that Fred Snodgrass dropped. The famous Snodgrass muff. It could happen to anybody.

I was up next and I tried to bunt, but I fouled it off. On the next pitch I hit a line drive into left center that looked like a sure triple. Ninety-nine times out of a hundred no outfielder could possibly have come close to that ball. But in some way, I don't know how, Snodgrass ran like the wind, and dang if he didn't catch it. I think he *outran* the ball. Robbed me of a sure triple.

I saw Snodgrass a couple of years ago at a function in Los Angeles, and I reminded him of that catch.

"Well, thank you," he said, "nobody ever mentions that catch to me. All they talk about is the muff."

I don't know about anybody else. But *I* remember that catch all right. I'm the one guy who'll never forget it.

After that, Steve Yerkes got a base on balls, and that brought up Tris Speaker. We're still behind, 2–1, and there's one out. Well, Spoke hit a little pop foul over near first base, and old Chief Meyers took off after it. He didn't have a chance, but Matty kept calling for him to take it. If he'd called for Merkle, it would have been an easy out. Or Matty could have taken it himself. But he kept hollering for the Chief to take

Hooper slides in to third. Is he safe or out? The Philadelphia third baseman is Home Run Baker.

it, and poor Chief—he never was too fast to begin with—he lumbered down that line after it as fast as his big legs would carry him, stuck out his big catcher's mitt—and just missed it.

Spoke went back to the batter's box and yelled to Mathewson, "Well, you just called for the wrong man. It's gonna cost you this ball game."

And on the next pitch he hit a clean single that tied the game, and a couple of minutes later Larry Gardner drove in Yerkes with the run that won it.

After that wonderful season, Joe Wood never pitched successfully again. He hurt his arm and never was able to really throw that hummer any more, the way he did in 1912. Joe kept trying to come back as a pitcher, but never could do it. He had a lot of guts, though. He couldn't pitch any more, so he turned himself into an outfielder and became a good one. He could always hit. He played with Cleveland in the 1920 World Series as an outfielder. I think he's the only man besides Babe

Ruth who was in one World Series as a pitcher and another as an outfielder.

Harry Frazee became the owner of the Red Sox in 1917, and before long he sold off all our best players and ruined the team. Sold them all

And now he slides home. Is he safe or out this time?

to the Yankees—Ernie Shore, Duffy Lewis, Dutch Leonard, Carl Mays, Babe Ruth. Then Wally Schang and Herb Pennock and Joe Dugan and Sam Jones. I was disgusted. The Yankee dynasty of the twenties was three-quarters the Red Sox of a few years before. All Frazee wanted was the money. He was short of cash and he sold the whole team down the river to keep his dirty nose above water. What a way to end a wonderful ball club!

I got sick to my stomach at the whole business. After the 1920 season I held out for $15,000, and Frazee did me a favor by selling me to the Chicago White Sox. I was glad to get away from that graveyard.

At Chicago they gave me a blank three-year contract and told me to fill in the figure.

"Well," I thought, "I'll be doing business with Mr. Comiskey for some years, and I don't want to start off on the wrong foot."

So instead of filling in $15,000—which was what I'd been holding out for with the Red Sox—I put down $13,250. Well, I had five darn-good years with the White Sox, best hitting years I ever had. Hit .328 one year, and .327 another. But in 1926 I got a contract in the mail calling for $7,000. That's right—$7,000!

So I wrote to Comiskey and reminded him that when I'd signed with him in 1921 I'd been more than reasonable in filling in a blank contract. I said I thought perhaps that should sort of be taken into account now. Ha! He wrote back that he never heard of anyone getting a guarantee of anything in this business, and sent me my release along with the letter. And they really needed me that year; they had nobody to play right field.

Well, that was early in 1926, and I was thirty-eight years old. So I went into the real-estate business for a while, coached baseball at Princeton for a couple of years, and then during the depression I took a fill-in job here at Capitola as postmaster—and didn't leave it until 25 years later. Supposed to be a *temporary* job.

I enjoyed the couple of years I coached at Princeton very much. Still go back there every once in a while. Beautiful spot, Princeton. Speaking about that, today they make such a big deal about all the college men in baseball, and about how baseball today has such a "better class" of people in it than the "rowdies" of the old days. But that's not true at all. With respect to college men, let me give you an idea of what it was *really* like.

I joined the Boston Red Sox in 1909, and when I got there Bill Carrigan was the regular catcher. He'd gone to Holy Cross. At first base was Jake Stahl, from the University of Illinois, and at third was Larry Gardner, from the University of Vermont. In the outfield, I had gone to St. Mary's, and so had Duffy Lewis. On the pitching staff was Marty McHale of the University of Maine (another civil engineering graduate), Chris Mahoney from Fordham, and Ray Collins from Vermont.

That was just the Red Sox. In general, I'd say that back in my day maybe as many as about one out of every five or six Big Leaguers had gone to college. I don't know how many of them graduated, but that isn't the point. The point is that they came from colleges into professional baseball.

Of course, it's ridiculous to think that only college men are gentlemen, or are intelligent. That isn't even worth discussing. But it should certainly be clear that the impression that we were an uneducated bunch of "rowdies" is a lot of nonsense.

Most people know that Mathewson went to Bucknell, but they don't realize that Frank Chance went to Washington University, Hal Chase to Santa Clara, Buck Herzog to the University of Maryland, Orvie Overall to the University of California, Eddie Plank to Gettysburg College, Chief Bender to Dickinson College, Art Devlin to Georgetown, and so on.

And there were more. Ginger Beaumont went to Beloit College, Andy Coakley and Jack Barry to Holy Cross, Eddie Collins to Columbia, Eddie Grant to Harvard, Fred Tenney to Brown, Bob Bescher and Ed Reulbach to Notre Dame, Jack Coombs to Colby, Harry Davis to Girard College, Chief Meyers to Dartmouth, Davy Jones to Dixon College, et cetera, et cetera.

Why, Miller Huggins and Hugh Jennings were both lawyers—Huggins was a graduate of Cincinnati Law School and Jennings went to Cornell. Both of them went to law school *after* they were in the major leagues. Even John J. McGraw went to St. Bonaventure for a while, also after he was in the majors. And do you realize that every one of these fellows I've named was in the majors in 1910 or earlier, and most of them were there *before 1905.*

If you take into account the proportion of the total population that went to college back in those days, I think it's pretty clear that we had *more* than our share of college men in baseball. And it's also pretty clear that the usual picture you get of the old-time ballplayer as an illiterate rowdy contains an awful lot more fiction than it does fact.

11 _Joe Wood_

Some of the most exciting early games I saw were in 1912, when the Boston Red Sox came to town. They won the pennant that year, and they always beat the White Sox when I went to the games. Smoky Joe Wood, who belongs in the Hall of Fame, won 34 and lost 5 that year. In memory it seems as though he hurled all those games against Chicago. With the shadows pushing over the ball park he would stand out there on the pitching mound in his red-trimmed gray road uniform, hitch up his pants, and throw. To this day, I have a recollection of a strange sensation as if my head had emptied, when he fired the ball in the shadowy park. The White Sox couldn't touch him.

Perhaps Walter Johnson was faster than Wood. Perhaps Grove and Feller were. But Wood threw smoke, and in 1912 if there was a better pitcher than Wood in baseball, even Walter Johnson or Christy Mathewson, the difference was merely academic. No pitcher ever depressed a little boy in the stands more than Joe Wood did me. Why did the Boston manager, Jake Stahl, always have to pitch him against my White Sox?

—JAMES T. FARRELL, _My Baseball Diary_

"Can I throw harder than Joe Wood? Listen, my friend, there's no man alive can throw harder than Smoky Joe Wood."

—WALTER JOHNSON, Interview in 1912

YOU KNOW, I often look back on it now . . . the Wild West . . . Buffalo Bill . . . cattle rustlers . . . outlaws . . . sheriff's posses. I see these western pictures on television and sometimes it just hits me: I actually _lived_ through all that in real life. Sort of hard to believe, isn't it?

At the turn of the century we lived in this little town of Ouray in the southwestern part of Colorado, not far from places with names like Lizard Head Pass and Slumgullion Gulch. And every day I'd see these big stage coaches go by, drawn by six horses, two guards sitting up there with rifles, guarding the gold shipment coming down from the mines. Dad was a lawyer there—his law partner was later the attorney general of Colorado—and he was involved in some big cases for the Western Federation of Miners. During several of these cases they had to send in the state militia to guard him. Feelings ran high about unions in

Colorado back then. He was a great trial lawyer. Hardly ever lost a case in front of a jury.

Later we moved to Ness City, Kansas, about 60 miles north of Dodge City, and that was rough country too. Dad represented the Missouri Pacific and Santa Fe Railroads there. Even though he was a lawyer, my father never could really settle down. In 1897 he got the gold fever and went to the Klondike in the gold rush. Not as a lawyer—as a prospector! He returned with his legs frozen, Yukon diarrhea, and lots of great stories, but no gold. Later he took off on another prospecting trip, this time to Nevada and California, but he didn't do any better there than he had in the Yukon.

He had such a full life! A brilliant man. He spent his last years in this very house, the house where he was born, and when he died in 1944 he was only one month short of being ninety years old. I had a special generator put in here to give him electricity, then they started stringing electric lines through this part of the country and we had to carry two motors for the different voltages. But he'd never have anything to do with any of it. Always used kerosene lamps, the old icebox, the wood stove. Wouldn't even use a coal furnace. He'd cut his own firewood for his little stove. All those chores kept him going until he was almost ninety.

It was while we were living in Ness City that I first really started to play ball. That was in 1906, when I was only sixteen. I pitched for the town team—it was only amateur ball, you know, but that was the big thing in those days. We'd play all the surrounding Kansas towns, like High Point, Ransom, Ellis, Bazine, Wa Keeney, Scott City—nearby places like that. The ball game between two rival towns was a big event back then, with parades before the game and everything The smaller the town the more important their ball club was. Boy, if you beat a bigger town they'd practically hand you the key to the city. And if you lost a game by making an error in the ninth inning or something like that—well, the best thing to do was just pack your grip and hit the road, 'cause they'd never let you forget it.

Anyway, when I was only sixteen I was Ness City's pitcher even though I was the youngest on the team by a good two or three years. Had a terrific fast ball with a hop on it even then. And I also played the infield when I didn't pitch.

A funny thing happened in September of 1906 that I'm not too keen

The Ness City team in 1906. Their star pitcher is little Joey Wood, sixteen years of age, in the dark shirt on the bottom right.

Joe Wood in 1909

about talking about, but I guess it wouldn't be exactly right to act like it never happened. In a nutshell, that's when I started my professional career, and I might as well just take a deep breath and come right out and put the matter bluntly: the team I started with was the Bloomer Girls.

Yeah, you heard right, the Bloomer Girls.

One day in September this Bloomer Girls team came to Ness City. In those days there were several Bloomer Girls teams that barnstormed around the county, like the House of David did 20 or 30 years later. The girls were advertised on posters around Ness City for weeks before they arrived, you know, and they finally came to town and played us and we beat them.

Well, after the game the fellow who managed them asked me if I'd like to join and finish the tour with them. There were only three weeks left of the trip, and he offered me $20 if I'd play the infield with them those last three weeks.

"Are you kidding?" I said. I thought the guy must have been off his rocker.

"Listen," he said, "you know as well as I do that all those Bloomer Girls aren't really girls. That third baseman's real name is Bill Compton, not Dolly Madison. And that pitcher, Lady Waddell, sure isn't Rube's sister. If anything, he's his brother!"

"Well, I figured as much," I said. "But those guys are wearing wigs. If you think I'm going to put a wig on, you're crazy."

"No need to," he says. 'With your baby face you won't need one anyway."

So I asked Dad if I could go. He thought it was sort of unusual, but he didn't raise any objections. I guess it must have appealed to his sense of the absurd.

Fact is, there were four boys on the team: me, Lady Waddell, Dolly Madison, and one other, the catcher. The other five were girls. In case you're wondering how the situation was in the locker room, we didn't have clubhouses or locker rooms in those days. We dressed in our uniforms at the hotel and rode out to the ball park from there. I think everybody except maybe some of the farmer boys must have known some of us weren't actually girls, but the crowds turned out and had a lot of fun anyway. In case you're interested, by the way, the first team Rogers Hornsby ever played on was a Bloomer Girls team, too. So I'm not in such bad company.

It was the next year, 1907, that I *really* got started in organized ball, with Hutchinson in the Western Association. It all came about by accident. My brother Harley was going to the University of Kansas at the time, and he happened to tell a friend of his about me. This friend knew Belden Hill, who ran the Cedar Rapids club in the Three-I League, and as a result I was offered a contract with Cedar Rapids in January of 1907. Ninety dollars a month, that's what it called for. Before it came time to report to Cedar Rapids, however, Mr. Hill decided he didn't really need me after all, and he gave my contract to his friend Doc Andrews, who managed the Hutchinson club in the Western Association. He didn't sell me, he just *gave* me away.

So, in the spring of 1907 Dad and I got on the train for Hutchinson, Kansas. My father didn't have any objections to me playing baseball, but I was only seventeen years old and he wanted to make sure this was a proper environment. So he came to Hutchinson with me to make sure everything was all right. Hutchinson's only a little over a hundred miles from Ness City, so it wasn't too far from home.

I had a pretty good year there, won about 20 games and struck out over 200 men, and after the 1907 season was over I was sold to Kansas City in the American Association. I pitched there until the middle of the 1908 season, when John I. Taylor bought me for the Boston Red Sox, and I reported to the Red Sox that August.

Rube Marquard came up to the Giants from Indianapolis a month later. We'd pitched against each other many and many a time when he was with Indianapolis and I was with Kansas City, and we both went up to the Big Leagues at practically the same time. Neither one of us was nineteen years old yet: Rube turned nineteen on October 9 of that year, and me 16 days later. Four years later we faced each other again in the 1912 World Series, and then again eight years after that in the 1920 World Series. By then both of us had been around a long time, but neither one of us had reached our thirty-first birthday.

Of course, that Red Sox team I joined in 1908 turned out to become one of the best teams of all time. Tris Speaker had been on the club earlier that year but had been farmed out to Little Rock, where he hit .350 and led the league. He came back up a few weeks after I got there and we started to room together, and we roomed together for 15 years, first with the Red Sox and later with Cleveland. All the years I was in the American League my roommate was Tris Speaker.

There was nobody even close to that man as an outfielder, except maybe Harry Hooper. Speaker played a real shallow center field and he had that terrific instinct—at the crack of the bat he'd be off with his back to the infield, and then he'd turn and glance over his shoulder at the last minute and catch the ball so easy it looked like there was nothing to it, nothing at all. Nobody else was even in the same *league* with him.

Harry Hooper joined the Red Sox the next year. He was the closest I ever saw to Speaker as a fielder. It's a real shame Harry was on the same club as Spoke, having to play all those years in his shadow. Just like Gehrig with Ruth, or Crawford with Cobb.

Won 11 games for the Red Sox in 1909, 12 in 1910, and then 23 (including a no-hitter) in 1911 and 34 in 1912. That was my greatest season, 1912: 34 wins, 16 in a row, 3 more in the World Series, and, of course, beating Walter Johnson 1–0 in that big game at Fenway Park on September 6, 1912.

It was on a Friday. My regular pitching turn was scheduled to come on Saturday, and they moved it up a day so that Walter and I could face each other. Walter had already won 16 in a row and his streak had ended. I had won 13 in a row and they challenged our manager, Jake Stahl, to pitch me against Walter, so Walter could stop my streak himself. Jake agreed, and to match us against each other he moved me up in the rotation from Saturday to Friday.

The newspapers publicized us like prizefighters: giving statistics comparing our height, weight, biceps, triceps, arm span, and whatnot. The Champion, Walter Johnson, versus the Challenger, Joe Wood. That was the only game I ever remember in Fenway Park, or anywhere else for that matter, where the fans were sitting practically along the first-base and third-base lines. Instead of sitting back where the bench usually is, we were sitting on chairs right up against the foul lines, and the fans were right behind us. The overflow had been packed between the grandstand and the foul lines, as well as out in the outfield behind ropes. Fenway Park must have contained twice as many people as its seating capacity that day. I never saw so many people in one place in my life. In fact, the fans were put on the field an hour before the game started, and it was so crowded down there I hardly had room to warm up.

Well, I won, 1–0, but don't let that fool you. In my opinion the greatest pitcher who ever lived was Walter Johnson. If he'd ever had a good ball club behind him what records he would have set!

You know, I got an even bigger thrill out of winning three games in the World Series that fall. Especially the first game, when we beat

Joe Wood and friend: "All the years I was in the American League

my roommate was Tris Speaker"

Joe Wood getting ready for the big game against Walter Johnson. "The fans were put had room to warm up"

on the field an hour before the game started, and it was so crowded down there I hardly

the Giants, 4–3. In the last of the ninth they got Chief Meyers on second base and Buck Herzog on third with only one out, and I started to get a little nervous. Only one run ahead and two Giants in scoring position. A sacrifice fly would have tied it and a hit would have beaten us. But I struck out both Art Fletcher and Otis Crandall and we won it. They say that was the first time Crandall ever struck out at the Polo Grounds. I fanned him with a fast ball over the outside corner. I doubt if he ever saw it, even though he swung at it. The count was three and two and that pitch was one of the fastest balls I ever threw in my life.

That was the Series we won in the tenth inning of the last game. In that last game you always hear about Snodgrass dropping that fly ball,

The victory parade through Boston after the 1912 World Series. In the head car are Mayor Fitzgerald (standing in front, with hand on windshield) and Joe Wood (perched on the rear seat, with bow tie).

but you never hear about the incredible catch that Harry Hooper made
in the fifth inning that saved the game for us. That was the thing that
really took the heart out of the Giants. Larry Doyle hit a terrific drive
to deep right center, and Harry ran back at full speed and *dove* over
the railing and into the crowd and in some way, I'll never figure out
quite how, he caught the ball—I think with his bare hand. It was
almost impossible to believe even when you saw it.

Boy, if there was any one characteristic of Harry Hooper's, it was
that he was a clutch player. When the chips were down that guy played
like wildfire. In the 1915 World Series, you know, he got two home runs
in the last game of the Series, and the second one won the game and the

Series for us. Just to give you an idea of how Harry played in the clutch: those two homers in that one Series game matched the total number he'd hit all season long!

So there I was after the 1912 season—including the World Series I'd won 37 games and lost only 6, struck out 279 men in days when the boys didn't strike out much, and I'd beaten Walter Johnson and Christy Mathewson one after the other. And do you know how old I was? Well, I was twenty-two years old, that's all. The brightest future ahead of me that anybody could imagine in their wildest dreams.

And do you know something else? That was *it* That was it, right then and there. My arm went bad the next year and all my dreams came tumbling down around my ears like a damn house of cards. The next five years, seems like it was nothing but one long terrible nightmare.

I was fine that winter of 1912. After the Series we went back to Boston and got a reception that would make your head spin. I rode through the city in the same car with manager Jake Stahl and Mayor John F. Fitzgerald. That was Honey Fitz, President Kennedy's grandfather. He was the mayor of Boston then.

Honey Fitz had gone back and forth on the train with us between Boston and New York so as not to miss a single game of the World Series. The Red Sox had a contingent of fans called the Royal Rooters, and their theme song was something called *Tessie*. Old Honey Fitz used to sing *Tessie* louder than anybody. Then I went down to Texas with Tris Speaker for a few days, and after that he came home with me for a few days around here.

Then it happened. In the spring of 1913 I went to field a ground ball on wet grass and I slipped and fell on my thumb. Broke it. The thumb on my pitching hand. It was in a cast for two or three weeks. I don't know whether I tried to pitch too soon after that, or whether maybe something happened to my shoulder at the same time. But whatever it was, I never pitched again without a terrific amount of pain in my right shoulder. Never again.

I expected to have such a great year in 1913. Well, I did manage to win 11 games, with only 5 losses, and I struck out an average of 10 men a game. But it wasn't the same. The old zip was gone from that fast ball. It didn't hop any more, like it used to. The season after that I won 9 and lost 3, and in 1915 I won 14 and lost 5. But my arm was getting worse and worse. The pain was getting almost unbearable. After each game I pitched I'd have to lay off for a couple of weeks before

I could even lift my arm up. Still, in 1915 I led the league with an earned run average of 1.49.

In the winter of 1915 I was desperate. I must have gone to hundreds of doctors over the previous three years, and nobody seemed able to help me. Nowadays a shot of cortisone would probably do the job in a flash, but that was over 50 years ago, you know. Hell, they didn't even know about insulin back then, not to mention cortisone.

Finally, somebody told me about a chiropractor in New York, so every week that winter of 1915–16 I took the train in to New York and this fellow worked on my back and my arm. All very hush-hush—an unmarked office behind locked doors—because in those days it wasn't legal for a chiropractor to practice.

After each treatment this chiropractor wanted me to throw as long and as hard as I possibly could. He said it would hurt, but that's what he wanted me to do. So after he was through working on me I'd go up to Columbia University, where Andy Coakley was the baseball coach, and I'd go into a corner of the gym and throw a baseball as hard as I could. I'd do that until I just wasn't able to stand the pain anymore. And I do mean pain. After about an hour I couldn't lift my arm as high as my belt. Had to use my left hand to put my right into my coat pocket. And if I'd go to a movie in the evening I couldn't get my right arm up high enough to put it on the arm rest.

So in 1916 I didn't play at all. I retired. I stayed on the farm here, fed the chickens, and just thought and thought about the whole situation. Only twenty-six years old and all washed up. A has-been. I put up a trapeze in the attic and I'd hang on that for hours to stretch my arm out. Maybe that would help—who could say? But it didn't.

I stayed on the farm all through the 1916 season. That fall, though, I began to get restless. Well, that's putting it mildly. What it was, I was starting to gnaw on the woodwork I was getting so frustrated. Maybe I could come back. So what if I couldn't pitch anymore. Damn it, in 1912 I'd hit .290 in addition to winning 34 games. I could hit and I could run and I could field, and if I couldn't pitch why couldn't I do something else? Doggone it, I was a *ballplayer*, not just a pitcher.

I phoned my best friend, Tris Speaker, and told him I wanted to try again. Spoke had been traded from the Red Sox to Cleveland just before the 1916 season started. Tris said he'd see what he could do. Meanwhile, the Red Sox had given me permission to make any deal for myself I wanted, provided it was satisfactory with them. So on February 24,

Manager Jake Stahl and Smoky Joe Wood in 1912

1917, I was sold to the Indians for $15,000, and once again I went to spring training, this time with the Cleveland Indians, all of twenty-seven years old and a relic from the distant past.

I'd hear fathers tell their kids, "See that guy over there? That's Smoky Joe Wood, used to be a great pitcher long ago."

Lee Fohl was managing Cleveland at the time, and he encouraged me every way he could. And for my part I tried to show him that I could do more than pitch. I played in the infield during fielding practice, I shagged flies in the outfield, I was ready to pinch-run, to pinch-hit—I'd have carried the water bucket if they had water boys in baseball. The hell with my pride. I wasn't the Invincible Joe Wood anymore. I was just another ballplayer who wanted a job and wanted it bad.

And it paid off. My arm never did come back, but the next year, 1918, they got short of players because of the war and I was given a shot at an outfield job. Well, I *made* it. I hit .296 that season, and for *five* years I played in the outfield for Cleveland. In 1921 I hit .366. Could have played there longer, too, but I was satisfied. I figured I'd proved something to myself. So in 1923 when Yale offered me a position as baseball coach at the same salary as I was getting from Cleveland, I took it. Coached there at Yale for 20 years, from 1923 to 1942.

My biggest thrill came one day in 1918, shortly after they gave me a chance in the outfield. That day we beat the Yankees, 3–2, in a game that lasted *19 innings*. It was at the Polo Grounds, the same ball park where six years before I'd won three World Series games as a pitcher for Boston. But now, as an outfielder for Cleveland, I hit two home runs and the second one came in the 19th inning and broke up the ball game.

What a wonderful day that was! That game is still the longest game ever played at the Polo Grounds, and even today only five games in the history of the American League have lasted longer. Stanley Coveleski pitched the whole game for us, all 19 innings of it. In the top of the seventh I slammed one into the left-field bleachers, in the 9th inning I saved the game with a catch I didn't think I could make myself, in the 12th I threw a man out at second, and then in the top of the 19th I cracked *another* one into the left-field seats. Covey set the Yankees down one-two-three in the bottom of the nineteenth and we'd won it, 3–2.

That was one of the biggest days of my life. May 24, 1918. The season was pretty young yet and I hadn't been in the outfield very long. It was up to me to show Lee Fohl I could do the job. But from that day on he knew I could do it, and so did I. And the worst was finally over.

12   *Chief Meyers*

The Cahuilla Valley is high up among the peaks and spurs of the San Jacinto Mountains; a wild, barren, inaccessible spot. The Cahuilla village, situated there, was one of the most interesting that we visited. The Cahuillas seemed a more clear-headed, more individual, and more independent people than any other tribe we saw.

This is partly due to their native qualities, the tribe having originally been one of the most warlike and powerful in the country. The isolation of this village has also tended to keep these Indians self-respecting and independent. There is no white settlement within 10 miles, there being comparatively little to tempt white men into these mountain-fastnesses. The houses are of adobe, thatched with reeds; three of the houses have shingled roofs, and one has the luxury of a floor.

The Cahuillas are a particularly proud and spirited people. They will endure a great deal before they ask for help. Last winter they were for many weeks without sufficient food, due to crop failures. The teacher of their school repeatedly begged them to let her write to the Indian Agent for help, but they refused. At last, one night, two of the head men came to her and said she might write. They could no longer subdue the hunger. She wrote the letter. The next morning, at daylight, the Indians were at her door again. They would not permit her to send the letter. They had reconsidered, they said, and would not beg. They would rather starve.

—HELEN HUNT JACKSON, *On the Condition & Needs of the Mission Indians of California*, 1883

THE BIGGEST REGRET of my life is that I never finished my college education. I was born in 1880 in a small Cahuilla village, and I went to school there. We're one of the tribes that make up what are usually called the Mission Indians of Southern California. Far back in the past, however, the Cahuillas are descended from a Shoshone background.

Then my family moved here to Riverside when I was about eleven or twelve, and I went to the public schools here. I didn't even think of going to college right away after high school. Instead, I caught for various semipro teams around here, in Southern California and Arizona and New Mexico. Not in organized ball, you know, just bush-league ball, semipro, although I made a living of sorts at it.

However, after a few years of that I applied for admission to Dartmouth, and was accepted. I was a few years older than the average college student, and getting accepted at Dartmouth was a great thrill for me. You know that Dartmouth originally started back in King George's time as Moor's Indian Charity School. It was a missionary school, staffed by missionaries sent over from England to convert and educate the Indians. That was when America was still an English colony.

Eleazar Wheelock was the founder of the school—Moor's Indian Charity School—and he convinced King George III of the good work that was being done, so the Crown made large sums of money available for its continuance. However, the Earl of Dartmouth was even more impressed, and he set up a sizable fund with the stipulation that it was to be used only for the purpose of teaching any Indian who was qualified to matriculate at the school.

That fund still exists today, although few Indians know anything about it. I didn't know about it myself until I came in contact with Ralph Glaze while I was playing in a tournament in Albuquerque late in 1904. Ralph was on Walter Camp's All American Football Team when he was at Dartmouth, and later he became a pitcher with the Boston Red Sox.

Ralph told me about Dartmouth, and through his efforts and the information he obtained for me I eventually got admitted myself. I was the first Cahuilla to ever get such a wonderful chance, so in September of 1905 I left home and went East to Hanover, New Hampshire, to avail myself of the opportunity.

However, I never got to finish. I regret it to this day. In 1906, after my freshman year, I went to Harrisburg, Pennsylvania, to play summer ball. I was ineligible for baseball at Dartmouth, anyway, because I'd already played professionally, and I had a chance to make a little money over the summer playing for the Harrisburg club in the Tri-State League. That was my first club in organized baseball.

When the season was over and it was time to go back to college, my mother got very ill out here in California. My brother wrote me that she wanted me home, so I came back. Mother eventually recovered, but by the time she did it was too late to go back to Dartmouth. That was an unfortunate thing. Then . . . well, there was nothing else to do but go on with baseball, at least temporarily.

From Harrisburg I went to Butte, Montana, in the Northwestern League, from Butte to St. Paul in the American Association, and from St. Paul I was sold to the New York Giants. That was in 1908. I have no regrets about it. I liked playing ball, and I made good at it. But I do wish I had finished my college education.

You know, Dartmouth is just like the Giants: once a Giant, always a Giant. Mr. McGraw instilled a spirit there that never left you. And this is quoted from Chaucer: once a Dartmouth, always a Dartmouth. You never lose that affection for the old school, regardless if you just get in there and get a cup of coffee. They instill that spirit into you that lasts. Dartmouth men are very, very close, all over the world. They'll never turn you down.

In those days, of course, baseball was different than it is today. I don't mean as a game, although that was different, too. I mean it was not well thought of, like it is today. Ballplayers were considered a rowdy bunch. We weren't admitted to hotels, that is first-class hotels. Like the sailors in Boston, on the Commons—"No Sailors Allowed." We were in that class. We were just second-class citizens, even worse.

Mr. McGraw was the one who changed all that. He was the one who paid the price, and even more than the price, to get his ball team into the best hotels. Now, the ballplayer is respected. But it wasn't like that when I started. You have to realize that I began playing ball—in the bush leagues, that is—when Dewey took Manila. That was in the late 1890's, quite a while back.

Of course, they didn't have scouts in those days, or bonuses. Nothing like that. It was a situation where you needed them more than they needed you. Today, it seems to be just the opposite. But in those days, you just pushed yourself in. If you liked to play ball and they saw you, they took you, that's all. And then it was up to you to prove yourself.

Ballplayers in those days didn't take too kindly to rookies, either. Not those tough babies! They figured a youngster was in there after one of their jobs. That's the only way they looked at a youngster. And I don't like to say this, but in those days, when I was young, I was considered a foreigner. I didn't belong. I was an Indian.

I remember when I broke in with that Harrisburg club in 1906 there were a lot of old-timers on that team. That was my first club in organized ball. I joined them in the middle of the season, after school was over at Dartmouth. Soon after I got there the catcher got hurt in the late innings of a game. Broke his finger and couldn't catch. So the manager—Billy Hamilton, remember him?—he told me to put the stuff on. Which I did. The pitcher was a spitball pitcher, and I checked the signs out with him. But the first ball he pitched, he hit me right in the belly with it.

Chief Meyers in 1910

I'd called for a fast ball, but he threw me a spitter. Crossed me up all the way. So there I was, a young fellow behind the plate, being crossed up in my very first game.

After that I didn't give him any signs at all. Because I was on my own then, I wasn't expecting anything, and I could catch him.

"What's the matter, you're not giving any signs?" he yelled in at me.

"What's the use?" I said. "You go ahead and pitch." And I caught him.

When it came time for me to hit, I had no bat. I had just reported, and for some reason I didn't have my bat. So when it came my turn to hit I went to pick up a bat, and some guy growls at me, "Hey, Busher, drop that bat!" Just like that.

So I looked at the manager, and told him I didn't have any bat. Well, he went over and grabbed a bat and handed it to me. Of course, I had no choice of bat or anything. And when I got up to the plate, the first pitch came whistling in sort of high and inside—right at the old head, you know. Kind of tamed me down. But I'd figured it. I'd figured it would be like that. It was tough, don't think it wasn't. In those days you had to have guts. That's all there was to it.

However, on the next pitch I hit one over the fence, clear into the Susquehanna River. There were two men on base at the time, and that won the ball game. And the next day the papers came out and gave me credit for it, and after that things started to get better.

Two years later, in 1908, I was on the New York Giants. I did pretty well at St. Paul in the American Association that year, and late in the season St. Paul sold me to the Giants. I didn't get in any games with the Giants during the little that remained of the 1908 season. Heck, they had Roger Bresnahan there, the best catcher in the league. But the next year Roger was traded to St. Louis, where he had the opportunity to manage the team, and George Schlei and I divided the catching.

By 1910, however, I was the regular Giant catcher and, as you know, I stayed as the regular catcher until 1916. Batted over .300 for that seven-year period on the Giants, including .358 in 1912. And then in 1916 I was traded to the Dodgers.

But once a Giant, always a Giant. That's the truth. It was because of Mr. McGraw. What a great man he was! Oh, we held him in high esteem. We respected him in every way. According to Mr. McGraw, his ball team never lost a game; he lost it, not his players. He fought for his ballplayers, and protected them. You couldn't come around and second-guess McGraw's players in his presence without having a fight on your hands right there. He stood up for us at all times.

Of course, errors of judgment—not thinking and not being alert—were taboo with him. He wouldn't stand for that. But regular errors—he often said errors are part of the game, and if there weren't any the game would be perfect and no one would come out and see us. "But don't make too many of them," he'd say, "or else you won't stay here very long!"

And how he hated lies. Don't ever come in with some alibi. That didn't go with him. No, he loved the truth, and you'd better come with the truth and nothing else. I remember one time a young player was on second base, and the next batter singled. This kid came tearing around third base and scored, but on the way around he missed the base. The third baseman shouted for the ball and touched the base, and the umpire called the youngster out.

"What's the matter, didn't you touch that base?" McGraw asked him.

"Yes, I did," the kid said. "I stepped right on it."

"You know something," McGraw said, "that'll cost you $100. For *stepping* on that base. Any time that umpire says you didn't touch the base, you didn't touch it. They never call that play any other way."

That was McGraw. What a wonderful man he was. Honest and forth-right and charitable in the deepest sense of the word. We always called him *Mr.* McGraw. Never John or Mac. Always Mr. McGraw. And how he hated to be called "Muggsy!" That was a sore spot with him. Sometimes we'd call him that behind his back, but if he ever heard you, he wasn't your friend any more.

It was the same way with Bill Klem, that great old umpire. If Klem was umpiring behind the plate, all you had to do was call him "Catfish" and out of the game you'd go. That's all. Just that one word and you were out. I'm not quite sure why. Maybe it was because he had rather prominent lips, and when he'd call a ball or a strike he'd let fly a rather fine spray from his mouth. Sort of gave the general impression of a catfish, you know. He was a little sensitive about it, to say the least!

Those were great Giant teams the years I was there. Take, for instance, Mathewson. I caught almost every game he pitched for seven

Bill Klem: ". . . all you had to do was call him 'Catfish' and out of the game you'd go"

years. What a pitcher he was! The greatest that ever lived. He had almost perfect control. Really, almost perfect. In 1913 he pitched 68 consecutive innings without walking a man. That record is still standing, I think. That season he pitched over 300 innings and I doubt if he walked 25 men the whole year. Same thing in 1914. I don't think he ever walked a man in his life because of wildness. The only time he might walk a man was because he was pitching too fine to him, not letting him get a good ball to hit. But there was never a time he couldn't throw that ball over the plate if he wanted to.

How we loved to play for him! We'd break our necks for that guy. If you made an error behind him, or anything of that sort, he'd never get mad or sulk. He'd come over and pat you on the back. He had the sweetest, most gentle nature. Gentle in every way. He was a great checker player, too. He'd play several men at once. Actually, that's what made him a great pitcher. His wonderful retentive memory. Any time you hit a ball hard off of him, you never got another pitch in that spot again.

You know, those fellows back there, they *thought*, they used their head in baseball, a whole lot. They talked baseball morning, noon, and night. Baseball was their whole life. We had old pitchers, like Joe McGinnity, who'd go out and pitch two games in an afternoon. Pitch a doubeheader! He did that a number of times.

Nowadays, the pitcher wastes so much time out there it's ridiculous— fixing his cap . . . pulling up his pants . . . rubbing his chin . . . wiping his brow . . . pulling his nose . . . scratching the ground with his feet. And after he does all that he looks all around at the outfield, and then he st-a-a-a-res in at the catcher giving the sign. Why, he's afraid to throw the darned ball! And with this modern jackrabbit ball, I don't know as I blame him.

They waste an hour or so every day that way. We *always* played a game in less than two hours. Never longer. Two hours used to be considered a long game, really a long game. We played a lot of games in an hour and a half. I played in one that took only 58 minutes. Nowadays, a three-hour game isn't at all unusual.

At the Polo Grounds then, you know, the Giants didn't even *start* home games until four o'clock in the afternoon. That was because of Wall Street. The stock market didn't close until three o'clock, and then two or three thousand people who worked down at Wall Street would take the elevated train up to the Polo Grounds. They were all good

Christy Mathewson:
"We'd break our necks
for that guy"

fans, and that was the only way they could get in to see the game if it was on a weekday. Of course, we played only day games then. If we didn't start until four o'clock, and we didn't have any lights in those days, you know we just *had* to play a game in less time than they do today. In those days, the pitcher simply pitched, and that was that.

I'm not saying anything disparaging about the athletes of today. They're just as good and just as fast now as they ever were. In fact, I think they're faster. But they've got so much to work with that we didn't have. The equipment and the fields, for instance. It's just like the pole-vaulters today. Like Sunny Jim, high over the fence he goes! He just *boosts* over. In those days we didn't have anything. Our gloves were like a motorman's mitt. Now they're similar to a lacrosse net. You just catch the ball in the net.

And they strike out so much today. A lot of players with 100 strikeouts, 150 strikeouts. It's hard to believe! As old Al Smith used to say there in New York, "Let's take a look at the record." If you do, you'll find out that I'd only strike out two or three times a season. We didn't strike out, that's all. We hit the ball. We had big, hefty bats. Mine weighed about 47 or 48 ounces. A modern ballplayer wouldn't have anything to do with a bat like that. They don't have bats now. They have whips. Thin-handled things that weigh about 30 or 32 ounces. Because they're not trying for singles and doubles. They're not trying to just meet the ball. They're all trying for that home run, even the little shortstops and second basemen.

Another big difference between today and yesterday is that the ball-players are all businessmen now. They've got agents and outside interests and all that sort of thing. We played for money, too. Naturally. That's how we made our living. But mostly we played just for the love of it. Heck, most of us would have paid *them* just to let us play. We loved baseball.

I don't blame the modern players for making it while the making's good. I'm not belittling them. Why shouldn't they get the money? We never got it. I guess in a way we were just dumb eggs. We played for practically nothing. My top was about $6,000. Matty never made more than about eight. Well—that's the way it was then.

But we sure did have some ballplayers in those days. Old Grover Cleveland Alexander. Boy, he had stuff, don't think he didn't. And Walter Johnson, what a pitcher he was. That Walter could buzz it by you, he sure could. He was wonderful, the fastest I ever saw. And Rube

Marquard. The record books say he won 19 straight games in 1912, but they're wrong. He actually won 20 straight, but they didn't give him credit for one of them. I caught just about every one of those 20 games. And do you know that of those 20 straight wins, 16 or 17 were complete games?

The one they didn't give him credit for was one where he came in as a relief pitcher and we scored the winning run after that. Under modern rules Rube would get credit for that victory, but then they gave it to the starting pitcher, Jeff Tesreau. At that, Rube's record was 19 wins and no losses in mid-July of that year!

And catchers: Johnny Kling, Jimmy Archer, George Gibson, Roger Bresnahan. The best throwing catcher of them all was Jimmy Archer of the Cubs. He didn't have an arm. He had a rifle. And perfect accuracy.

You know, one player who never got the credit he deserved was Nap Rucker, the great Dodger left-hander. He was terrific. One of the smartest pitchers I ever saw, and with plenty of stuff, too. I caught him when he was about through, when I went to the Dodgers. That was in 1916. Heck, I was practically through by then myself. I was thirty-six years old. I didn't get into the Big Leagues until I was twenty-eight. And I didn't get to play regularly for the Giants until 1910, when I was thirty. I cheated a little on my age, you know, so they always thought I was a few years younger. But when the years started to creep up on me I knew how old I was, even if nobody else did.

That Brooklyn ball club in 1916 was full of ex-Giants. Myself and Marquard and Fred Merkle. And, of course, old Robbie was the manager. He didn't have to do much managing, though, because it was a team of veterans. Nap Rucker, Jake Daubert, Colby Jack Coombs, Rube, Zack Wheat, Hi Myers—we'd all been around a long time. And, of course, Casey Stengel. He was one of the few younger ones on that team. We won the pennant that year by just outsmarting the whole National League, that's all. It was an old crippled-up club, and you might say, figuratively, they had to wrap us up in bandages and carry us out to play the World Series. We were all through.

I always maintained that Stengel won one more pennant than the record books show. That was in 1916, with Brooklyn. Of course, Robbie was the manager. But Robbie was just a good old soul and everything. It was Casey who kept us on our toes. He was the life of the party and kept us old-timers pepped up all season. And we knew so much baseball that we just outsmarted the rest of the league and walked off—or, you might say, limped off—with the pennant.

But, of course, the years that stand out most in my memory are when I was with the Giants, from 1908 through 1915. So many unforgettable things happened during those years. Like the time Fred Merkle failed to touch second base and we lost the pennant, in 1908. It was a technicality. The New York club *won* that pennant, and it was taken away from us on a technicality. As the years went by, the smartest man on the club was the "bonehead," Mr. Merkle. McGraw never consulted anybody except Merkle on a question of strategy or something of that sort. He never asked Matty, he never asked me. He'd say, "Fred, what do you think of this?" The bonehead! What a misnomer! One of the smartest men in baseball, Fred Merkle. Isn't that something! It's the truth. It shows what the newspapers can do to you.

And the 1911 World Series, the Giants against Connie Mack's Athletics. Chief Bender was there with the A's. I knew Charlie quite well. He was a Chippewa from Minnesota, one of the nicest people you'd ever meet. He graduated from Carlisle and went to Dickinson College for a while, and from there he went straight to the Athletics in about 1902 or so. He didn't go to the minors at all. Straight to the Big Leagues. He was still with the A's, as a coach or a scout or something, when he died in 1954 at the age of about seventy.

That was the Series that didn't end until about the start of November. We had six straight days of rain in Philadelphia between the third and fourth games. We were behind two games to one at the time, and don't think that wasn't hard on the nerves! Superstitious McGraw, he had us dressed in black uniforms, because that's the way the Giants had been dressed when they beat the A's in the 1905 World Series.

But it didn't work this time. Matty beat Bender in the first game, 2–1, even though Charlie gave us only five hits and struck out 11. I scored the winning run myself in the seventh inning, after I got a double off Charlie. In the second game, though, Eddie Plank beat Rube Marquard when Frank Baker hit a home run to win the game. That's the Series that gave Baker his name, "Home Run" Baker. He hit one off Rube in the second game and another off Matty the next day. And all the while there was a big rumpus because the newspapers were claiming that Snodgrass was trying to spike Baker to get him out of there. Which wasn't so.

Anyway, they beat us, four games to two. They were a great team, there's no doubt about that. Especially that "$100,000 infield" of Stuffy McInnis at first, Eddie Collins at second, Jack Barry at short, and Frank Baker at third. But I still think we were the better club. They had our signs, or could read our pitchers, or something. They knew what Marquard was pitching. Matty, too.

"They're getting our signs from someplace," I told McGraw. "That coach on third base, Harry Davis, is calling our pitches. When he yells 'It's all right,' it's a fast ball."

"He must be getting them off you," McGraw said.

But they weren't getting them from me. I went to Rube and to Matty and said, "Pitch whatever you want to pitch. I'll catch you without signals." And still the guy was hollering "It's all right" for the fast ball. He knew something. I never did find out how he did it.

The next year we lost the World Series again, this time to the Boston Red Sox. That's the Series they blame on Fred Snodgrass because he dropped that fly ball. The newspapers blamed him, that is. But we didn't. That was just a simple error. It could happen to anybody. Neither Mr. McGraw nor anybody on the club ever censured Fred Snodgrass. He was another gentleman, a very fine fellow, proven so throughout his life. We always held him in high esteem, and still do today.

Chief Meyers of the Giants and Chief Bender of the Athletics before the 1911 World Series: "Superstitious McGraw, he had us dressed in black uniforms"

Jim Thorpe, at the start of his triumphant parade up Fifth Avenue after returning from the 1912 Olympics

Heck, right after that muff he made the greatest catch you ever saw on a line drive hit by Harry Hooper. After that, Tris Speaker hit a foul pop-up that should have been the second out. It fell practically in the first-base coach's box, and Fred Merkle or Matty could have taken it easily. But nobody did, and then Speaker singled and drove in the tying run. I gave that pop-up the old college try, but it was too far away for me to get. Matty came over, too, but waited for Merkle to take it, and it fell right between all of us. I think the Red Sox dugout coached Merkle off it. The Boston bench called for Matty to take it, and called for me to take it, and I think that confused Fred. He was afraid of a collision. You see, the Red Sox bench was right there, near where the ball fell, and they just coached him off of it. Well, that's all right. It's all part of the game.

The year after that was the year Jim Thorpe joined us. Jim was a Sac and Fox, from Oklahoma originally. I roomed with him. Gee, he was an Adonis! Built like a Greek god. The greatest all-around athlete who ever lived. Agreed by all the experts as one of the greatest and most wonderful athletes the world has ever known. They may top his records. You always get topped, you know. But in his day he had no equal. All-American football player at Carlisle, and winner of everything in sight at the 1912 Olympics in Stockholm. He wasn't as good in baseball as he was in football and track, where he was in a class all by himself. However, he was good enough to stay in the Big Leagues almost ten years.

Boy, could that guy ever eat! For breakfast he'd order a beefsteak smothered in pork chops. And corned beef and cabbage, that was his favorite. He could down four servings in one sitting. Jim was very proud of the great things he'd done. A very proud man. Not conceited, he never was that. But proud.

When King Gustav of Sweden pinned the last Olympic gold medal on Jim, he looked at that American Indian, and shook his hand, and said, "Sir, you are the greatest athlete in the world."

Jim never forgot that. And he never got over what happened after the Olympics were finished. When they took all his medals and trophies away from him. They claimed he had violated his amateur status by playing semipro ball during summers, when he was going to Carlisle. They made him return every one of his Olympic medals and trophies, and that broke his heart. It really did.

I remember, very late one night, Jim came in and woke me up. I remember it like it was only last night. He was crying, and tears were rolling down his cheeks.

"You know, Chief," he said, "the King of Sweden gave me those trophies, he gave them to me. But they took them away from me, even though the guy who finished second refused to take them. They're mine, Chief, I won them fair and square." It broke his heart, and he never really recovered.

In those days, you know, the Indian was in the position of a minority group. Still is, for that matter. Nowadays, you can't ridicule an Irishman on the television, you can't ridicule a Jew, and you can't ridicule a Negro. But they can kill us all the time—make everything out of us they want. Every night you see them on the television—killing us Indians. That's all they do.

That's one reason I don't look at anything but a ball game or the news on the television. I like the ball games and the news, but after the news, then comes the killing. Those things I don't like to talk about. I see them . . . I know them . . . but I don't like to talk about them.

The world seems to be turned all upside down today. Progress, they call it. The radio and the television and all, brainwashing the children and teaching them to cheat and steal and kill. Always violence and killing. I think it's an awful bad example for the youngsters. Why can't they teach people about the good things of life, instead?

In the old days, you know, a shake of your hand was your word and your honor. In those days, if anything was honest and upright, we'd say it was "on the square." Nowadays, they've even turned that word around: now it means you don't belong, you're nothing. "Square deal" is no more. You're a "square." Where do they get that stuff, anyhow? It just doesn't make sense—at least not to me, it doesn't.

I guess I'm like the venerable old warrior Chief of the Great Six Nations, who announced his retirement by saying, "I am like an old hemlock. My head is still high, but the winds of close to a hundred winters have whistled through my branches, and I have been witness to many wondrous and many tragic things. My eyes perceive the present, but my roots are imbedded deeply in the grandeur of the past."

13 *Hans Lobert*

Poised between going on and back, pulled
Both ways taut like a tightrope-walker,
Fingertips pointing the opposites,
Now bouncing tiptoe like a dropped ball
Or a kid skipping rope, come on, come on,
Running a scattering of steps sidewise,
How he teeters, skitters, tingles, teases,
Taunts them, hovers like an ecstatic bird,
He's only flirting, crowd him, crowd him,
Delicate, delicate, delicate, delicate—*now!*
—ROBERT FRANCIS, "The Base Stealer"

No KIDDING, are you sure that's right? That except for Connie Mack
I've been in baseball longer than anybody else in the whole history of the game? That's really hard to believe.

Let's see, I started with the Pittsburgh Pirates in 1903. They sent me
to Des Moines in the Western League in 1904, in 1905 I jumped to
Johnstown in the Tri-State League, and came up with the Chicago Cubs
in the fall of that same year. In 1906 the Cubs traded me to Cincinnati
for Harry Steinfeldt, which rounded out that great infield they had for
so many years after—Chance, Evers, Tinker, and Steinfeldt. If that
trade hadn't been made it would have been Chance, Evers, Tinker, and
Lobert, I guess. I played third for Cincinnati from 1906 through 1910,
for the Phillies from 1911 through '14, and then finished up with three
years under McGraw on the Giants.

After my playing days were over I coached at West Point from
1918 to 1925—four of those years were under MacArthur—and then
went back to the Giants as a coach for four years. The Giants sent me
to manage their farm club at Bridgeport in the Eastern League in
1929, '30, and '31, then I managed Jersey City for a while, and from
1934 to 1941 I was a coach with the Phillies. I managed them in
1942, and that was enough to end a beautiful friendship, so in '43 and
'44 I coached for Cincinnati. Since '45 I've been a scout for New York
and San Francisco.

185

So that's it. Sounds more like a travelogue than a life history, doesn't it? It really isn't as much traveling as it sounds, though—it's mostly the Giants, the Phillies, and the Reds, once you stop to think about it. But it does add up. Over 60 years in baseball. That's almost impossible for me to believe.

I still remember back in Williamsport, Pennsylvania, where I grew up, there was a team called the Demarest Sewing Machines that played only a few blocks from where we lived, and I used to sneak into the games all the time. I used to crawl under the fence, so I wouldn't have to pay my ten cents. I must have been about ten years old, which means it was around 1890 or so.

Well, the day I'm thinking of is the day the ticket-taker caught me. He'd seen me crawling under the fence before, but he'd never been fast enough to catch me. But this time I must have been careless. He grabbed me and dragged me up in front to the ticket office, where they had a great big ugly bulldog chained to a post. He chained me to another post, right next to the bulldog, but just beyond his reach. Just barely. That was to teach me a lesson, so I wouldn't do it again, I guess.

He kept me there for about four innings, and all the while I'm getting more and more scared. I could see myself in jail, with my father coming down to get me out, and a whole lot worse. Although at the age of ten I'm not sure what could possibly be worse than that. Finally he unchained me, and he says, "Well, what are you going to do now?"

"I'm going to watch the game," I said, and I ran like the devil. But the next day I was right back, crawling under the fence again.

A few years later we moved to a little town right outside of Pittsburgh. My father was a cabinetmaker, but we had about 10 cows too, and every morning brother and I would get up at four in the morning and milk the cows and deliver the milk and take the cows to pasture before we went to school. We had the cows, but we didn't really live on a farm. We'd take them to pasture on a big farm nearby.

There's where I got my first baseball uniform. I was about fifteen, I guess. I was playing on some little amateur team and they got us uniforms. Boy, I'll never forget it. I slept in it that night. They couldn't get that thing off my back.

But I still didn't have a pair of baseball shoes. That same year my Dad gave me $3.50 for Christmas.

"What are you going to do with all that money?" he asked me.

"I'm going to buy a pair of the best baseball shoes I can find," I told him.

And I went downtown to Pittsburgh and got a pair of Spalding Featherweights, which were just $3.50 at that time. When I got back home it was snowing out, but I couldn't wait to try them on. I put the whole uniform on, and the new shoes, and ran outside as quick as I could. I can still see my Mom and Dad watching me out the front window—I could hardly see them it was snowing so hard—with me out there dancing in the snow in those beautiful shoes.

I played every chance I could get, and late in my teens I started to play third base with a semipro club in Pittsburgh, the Pittsburgh AC's. Naturally, living near Pittsburgh and all, my idol was Honus Wagner, and I tried to do everything just like he did. I even tried to walk like him. Wagner lived in Carnegie, which wasn't far from where we lived, and lots of times I'd see him out there playing baseball with the kids after the Pirates' game was over. A wonderful man, he was.

One day in September of 1903, after I'd been playing with the Pittsburgh AC's for a few seasons, we took a trip to Atlantic City to play a game there. It so happened that Barney Dreyfuss, who was president of the Pittsburgh Pirates, happened to be in Atlantic City at the time, and he watched the game from the stands. After it was over, he buttonholed me.

"Where do you live, young man?" he says to me.

"In Pittsburgh, sir," I said.

"Is that so?" he says. "How would you like to come out to Exposition Park and have a trial with the Pirates?"

What could I say? I gulped and stammered something, and I guess he got the idea, because next week there I was, at Exposition Park over in Allegheny, which was where the Pirates used to play in those days. This was in September of 1903. I remember the year because that was the year the Pirates won their third pennant in a row, and they had the first World Series ever, the Pirates and the Red Sox. I sat on the Pittsburgh bench during that World Series.

So I went over to Exposition Park, like Mr. Dreyfuss asked me to, and started to go into the clubhouse. There was a big fellow at the door who turned out to be the trainer.

"What do you want here?" he says, real gruff and tough. Scared the tar out of me. I told him why I was there, and he finally let me in.

Honus Wagner:
"From then on he
always called me
Hans Number Two"

When I got inside I didn't know what to do, so I began to look for Fred Clarke, the manager. All the players were there, you know, getting dressed and everything, and I felt like a real big shot and a nobody both at the same time. While I'm looking for Mr. Clarke I'm mostly looking out of the corner of my eye at the players to see who I recognize and what they *really* look like—like Honus Wagner and Tommy Leach and Ginger Beaumont and the rest. I guess I must have looked sort of lost, because all of a sudden Wagner, of all people, yells out to me, "Hey, kid, come on over here and use my locker!"

"Oh, no, Mr. Wagner," I says, "I have to find Mr. Clarke."

"He won't be here for twenty minutes yet," Wagner said. "Meanwhile come on over and get dressed here."

So I did, and I really felt like a big shot then. Wagner asked me where I was from, and when he found out I lived near him and my name was John, or Johannus, the same as his, he started calling me Hans Number Two. Actually, we did look a little bit alike. Especially our noses! From then on he always called me Hans Number Two, for all the fifty years we knew each other. I've always been proud of that.

I stayed with Pittsburgh the rest of the season and got in about five games. The first one was against the Giants and Joe McGinnity was the pitcher. Boy, he was at his peak then. He won over 30 games in 1903 and 1904 both, and that's when he was pitching double headers and all. I think he pitched at least three doubleheaders that year, 1903, and won both of the games each time.

Well, in that first game I didn't get any hits until about the eighth inning. I came up for the fourth time and McGinnity got two quick strikes on me, both curve balls. That's all he threw, underhand curve balls, one after the other. But with two strikes on me I bunted down the first-base line and beat it out. When I went out to my position the next inning, Giant manager John McGraw was coaching at third base, which was where I was playing.

"Say, young man," he said, "who ever taught you to bunt with two strikes on you?"

"Nobody did," I said, "but I like to bunt and nobody was looking for a busher to do that."

"Well, you keep it up," he said. "That's the way to keep them on their toes."

And he and I became friends from that day on, until he died.

After that season, the Pirates sent me to Des Moines in 1904, and in 1905 I was with Johnstown. I hit .337 there and stole 57 bases, so at the end of that season the Chicago Cubs bought me. Like I said, though, they traded me to Cincinnati before the 1906 season began in order to get Harry Steinfeldt.

So in 1906 I started to play regular in the Big Leagues, at shortstop and third base with Cincinnati. Ned Hanlon, who used to manage the old Baltimore Orioles, was the manager of the Reds when I came up, and later it was Clark Griffith. That was before Griff bought the Washington club. Cy Seymour was there, and Miller Huggins, and Jimmy Delahanty, and later Bob Bescher and Dode Paskert. That was a very fast team around that time, you know. One year Bob Bescher stole about 80 bases, Paskert stole about 50, and I stole about 40.

Andy Coakley was a pitcher on that Cincinnati team, too. Quite a guy. Andy had graduated from Holy Cross, and he was a great fellow

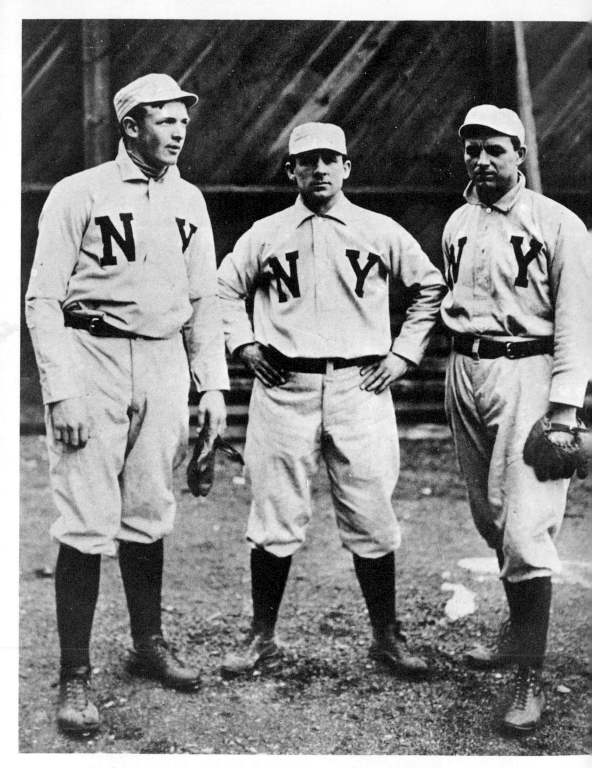

Mathewson, McGraw, and McGinnity in 1903. That year Matty won 30 games and McGinnity won 31. Three times that season "Iron Man" Joe McGinnity pitched—and won—both games of a double-header.

to have around. In the middle of an argument he'd come out with, "Being unable to assume an initial premise with any tolerable degree of accuracy, I am loathe to assert a conclusion fearful lest I should err."

Andy and I saw a lot of each other many years later, when he was coaching at Columbia and I was at West Point, and every time we got together one or the other of us would spout that out before we'd even said hello.

Of course, I'm making it all sound like it was just a joy ride. But those were very rough days. It wasn't easy to break into the Big Leagues. I still remember the famous day Rube Marquard made his debut with the Giants. We were the opposition. It was in 1908, very late in the season, only a couple of days after the Merkle incident. I think the Merkle incident happened on September 23, and on Friday the 25th McGraw started Marquard against us in the first game of a doubleheader.

New York was in an uproar over the Merkle thing, and everybody was also all excited about Marquard, the "$11,000 beauty" that McGraw had just bought from Indianapolis. The Polo Grounds was jammed to the rafters. Well, this kid—I don't think Marquard was nineteen years old yet—was so nervous he couldn't do a single thing right. He hit the first man up in the ribs, then I tripled, then Bob Bescher tripled, all in the first inning, and suddenly they started calling the "$11,000 beauty" the "$11,000 lemon." Just a kid, you know. It was rough. He showed them a few years later, though, that he had the stuff.

Also playing conditions were very primitive then. The fields were bumpy and the gloves were nothing compared to today. And you know we were only permitted to have 17 men on a club, not 25 like they have now. If you got banged up, it was just too bad. You had to play. Actually, I believe there are a greater number of better players around today, but they're not as rugged as we used to be. We didn't have any choice, you see.

For instance, we didn't have any training facilities to speak of. The trainer in those days had to take care of the uniforms and the equipment and everything else. Just one man. He didn't know any more about health or medicine than the man in the moon. And no doctors, of course. If somebody got hurt the old cry would go out, "Is there a doctor in the stands?"

I remember once, in 1907 I think it was, I got hit in the head with a pitched ball. We were playing the Cubs and Orvie Overall was pitching for them. He and I had roomed together the year before, when I first came to Cincinnati, and then he'd been traded to the Cubs. I had three balls and one strike on me, and Ned Hanlon yelled, "Make him pitch to you, Hans."

Well, if Hanlon called your first name, that meant to hit. So as soon as I heard "Hans" I knew I was to hit the next pitch. Overall let go with a high fast one and it hit me smack on the temple. I thought I was down about five seconds, but it was about ten minutes. Even so, when I came to, I had to stay in the game. They didn't have anybody else to put in. Every step I took I felt the ground was coming up to meet my feet, or I was stepping into a hole. But I had to stay in there.

I thought I was getting over it after a week or two, but then suddenly I started to get plate shy. I couldn't stand up there at the plate and I began to get terrible headaches every night. I couldn't see the ball very well, either. It was September by then, and our position was pretty set, so I finally asked Mr. Hanlon if I could go home for the rest of the season. When I got home I went to a doctor for the first time, and he said I had a concussion.

So it was a different setup then. The boys were pretty rough. They were beer drinkers. They never drank hard liquor. After the game we'd go and have a couple of glasses of beer. Very few drank anything else. It wasn't until prohibition came in, years later, that there was very much drinking besides a beer or two. There was lots more drinking *during* prohibition than before or since.

I didn't even drink beer when I first came up. I'll never forget in Cincinnati, we were sitting in a restaurant—Joe Kelley, Jimmy Delahanty, Cy Seymour, Shad Barry, Larry McLean, and myself—and they wanted me to join them and have a beer.

"No," I said, "I don't drink beer. I've never tasted it."

Boy, they all grabbed me and held me and started pouring this beer in my face. I kept my mouth closed, and soon I had beer all over me. Finally, I'd had enough.

"OK," I said, "cut it out. I'll take a glass of beer."

In the spring of 1911 Dode Paskert and I were traded to the Phillies, and a new rookie in the Phillies' camp for the first time that spring was a big fellow by the name of Grover Cleveland Alexander. As you know, Alex got to drinking very heavily later in his career, but to the best of my knowledge he didn't drink at all at that time. He was really something back then. I was with the Phillies for four years—1911 through

Grover Cleveland Alexander
as a rookie pitcher in 1911

1914—and he was terrific every one of those years. In his rookie year, 1911, Alex won 28 games and at one point that season he pitched four shutouts in a row. And the thing is he wasn't at his peak yet.

In 1915, '16, and '17 he won 30 or more games each season, and in 1916 he had 16 shutouts. For a right-handed pitcher in Baker Bowl in Philadelphia, where we played then, that was almost impossible to believe. The right-field fence was only 280 feet away and cut straight over to center field. That park was heaven for a left-handed hitter.

Alex was really an amazing pitcher. He had little short fingers and he threw a very heavy ball. Once, later on, when I'd moved over to the Giants, Alex hit me over the heart with a pitched ball and it bore in like a lump of lead hitting you. I couldn't get my breath for ten minutes afterward. Matty was just as fast, but he threw a much lighter ball.

Anyway, like I said, Alex didn't drink when he first came up. He didn't really start to drink heavily until after he came back from the war in 1919. He wasn't any youngster when he first came up, either. He must have been twenty-four or twenty-five by then. I guess he started in baseball late.

He was a great big guy, with a fine build. Now, you know, they always seem to remember Alex as an old man, and the only thing you hear about him is that he came in at the age of thirty-nine and struck out Tony Lazzeri to save the 1926 World Series for the Cardinals. But in those days he wasn't any thirty-nine years old. He was in his twenties and he had a wonderful constitution. Funny thing, he never ran, like pitchers are supposed to. He'd get around third base and field some ground balls, and that would be that.

Alex's big problem was that he took epileptic fits on the bench, and that continued all the years we played together. Maybe two or three times a season he'd have an epileptic seizure on the bench. He'd froth at the mouth and shiver all over and thrash around and sort of lose consciousness. We'd hold him down and open his mouth and grab his tongue to keep him from choking himself. It was awful.

After we'd gotten him down we'd pour some brandy down his throat and in a while he'd be all right. It always happened on the bench, though, never out on the pitching mound. We always kept a bottle of brandy handy because there never was any warning.

Alex wasn't the only epileptic on the Phillies at that time. Sherry Magee in the outfield had epilepsy, too. And Tony Lazzeri with the Yankees, later on.

I remember one Sunday when I was on the Phillies we all went over to Atlantic City. We didn't play Sunday baseball in those days in Philadelphia. Monday, when we got back, was a beastly hot day, and Sherry Magee had been drinking and had a hangover. We played St. Louis that day and Bill Finneran was umpiring behind the plate. He called a bad strike on Sherry, and we could all see that Magee was about to go into a fit. He started frothing at the mouth and he went at Finneran like a crazy man. Finneran had his mask off and Sherry hit him in the mouth and knocked him down before we could get out there and stop him. Sherry was suspended 30 days for that.

In 1915 I was traded to the Giants, and after ten years in the Big Leagues I finally got to play under McGraw. That was a great thrill for me. Actually, I already knew McGraw pretty well, because he'd taken me on his world tour in 1913.

He took two teams around the world that winter. We were called the Giants and the White Sox, but we weren't really. I was on the Phillies then, and I went along, and so did Sam Crawford, who was on the Tigers, and Tris Speaker from the Red Sox, Germany Schaefer from the Senators, and a few others who weren't on either the White Sox or the Giants.

We left in 1913 on October 18, which is my birthday, and got back March 6, 1914. That was my honeymoon trip, too. We all took our wives and had a great time. First we toured the United States for a month and then went to Japan, China, Australia, Egypt, Italy, France, England, and Ireland.

When we were almost finished with the American part of the tour we played a game in Oxnard, California, which was Fred Snodgrass' home town, and that was something I'll never forget. It was one of the most bizarre incidents I ever took part in.

We arrived in Oxnard at about seven in the morning and were met at the train by about ten stagecoaches, in which they took all of us out to this big ranch for a huge barbecue. That was great cattle and lima-bean country around there then. They had this tremendous ox roasting, been roasting it for a couple of days, and lima beans with onions, and beer. That was our breakfast! Did you ever try roasted ox and beer for breakfast? Not bad. Puts hair on your chest, to say the least.

Well, after we had finished all this great food the mayor of the town got up and put me on the spot. He asked me if I would race a horse around the bases that afternoon.

"Lord," I said, "I'm not here to run horses around the bases. I'm here to play baseball."

But he wouldn't take no for an answer, and McGraw finally talked me into agreeing to it. See, I was very fast in those days. In a field day at Cincinnati, a couple of years before, I had circled the bases in 13 4/5 seconds from a pistol start. As far as I know, that's still a record. Tommy Leach held the record before that, 14 1/5 seconds, which he had made in 1907.

The idea was that first we'd play the game, and then after the game I'd race the horse. Well, afternoon came and we started the game, but it was very difficult to play. Nobody wanted to see the game. They all wanted to see this race between the man and the horse. There was a huge crowd there, maybe 5,000 people packed into those little rickety stands, and out in the outfield there must have been several hundred cowboys on horseback watching the game. (I learned later that there was a terrific amount of local wagering among the cattlemen and the cowboys on who would win, me or the horse.) The cowboys kept creeping in closer and closer, till we hardly had any room left to play.

So along about the seventh inning McGraw came to me and said, "John, we can't finish this game. You might as well get ready to run the horse around the bases."

Then, from this mass of cowboys encircling the outfield, out steps the most beautiful black animal you ever saw, with a Mexican cowboy on him all dressed up in chaps and spangles. Both he and the horse were glittering like jewels in the sunlight. The horse was a beautiful coal-black cow pony that was trained to make very sharp turns.

The cowboy couldn't speak English, so I said, "Señor, practico. We'll take a practice walk around the bases."

So around we walked, the crowd roaring and the moving-picture cameras whirring—Pathé News was there. I was to touch the inner corner of each base, and he was to go around the outside, so as not to run me down.

Finally, everything was all set. Bill Klem was to be the referee and we were ready to go. A pistol started us, and off we went. I led at first base by at least five feet, and by second base I had picked up and was at least ten feet ahead. I was in perfect stride, hitting each bag with my right foot and going faster all the time. But instead of the horse keeping his distance, he crowded me between second and third and I had to dodge to avoid being knocked down. I broke stride, and that was the

Hans Number Two:
Hans Lobert in 1906

end. I was still in front as we rounded third, but not by much, and on the home stretch the horse just did beat me in. I still think I would have won if I hadn't been practically bowled over at shortstop.

Bill Klem said the horse won by a nose. But, as you can plainly see, that was highly unlikely.

14 *Rube Bressler*

It is, as a rule, a man's own business how he spends his money. But nevertheless we wish to call attention to the fact that many men do so in a very unwise manner. A very glaring instance of this among baseball players is the recent evil tendency to purchase and maintain automobiles.

Put the money away, boys, where it will be safe. You don't need these automobiles. That money will look mighty good later on in life. Think it over, boys.　　　　　　　　　　　　　　—Editorial in *Baseball Magazine,* 1914

HOW CAN YOU EXPLAIN the way things happen in this world? Some things you just can't account for, that's all.

I grew up in Flemington, Pennsylvania, and in 1912 I was a seventeen-year-old kid swinging a sledge hammer in a railroad shop. Had never pitched a game of professional ball in my life. Two years later I was a starting pitcher on Connie Mack's World Champion Philadelphia Athletics, one of the greatest aggregations of talent to ever walk out on a baseball field at one and the same time. I won 14 games for them, lost only 3, and had a terrific earned-run average. And less than two years after that I was back in the bushes again. Couldn't win a game to save my life. Twenty-one years old and evidently all washed up.

Well, I've heard of people aging quickly, but that was ridiculous. When I was a kid, George M. Cohan used to sing a song that I've never forgotten. It ended with: "Life's a pretty funny proposition . . . *after all.*"

It all began because I used to pitch for the Pennsylvania Railroad shop team where I worked, at Renovo, Pennsylvania. One day Earle Mack, Connie's son, came up with his All-Stars, and I beat them. I guess he told his Daddy, because the next year I was pitching for Harrisburg in the Tri-State League. That was 1913. And the year after that I went up with the Athletics.

The only pitchers I had to compete with when I got up there were Eddie Plank, who's in the Hall of Fame, Chief Bender, who's in the Hall of Fame, Herb Pennock, who's in the Baseball Hall of Fame, Bullet Joe

Bush, Colby Jack Coombs, and Bob Shawkey. Also Weldon Wyckoff. What a pitching staff! That's what I had to cope with.

I guess Connie liked me, though, because he let me stay. I hung around until the middle of the season, hardly pitching at all, and then one day he started me. No warning at all. We were playing the Boston Red Sox, and Ray Collins was scheduled to pitch against us. He beat us regularly. Just tossed his glove on the mound and we were finished. Connie probably figured why waste a regular starter when Collins was going against us, so he threw me in there. And I won.

Connie Mack. There was a wonderful person. A truly religious man. I mean *really* religious. Not a hypocrite, like some are. He really respected his fellow man. If you made a mistake, Connie never bawled you out on the bench, or in front of anybody else. He'd get you alone a few days later, and then he'd say something like, "Don't you think it would have been better if you'd made the play this way?"

And you knew damn well it would have been better. No question about it. He knew what he was talking about. Never raised his voice. Never used profanity of any sort. Oh, he might say, "Good grief, look at that!" Never anything stronger than that.

In my opinion, Connie Mack did more for baseball than any other living human being—by the example he set, his attitude, the way he handled himself and his players. You know, like you're playing a great game and you're heroes to the children of this country. Live up to it, conduct yourself accordingly. Over a period of years others followed, and baseball became respectable. He was a true gentleman, in every sense of the word. Not many men are.

And, of course, those 1914 Athletics were one of the greatest baseball teams ever assembled, if not *the* greatest. That "$100,000 infield"— Stuffy McInnis, Eddie Collins, Jack Barry, Frank Baker. I don't know of any better infield ever played together. Wally Schang and Jack Lapp catching, Eddie Murphy, Amos Strunk, and Rube Oldring in the outfield, and you know the pitching staff. Three future Hall of Famers, that's all. Plus a few more who should be there, like Bush and Coombs and Shawkey. Well, they won four pennants in five years, and *three* World Championships. Can't do much better than that, can you?

The only World Series they lost was that 1914 one—to George Stallings' "miracle" Boston Braves, of all teams. The weakest of them all. And we lost it in four straight games, too. Overconfidence was the thing

Rube Bressler in 1914

that did us in more than anything else. We thought it would be a push-over. Also, Connie sent Chief Bender and Eddie Plank home to Phila-delphia a week before the Series, to rest up, and they lost that fine edge. Their control was off.

You know, baseball is a matter of razor-edge precision. It's not a game

Chief Bender:
"One of the kindest and
finest men who ever lived"

of inches, like you hear people say. It's a game of *hundredths* of inches. Any time you have a bat only that big around, and a ball that small, traveling at such tremendous rates of speed, an inch is way too large a margin for error.

Bender and Plank, the old war-horses! When I got there in 1914, a nineteen-year-old kid, Bender had been with the A's for 11 years and Plank for 13. Hell, I'd been reading about those guys since I was in the third grade. And how do you think they treated me? Well, I'll tell you: wonderful. Just wonderful. Two of the finest guys who ever lived.

I used to try to get near them and listen to what they were talking about, and *every question* I'd ask they'd pay attention and tell me what they thought. I used to put sticks behind my ears so they'd stand out further. Boy, I wanted to hear what those guys had to say. (Today, they tell me, the rookies put cotton in their ears.)

I roomed with Bender that first year. One of the kindest and finest men who ever lived. See, Connie roomed a youngster with a veteran. He didn't room two youngsters together, where they could cry on each other's shoulders and commiserate with each other. ("Oh, you'll do better, dear, tomorrow.") No, sir. He had an old pitcher in there with a young one.

You never could tell whether Bender won or lost. One day in Washington Walter Johnson beat me, 1–0, and as Bender and I went up to the room that evening I said, "Gee, that sure was a tough one to lose."

"Are you talking about today's game?" Bender asked me.

"Of course," I said.

"Did you hear the boys yelling when we came into the hotel?"

"What boys?"

"The newsboys," he said.

"Oh, I guess so."

"What were they saying?"

"They were saying 'Washington Wins, 1–0,'" I said.

"That's right," he said. "It's a matter of record now. Forget about that game. Win the next one." That's all he said.

Well, after I beat Ray Collins I started in the regular rotation, and, as I said, I had a terrific season. Earned-run average was about 1.76 and all. But I pitched so much the second half of the season that I hurt my arm. It never ever really came back the way it had been.

The next year, 1915, I won 4 games and lost 17. Yeah, that's right, 4 and 17. Of course, that wasn't *too* bad. The real battle was between Tom Sheehan and Jack Nabors the year after that. Nabors won. He won 1 game all season and lost 21. Sheehan also won 1, but he was only able to lose 15.

Well, you know what happened. It wasn't just my arm went bad. After losing the 1914 World Series, Connie broke up the whole team. Eddie Collins was sold to the White Sox for $50,000, Jack Barry and Herb Pennock were sold to the Red Sox, Home Run Baker and Bob Shawkey to the Yankees, Jack Coombs to the Dodgers, and so on. Bender and Plank both jumped over to the Federal League. The whole team was scattered to the four winds, and the A's ended last *seven* years in a row after that.

As for me, after that great 4 and 17 year in 1915, I found myself with Newark in the International League on May 15, 1916. I was no world-beater there, either, and by June I was pitching for New Haven in the Eastern League. So there I was, struggling along in the Eastern League, less than two years after beating Ray Collins and winning 14 games with the World's Champions. I forget who was my roommate in New Haven, but I'll tell you one thing: it wasn't Chief Bender.

Well, there was only one way to go from there, and that was up. After all, I was still only twenty-one years old. Although, to tell the truth, I wasn't sure whether that was good or bad. Anyway, the next year I wound up in the Southern Association, with Atlanta, and wouldn't you know it, I snapped back and won 25 games. We won the pennant, and before the 1917 season was over I was back in the Big Leagues, this time with the Cincinnati Reds—with Eddie Roush, Heinie Groh, Ivy Wingo, Larry Kopf (my brother-in-law), Jake Daubert, Greasy Neale— a good team. Christy Mathewson was the manager, then later it was Pat Moran. And, believe it or not, two years later we won the National League pennant and the 1919 World Series, and I was playing on a World's Champion once again. Yessiree, life's a pretty funny proposition, after all.

This time, though, I was up there to stay. Until 1932, anyway, when I was thirty-seven years old. It required a bit of doing, however, because in 1920 my arm gave out again, this time for good as far as pitching was concerned. What happened was that I fractured my ankle in 1920, and instead of quitting and never touching a ball the rest of the season I tried to pitch a little bit late in September. By favoring my leg I pitched unnaturally, and that did it. That was the end of my pitching days.

So I was up that familiar creek again, without a paddle. This time I decided the thing to do was give up the pitching business and take up the hitting business. Why not? Other guys could hit. Why not me?

Whereupon I became an outfielder and a first baseman. In the outfield I played alongside Eddie Roush. Oh, what a beautiful and graceful outfielder that man was! The more I played next to him the more I realized his greatness. Well, he's in the Hall of Fame, right? And he got there on his hitting and his fielding *both*. The first thing I did was go to him and tell him my problem.

"If I can help you in any way, Rube," he said, "I'll be tickled to death."

Hah! The understatement of the century. The greatest center fielder in the game saying to me "*if* I can help you." Terrific!

So he taught me: how to play hitters, how to judge line drives, how to yell for the ball, how to shift on different hitters and even on the same hitter, how to run out after a fly instead of backing up, where to throw in different situations. He taught me and I listened and I practiced and I learned. I *know* I learned, because I still remember the first ball I ever caught as an outfielder. I tried to back up and I tripped and caught the darn thing while lying flat on my back. If I hadn't caught it, it would have landed on my nose. Now I know that in subsequent years *some* improvement was clearly evident.

At first base, Jake Daubert taught me how to make the plays. Another wonderful fielder. As good a fielding first baseman as Chase or Sisler. In those days, of course, we didn't have the gloves at first base like they have today. Our gloves were much smaller, so we had to use our hands and our fingers when we caught the ball. Today the first baseman doesn't catch the ball. The *glove* catches it. That thing just reaches out and wraps itself around the ball and *swallows* it, in one huge gulp. Flap! And the ball disappears.

And I made myself into a hitter. I changed my whole style of batting. Went into a deep crouch. High fast balls inside were my weakness, so I adopted this crouch, leaning way over the plate, and when I'd straighten up that ball would be out there and I could whack it. It wasn't in close any more, see.

Many a time the ball would shoot in over the inside corner and I'd drop my bat and fall back, and the umpire would shout, "Ball." The catcher would grumble and fume.

"Jeez," he'd say to the umpire, "can't you see? That damn ball got three inches of the plate." And he'd look at me and say, "That was a good strike, Rube. What more do you want?"

I never said a word. It *was* a strike. I knew it. I could see it. But that was the one pitch I didn't like, and the way I crouched it looked like it was too close to me to be a strike. Well, 19 years in the Big Leagues and a lifetime .302 batting average. I hit .357 in 1926—highest batting average in the National League—and .351 for the three-year period, 1924–26. Not bad for a reformed pitcher, huh?

Of course, I didn't try to hit the long ball. I held the bat like Cobb, with my hands apart, and hit the ball where it was pitched. I tried to *control* the bat, swing in a short arc, not get fooled. It was a matter of manipulation, see, not power. You don't have to swing with all your might every time you get up at bat. All your great artists of the old days maneuvered. It was manipulation then; today it's power. Manipulation and power, two entirely different things.

Take Ty Cobb, for instance. He did everything—except steal first base. And I think he did that in the dead of night. He'd be in his glory today, wouldn't he? I think he'd steal first base every night, because that's when they play now, at night.

Cobb could hit the long ball—when he wanted to. Of course, that dead ball . . . we didn't have a baseball to hit in those days. We had a squash. Sounded about like hitting a squash. *Plunk*. Still, Cobb could hit them a distance when he wanted to. But he didn't. He manipulated. Drove infielders crazy. I think Eddie Collins was the smartest ballplayer who ever lived, but Cobb was right next to him. Infielders didn't know what the hell he'd do next, and neither did he until the last split second. You couldn't figure Cobb. It was impossible.

And Cobb had that terrific fire, that unbelievable drive. He wasn't too well liked, but he didn't care about that. He roomed alone. They made it pretty tough on him when he first came up, but he showed them. His determination was fantastic. I never saw anybody like him. It was *his* base. It was *his* game. *Everything* was his. The most feared man in the history of baseball.

Ruth was great too, but he was different. Totally different—easygoing, friendly. There was only one Babe Ruth. He went on the ball field like he

Ty Cobb with his new Owen in 1910

was playing in a cow pasture, with cows for an audience. He never knew what fear or nervousness was. He played by instinct, sheer instinct. He wasn't smart, he didn't have any education, but he never made a wrong move on a baseball field.

One of the greatest pitchers of all time, and then he became a great judge of a fly ball, never threw to the wrong base when he was playing the outfield, terrific arm, good base runner, could hit the ball twice as far as any other human being. He was like a damn animal. He had that instinct. They know when it's going to rain, things like that. Nature, that was Ruth!

Anyway, I played the outfield and first base with Cincinnati through 1927, and then I went to the Brooklyn Dodgers for four years. Talk about pretty fair country hitters: in 1929 and '30 I batted about .310, Johnny Frederick about .330, and Babe Herman about .385. All of us in the same outfield.

And even with that we wound up in sixth place in 1929, and I think maybe fourth the next year. No pitching. Plenty of hitting, but no pitching. Well, not really no pitching at all, because one of the best was right there all the while, namely Clarence Arthur Vance—who preferred the name Arthur Charles Vance, but who was nevertheless known to the world at large as Dazzy.

Oh, what a witty man he was, what fun to be with! I roomed with Dazzy Vance for four years, all the time I was with Brooklyn, and I loved every minute of it. He was one of the great storytellers of all time.

Do you remember the three men on third? The time three Dodgers wound up on third base? It started out with Babe Herman up at bat with none out and the bases loaded. Hank DeBerry was on third, Vance on second, and Chick Fewster on first. Babe hit a ball out to right field and it was hard to say whether it would be caught or would hit the wall. Turned out it hit the wall, and DeBerry came home from third easily. Vance held up so long on second, waiting to see if the ball would be caught, that he could only make it halfway to home—so at the last minute he decided to play it safe and scampered back to third. Chick Fewster kept on going from first and made it to third, so that as Vance came back to third Fewster was already there, standing on the base. And Babe Herman just kept on going as fast as he could, without looking up at anything. So as Vance slid *back* to third, and Fewster stood *on* the base, Babe slid *into* third from the second-base side!

It's a wonder Fewster didn't get spiked. Anyway, there was a rather

substantial amount of dust and confusion at third base. The third baseman didn't know what to do, so he tagged all three of them. And the
umpire hesitated, trying to decide which two of these guys are out and
which one is safe. Rather an unusual situation, doesn't exactly come up
every day, and they started arguing about who's what.

Well, while all this discussion is going on, Daz is still lying there flat
on his back, feet on third and head toward home. Then he lifts up his
head.

"Mr. Umpire, Fellow Teammates, and Members of the Opposition,"
he intones, "if you carefully peruse the rules of our National Pastime
you will find that there is one and only one protagonist in rightful occu-
pancy of this hassock—namely yours truly, Arthur C. Vance."

Impromptu speech. And he was right. The base always belongs to
the advance runner, which, in this case, was him. The umpire finally
declared Fewster and Herman out.

You might say that the reason I left Cincinnati and went to Brooklyn
in the first place was because Vance was there. If you can't hit 'em, join
'em! Every morning I'd wake up and see him there, and know damn
well I didn't have to hit against him that day.

Vance was by far the roughest guy I ever hit against. Even worse than
Walter Johnson. I mean, he was wicked. Oh, he had a curve, it started

*Dazzy Vance: "You couldn't hit
him on a Monday"*

here and broke right around your knees, and on account of the contour you couldn't see it. It was like an apple rolling off a crooked table. You couldn't hit him on a *Monday*. On a clear day on a Monday the batter never had a chance.

He'd cut the sleeve of his undershirt to the elbow, you know, and on that part of it he'd use lye on to make it white, and the rest he didn't care how dirty it was. Then he'd pitch overhand, out of the apartment houses in the background at Ebbets Field. Between the bleached sleeve of his undershirt waving and the Monday wash hanging out to dry— the diapers and undies and sheets flapping on the clotheslines—you lost the ball entirely. He threw balls by me I never even saw.

Of course, there are two kinds of pitchers, power pitchers—like Dazzy, Walter Johnson, Lefty Grove, Bob Feller—and manipulators—like Eddie Plank, Herb Pennock, Grover Cleveland Alexander, Eppa Rixey. The power pitchers are the toughest all the way through, for the simple reason that you're always hitting at terrific stuff. They overpower you. They can make a mistake and get away with it.

But the manipulators, oh brother! Rixey got behind a hitter *deliberately*, so he could throw him the change of pace. I roomed with Rixey six years at Cincinnati. (I only roomed with the best—Bender, Rixey, Vance. If I couldn't hit, at least I'd find out why.)

"How dumb can the hitters in this league get?" Rixey used to say to me. "I've been doing this for *fifteen* years. When they're batting with the count two balls and no strikes, or three and one, they're always looking for the fast ball. And they *never* get it. They get the change of pace every time—and they're always just as surprised to see it as they were the last time."

Rixey and I always felt that perhaps Grover Cleveland Alexander was the greatest of them all, because of the conditions under which he pitched. Sixteen shutouts in 1916 pitching in Baker Bowl, where there was practically only a running track between first base and the right field wall. Only a giant could do a thing like that.

Somebody said if Alex didn't drink he'd probably have won more games. I don't see how he could have been any *better*. My God, he won over 30 three years in a row. How much better can you get? Maybe drinking *helped* him. Maybe it let him relax.

And quick! An hour and a half, an hour and three-quarters, and the game would be over. Game after game he'd pitch in an hour and a half. No fussing around out there, no stalling, no waste motion, no catchers and infielders always running out to the mound to tell him he's in trouble, and just making matters all the worse.

Those conferences out there on the mound really get me. The pitcher *knows* he's in a jam. What can they say to him? They just remind him of it, that's all. Having pitched and played first base both, I know what they do. The catcher and the infielders run over to you and pick up your rosin bag, like they never saw one in their life before, and all they say is, "Bear down, buddy, you'll get out of this. Just bear down and work hard. You can do it." Then they give you a quick pat on the rear end and run back as far as they can get out of the line of fire.

Now just what do you learn from that? You already had a vague feeling that things weren't going just right. To tell the truth, you knew darned well that you were in a heck of a jam. And you've *been* bearing down, and you've *been* working hard. All it does is make you even more worried than you already were, which was plenty. There are mighty few pitchers who can survive those conferences on the mound, take it from me.

I remember one day I was playing first base for Cincinnati, and we were ahead by one run. We had a young rookie pitching for us that day, I can't recall his name. In the last of the eighth he got in a bit of trouble, two out and then men got on second and third. I saw the shortstop and second baseman start in to give him their usual inspirational message, so I ran over real quick, to get there ahead of them.

"Listen," I said, "after you get this guy out, be sure to take a good look at that blonde behind our dugout."

Well, you could just see this fellow's face brighten up. You know—relaxing—as if to say, "What the heck, I can't be in a very tough jam if this guy's talking about a blonde."

The batter popped a little foul to the catcher, and we're out of the inning. That's the last of the eighth. I went over to the water cooler in the dugout, and as I did I felt a tap on my shoulder. It was the pitcher.

"Yeah, she sure is good-looking," he says to me.

"What? Who's good-looking? What are you talking about?"

"The blonde!" he says.

"Oh," I said. I'd forgotten all about it.

So when I went out to my position in the ninth inning I took a look. And wouldn't you know it, there was one of the most gorgeous blondes I'd ever seen in my whole life! Well, I guess it's true: life *is* a pretty funny proposition . . . after all.

15 Babe Herman

What was to become the popular perception of the Brooklyn Dodgers—of the
Daffy Dodgers, clowns, buffoons, traffic jams on the basepaths, madcap fans rooting
zealously for chronic losers—began to take shape in the 1920's. Manager Wilbert
Robinson—Uncle Robbie—was at least partially responsible for the image. He
seemed to watch it all with a certain sense of detachment as though he might have
other, more serious business on his mind. He also seemed genuinely fond of his
athletes, like a grandfather with too many rascally grandchildren bounding mis-
chievously about, sighing at their boyish antics.

It was in the spring of 1926 that the most colorful Dodger of them all reported to
Brooklyn's Clearwater training camp. He was a tall, slim, light-haired, buck-
toothed, twenty-two-year-old slugger who was to become central to more incidents
quaint and bizarre than any other Dodger, and would finally emerge as the embodi-
ment of the total legend of Brooklyn baseball. His name was Floyd Caves Herman,
but nobody ever called him anything but Babe.

—DONALD HONIG, *The Brooklyn Dodgers*

ACTUALLY, when I was in high school I was more interested in playing
football than baseball. I got into baseball by sheer accident, and I mean
that more literally than figuratively.

Gus Gleichman, you see, was the playing manager and first baseman of
the Edmonton club in the Western Canada League. That was a Class B
minor league, pretty fast company in those days. Gus was down here in
southern California in the off-season, it must have been March or April of
1921, when he got into a pretty bad automobile accident. He was driving
to Ventura when his car skidded and flipped over, as a result of which Gus
wound up with a broken leg. So instead of enjoying a vacation, Gus found
himself searching for a first baseman.

As far as I was concerned, I was looking forward to finishing school at
Glendale High and then going on to the University of California at
Berkeley that fall on a football scholarship. About fifteen colleges had con-
tacted me about playing football, but I had my heart set on Berkeley.

A few days after Gus Gleichman's accident, though, I was in a local
sporting-goods store and the owner, Joe Rafferty, says to me, "Hey, do you
want to play professional baseball?"

"Gee, I don't know," I said. "What are you talking about?" I had something of a reputation as a first baseman because I played that position on a
lot of semipro teams in the area.

So Joe Rafferty told me about Gus Gleichman needing a first baseman
and how he'd recommended me to Gus. Pretty soon in came Gus himself,
on crutches, and after we talked a while he offered me $175 a month to
play for Edmonton that season. That was an awful lot of money to me. I
hadn't reached my eighteenth birthday yet. Before I really knew what I
was doing, I took the contract and signed my name on the dotted line.

Now I had to go home and tell Dad, which wasn't such an easy thing to
do. But that evening I braced myself and said, "Dad, I'm going to Canada
to play ball. They'll pay me $175 a month and I'll get a chance to see how
good I really am."

"Humph," Dad says, "they don't pay you to play in this world. You stay
with me and work and some day you'll have something." Dad was a building contractor.

"Well," I said, "I'd sure like to give it a try."

"I won't stop you," he said, "but you watch, pretty soon you'll be wiring
me for money to come home."

"No," I said, "if I have to, I'll come home riding the rails in a box-car."

So off I went. I hit .330 at Edmonton, led the league in triples and
batting average, and after the season was over was sold to the Detroit
Tigers. Detroit sent me to Omaha in the Western League in 1922, where I
hit .416. In those days, though, you had to pay your dues, put in four or
five years in the minors before they figured you were ready for the Big
Leagues. So it was 1926 before I got a real chance and then it wasn't with
Detroit but with the Brooklyn Dodgers, who'd acquired my contract.

I made it as a regular with the Dodgers the first year I was with them,
1926. Wilbert Robinson was the Dodger manager then, had been for many
years. Robbie had been a catcher with the old Baltimore Orioles in the
1890's, along with McGraw, Willie Keeler, Hughie Jennings, and that
crew. After that he'd been John McGraw's coach and right-hand man with
the New York Giants, and then he became manager of the Dodgers in
1914. In fact, most of the time I was there, we weren't called the Dodgers;
we were called the Brooklyn Robins, after Uncle Robbie.

Despite what you might have read, Uncle Robbie wasn't a clown. He
was a sound baseball man and a good manager, especially when it came to
handling pitchers. Of course, he had his idiosyncrasies, but who doesn't?
He liked to reminisce on the bench and talk about the good old days and

Babe Herman in 1927

about fishing and hunting. In the off-season he used to go to Dover Hall, a fishing and hunting place near Brunswick, Georgia, and sometimes he'd get so involved talking about the old Baltimore Orioles or about Dover Hall that he'd forget all about the ball game and forget to give his signs to the third-base coach.

Not that it mattered all that much. For a while we had old Joe Kelley as our third-base coach. A real nice fellow, Joe had been a teammate of Robbie's on the old Baltimore Orioles and was a great outfielder in his day, but obviously the only reason he was with us was because Robbie wanted to take care of a long-time friend. For instance, one day I hit a line drive over first base. The ball caromed into the Brooklyn bullpen and got tangled up under the benches there. As I was coming into second, I saw Joe Kelley, coaching at third base, motioning for me to hold up, so I put on the brakes and stopped at second. But then I saw that the right fielder was still scrambling around under the benches for the ball, so I headed for third. Coming into third, he stopped me again, or I could have scored.

"Gee, Joe," I said, when I got to third base, "what's going on? You stopped me at second while the outfielder was still trying to get to the ball."

He put his arm around my shoulder and whispered to me. "Babe," he says, "I want to tell you something. Without my glasses, I can't even see who's pitching. But I won't wear glasses on a ball field."

"Why not?" I asked.

"Pride," he says!

We had a catcher named Val Picinich, came to us from the Cincinnati Reds in 1929. The first time Robbie decided to use him in a game, he told Val he's catching, so Val goes and puts his gear on. Meanwhile, Robbie's making out the lineup card and he turns to me and says, "Hey, Babe, how do you spell that new guy's last name?"

"Don't you know how to spell it, Robbie?" I said.

Robbie thought a minute and then he mumbled, "Aw, the hell with it, I'll put DeBerry in to catch."

So now he's told two guys they're catching, and when the game starts Picinich and DeBerry both walk up to home plate with their gear on. When they get to the plate, they stop and look at each other, a little bit confused. They finally got it straightened out, though.

I wasn't the world's greatest fielder, as a lot of stories will attest, but I was always a pretty fair country hitter: .340 in 1928, .381 in 1929, and .393 with 35 homers and 130 runs batted in in 1930. The year I hit .393 I came into the last day of the season hitting .397. If I could have gotten three straight hits, it would have put me at .400. But we played a double-header, and I only went one for nine and dropped from .397 to .393. Didn't even lead the league because that's the year Bill Terry hit .401.

My salary was $19,000 in 1930, the year I hit .393. I tried to get a $1,000 raise that winter, but without success. They finally agreed to $800 "expense money"—whatever that meant—but they never gave it to me anyway.

Ruth was the highest paid at that time, at $80,000. That seemed like an enormous figure, but nobody begrudged him because we all knew he deserved it, and the more he got the more we would get. I think Al Simmons was the next highest; he had a three-year $100,000 contract with the White Sox. We always used to ask Al which year he'd get the extra cent in— because if they gave him $33,333.33 a year for three years, they'd still owe him a penny.

Speaking of Ruth, by the way, reminds me of a story that I was called "Babe" because when I came up to the Big Leagues with Brooklyn, I was supposed to have said that I was going to hit like Babe Ruth. As with so many stories that sound good, it's just not so. The fact is, I got the nickname "Babe" way back when I was playing with Edmonton in the Western Canada League, my very first year in organized baseball. There was a popular champion flyweight prize fighter at that time named Babe Herman, and a fog-horn lady fan at Edmonton started calling me "Babe" after Babe Herman the fighter, not after Babe Ruth. She'd yell, "Go get 'em, Babe," or "Get a hit, Babe" so loud you could hear her all over the ball park, and somehow the name stuck.

Oh, before I forget, there's one more story I've got to tell you about Uncle Robbie. It's about the time he agreed to catch a baseball dropped from an airplane as a publicity stunt. See, Gabby Street had just caught a baseball dropped from the top of the Washington Monument. So they were going to top that in Florida, in spring training, by having someone catch a ball dropped from an airplane flying over the ball park. With some reluctance, Robbie agreed to put on a mask and chest protector and be the hero of the hour. Heck, anything Gabby Street could do Robbie figured the catcher of the old Baltimore Orioles could do even better.

The first two times the plane flew over the ball park, Dan Comerford, the clubhouse man, dropped a baseball and both times he completely missed the field. The ball didn't come within half a mile of the ball park. Unfortunately, Dan had taken only two baseballs up with him, so he either

Uncle Robbie

had to come back down and get more or forget the whole thing. However, while he was trying to decide what to do, he noticed a sack of Florida grapefruit in the plane. In the early days in Florida, *everybody* had a sack of grapefruit. So the pilot circled around and made another approach, only this time Dan dropped a *grapefruit* instead of a baseball!

Well, down in the ball park, out near second base, Robbie is also circling around, getting a bead on this thing as it falls. As far as he knows—as far as *anybody* besides Dan knows—it's a baseball that's falling, not a grapefruit, and Robbie is determined to catch it.

"Get away, get away," Robbie yells, "I got it, I got it." And then *squash*, it smacks right into Robbie's mitt and literally *explodes*, juice and pulp splashing into Robbie's face and all over him. The force of the thing was so great that it knocked Robbie down, and all he knew was that he had all this liquid and stuff all over him.

"Help, help," he shouted, "I'm bleeding to death. Help me!"

Some players called him "Grapefruit" forever after. It was a nickname he never lost.

I was traded from Brooklyn after the 1931 season, partly because Uncle Robbie was let go at that time and partly because I was still feuding with the front office over the $800 "expense money" they'd promised me but never delivered, as well as over a proposed cut in salary. I played with the Reds and the Cubs for a few years, and then returned home here and played with the Hollywood Stars in the Pacific Coast League from 1939 through 1944. In 1945, near the end of World War II, I even came back to Brooklyn as a pinch-hitter for a few months at the age of 42.

The first time I came up as a pinch-hitter at Ebbets Field in 1945 the bases were loaded, and I hit one off the right-field screen to drive in two runs. However, I slipped rounding first, and wouldn't you believe the headline in the paper the next day never said a thing about the two runs I drove in. Instead, it read: SAME OLD HERMAN, TRIPS OVER FIRST BASE.

I guess the three men on third inspired more hilarity than anything else during those years. You know the old taxi-driver story, don't you? A cab is driving by Ebbets Field, and the cab driver sticks his head out of the window and yells up at a spectator, "How's the game going?"

"The Dodgers have three men on base," the spectator shouts back.

"Which base?" the cabbie asks.

Everybody blames me for three men winding up on third base, but it wasn't my fault. Actually, it was Dazzy Vance who caused the whole mess. We were playing the Boston Braves in 1926 and the score was tied, 1–1, in the bottom of the seventh inning. I came up to bat with the bases loaded: Hank DeBerry was on third, Vance on second, and Chick Fewster on first. Well, I hit a line drive to right field and slid safely into second with a double. But while I'm on the ground, I looked up and saw a run-down between third and home. Naturally, I figured Chick Fewster is caught in a run-down, so I get up and sprint for third, like I'm supposed to. That way we'll have a man on third even if Chick is tagged out.

But when I got to third, Fewster was *already* there, which surprised me. And then here comes Vance into third from the other side. That *really* surprised me, 'cause I thought he'd scored long ago. After all, he was on second, and even if you're slow as a turtle you should be able to score from second on a double! Especially when the first throw was to second base on me.

Anyway, there we were all on third at one and the same time. Vance was declared safe and Fewster and I were both out. If there was any justice, Vance would have been the one declared out because he's the one caused the traffic jam in the first place. But down through history, for some strange reason, it's all been blamed on me.

Ironic, isn't it, when you realize that I drove in the winning run with that hit. We won the game, 4–1, and that double scored DeBerry with the go-ahead run. Only time I can think of when a fellow drives in the winning run and the press makes him a goat instead of a hero!

Babe Herman and son Bobby at the 1933 All-Star Game in Chicago

16 Edd Roush

"Who is he, anyhow, an actor?"

"No."

"A dentist?"

". . . No, he's a gambler." Gatsby hesitated, then added coolly: "He's the man who fixed the World Series back in 1919."

"Fixed the World Series?" I repeated.

The idea staggered me. I remembered, of course, that the World Series had been fixed in 1919, but if I had thought of it at all I would have thought of it as a thing that merely *happened,* the end of some inevitable chain. It never occurred to me that one man could start to play with the faith of fifty million people—with the single-mindedness of a burglar blowing a safe.

"How did he happen to do that?" I asked after a minute.

"He just saw the opportunity."

"Why isn't he in jail?"

"They can't get him, old sport. He's a smart man."

—F. Scott Fitzgerald, *The Great Gatsby*

YES, I KNEW AT THE TIME that some finagling was going on. At least that's what I'd heard. Rumors were flying all over the place that gamblers had got to the Chicago White Sox, that they'd agreed to throw the World Series. But nobody knew anything for sure until Eddie Cicotte spilled the beans a year later.

We beat them in the first two games, 9–1 and 4–2, and it was after the second game that I first got wind of it. We played those first two games in Cincinnati, and the next day we were to play in Chicago. So the evening after the second game we were all gathered at the hotel in Cincinnati, standing around waiting for cabs to take us to the train station, when this fellow came over to me. I didn't know who he was, but I'd seen him around before.

"Roush," he says, "I want to tell you something. Did you hear about the squabble the White Sox got into after the game this afternoon?" And he told me some story about Ray Schalk accusing Lefty Williams of throwing the game, and something about some of the White Sox beating up a gambler for not giving them the money he'd promised them.

"They didn't get the payoff," he said, "so from here on they're going to try to win."

I didn't know whether this guy made it all up or not. But it did start me thinking. Later on in the Series the same guy came over to me again.

"Roush," he says, "you remember what I told you about gamblers getting to the White Sox? Well, now they've also got to some of the players on your own ball club."

That's all he said. Wouldn't tell me any more. I didn't say anything to anybody until we were getting dressed in the clubhouse the next day. Then I got hold of the manager, Pat Moran, just before the pregame meeting.

"Before you start this meeting, Pat," I said, "there's something I want to talk to you about."

"OK," he says, "what is it?"

"I've been told that gamblers have got to some of the players on this club," I said. "Maybe it's true and maybe it isn't. I don't know. But you sure better do some finding out. I'll be damned if I'm going to knock myself out trying to win this Series if somebody else is trying to throw the game."

Pat got all excited and called Jake Daubert over, who was the team captain. It was all news to both of them. So at the meeting, after we'd gone over the White Sox lineup, Moran looked at Hod Eller, who was going to pitch for us that day.

"Hod," he said, "I've been hearing rumors about sellouts. Not about you, not about anybody in particular, just rumors. I want to ask you a straight question and I want a straight answer."

"Shoot," says Hod.

"Has anybody offered you anything to throw this game?"

"Yep," Hod said. Lord, you could have heard a pin drop.

"After breakfast this morning a guy got on the elevator with me, and got off at the same floor I did. He showed me five thousand-dollar bills, and said they were mine if I'd lose the game today."

"What did you say?" Moran asked him.

"I said if he didn't get damn far away from me real quick he wouldn't know what hit him. And the same went if I ever saw him again."

Moran looked at Eller a long time. Finally, he said, "OK, you're pitching. But one wrong move and you're out of the game."

Evidently there weren't any wrong moves. Because ol' Hod went out there and pitched a swell game. He won two of the games in that Series.

A large crowd in Times Square follows the progress of the 1919 World Series

on a mechanical diamond

I don't know whether the whole truth of what went on there among the White Sox will ever come out. Even today nobody really knows exactly what took place. Whatever it was, though, it was a dirty rotten shame. One thing that's always overlooked in the whole mess is that we could have beat them no matter what the circumstances!

Sure, the 1919 White Sox were good. But the 1919 Cincinnati Reds were *better*. I'll believe that till my dying day. I don't care how good Chicago's Joe Jackson and Buck Weaver and Eddie Cicotte were. *We* had Heinie Groh, Jake Daubert, Greasy Neale, Rube Bressler, Larry Kopf, myself, and the best pitching staff in both leagues. We were a very underrated ball club.

I played center field for that Cincinnati club for 11 straight years, 1916 through 1926. I came to Cincinnati from the Giants in the middle of 1916, along with Christy Mathewson and Bill McKechnie.

Of course I started playing ball long before that, around 1909 or so, right here in Oakland City, Indiana. In those days every little town had an amateur club, and so did Oakland City. Never will forget it. I was only about sixteen at the time. Oakland City had a game scheduled with a neighboring town this day, and one of Oakland City's outfielders hadn't shown up. Everybody was standing around right on the main street of town—only a small town, you know—wondering what to do, when one of the town officials says, "Why not put that Roush kid in?"

I was kind of a shy kid, and I backed away. But the manager says, "Well, that's just what we'll do if he don't show up in five more minutes."

We waited for five minutes and the outfielder never did show, so they gave me a uniform and put me in right field. Turned out I got a couple of hits that day, and I became Oakland City's regular right fielder for the rest of the season.

The next year, of course, I was right in the middle of it. We reorganized the team—the Oakland City Walk-Overs, that's what we called ourselves—and had a pretty good club. In those days, you know, I used to throw with *either* hand. I'm a natural lefty, see, but when I was a kid I never could find a lefty's glove. So I just used a regular glove and learned to throw righty. Batted lefty, but got so I could throw with my right arm almost as well as with my left.

The year after that we got in quite a hassle. That would be 1911. Seems as though some of the Oakland City boys were getting $5 a game, and I wasn't one of them. So I started raising Cain about this under-the-table business and treating some different than others.

Two stars of the Oakland City Walk-Overs in 1910—Edd Roush (l.) and Pete Lowe

Wound up we had such an argument that I quit the home-town club and went over and played with the Princeton team. Princeton is the closest town to Oakland City, about 12 miles due west. And don't think that didn't cause quite a ruckus. Especially when Princeton came over to play Oakland City *at* Oakland City, with me in the Princeton outfield. A fair amount of hard feelings were stirred up, to say the least. I think there are still one or two around here never have forgiven me to this very day.

I played with Princeton about a year and a half, and then a fellow connected with the Evansville club in the Kitty League asked me would I like to play for them in professional baseball. Well, Evansville's only about 30 miles from Oakland City, almost due south, and the idea of getting paid for playing ball sounded real good to me. And Dad thought it was terrific. He'd played semipro ball himself, when he was young. William C. Roush was his name. A darn good ballplayer, too. So I signed with Evansville and finished the 1912 season with them.

I bought a lefty's glove when I started playing with Evansville, figuring I might as well go back to the natural throw. From then on I always threw left-handed, 'cause it didn't carry quite so well when I threw with my right. Wasn't really a natural throw.

After that, things moved quick. Evansville sold me to the Chicago White Sox—of all teams, considering what happened later—in the middle of the following season. I stayed with them a month—Cicotte was there then, and Buck Weaver, and Ray Schalk—and then they optioned me to Lincoln, Nebraska, in the Western League.

The next year the Indianapolis club in the new Federal League got in touch with me and offered me $225 a month, almost twice what I was getting at Lincoln. So I jumped to the Federal League for the next couple of years. That Federal League wasn't a bad league. Too bad it only lasted two years. Ran into a lot of financial troubles and folded in December of 1915. Of course, it was an outlaw league, you know, raiding the other leagues for its players. The established leagues threatened that anybody who jumped to the Feds would never be allowed back in organized ball, but once the Feds broke up they were glad to get us.

We had some good players there the two years the Federal League lived. A lot of old-timers jumped over, like Three-Fingered Brown, Chief Bender, Eddie Plank, Davy Jones, Joe Tinker, Jimmy Delahanty, Al Bridwell, and Charlie Carr, the old Indianapolis first baseman. They didn't care if organized ball never took them back, 'cause they were near the end of the trail anyway.

But there were also a lot of younger players, like Benny Kauff, Bill McKechnie, and myself. All three of us were sold to the New York Giants when the Federal League collapsed, and that's where we reported in the spring of 1916.

Me, I didn't like New York. I'm a small-town boy. I like the Midwest. Well, it wasn't *exactly* that. Not entirely, anyway. It was really McGraw I didn't like. John J. McGraw. I just didn't enjoy playing for him, that's all. If you made a bad play he'd cuss you out, yell at you, call you all sorts of names. That didn't go with me. So I was glad as I could be when he traded me to Cincinnati in the middle of the '16 season. I couldn't have been happier.

McGraw traded Mathewson, McKechnie, and me to Cincinnati for Wade Killefer and Buck Herzog, who had been the Cincinnati manager. Matty was to replace Herzog as the new manager. I still remember the trip the three of us made as we left the Giants and took the train to join the Reds. McKechnie and I were sitting back on the observation car, talking about how happy we were to be traded. Matty came out and sat down and listened, but he didn't say anything.

Finally I turned to him and said, "Well, Matty, aren't you glad to be getting away from McGraw?"

"I'll tell you something, Roush," he said. "You and Mac have only been on the Giants a couple of months. It's just another ball club to you fellows. But I was with that team for 16 years. That's a mighty long time.

William C. Roush,
Edd's father, as a semipro
ballplayer in the 1880's

To me, the Giants are 'home.' And leaving them like this, I feel the same as when I leave home in the spring of the year.

"Of course, I realize I'm through as a pitcher. But I appreciate McGraw making a place for me in baseball and getting me this managing job. He's doing me a favor, and I thanked him for it. And by the way, the last thing he said to me was that if I put you in center field I'd have a great ballplayer. So starting tomorrow you're my center fielder."

Well, we got to Cincinnati and sure enough, right off Matty puts me in center field. Greasy Neale was the right fielder. It was his first year with the Reds too, but he'd been there since the start of the season and, of course, I was a newcomer. The first game I played there, about three or four fly balls came out that could have been taken by either the center fielder or the right fielder. If I thought I should take it, I'd holler three times: "I got it, I got it, I got it." I'd holler while I was running for it, see.

But Greasy never said a word. Sometimes he'd take it, and sometimes he wouldn't. But in either case he never said a thing. We went along that way for about three weeks. What I finally did was watch *both* him and the ball. If it looked to me like I could catch the ball and get out of his way, I'd holler and take it. But if it looked like it was going to be a tie, I'd just cut behind him and let him take it. He still never hollered, and didn't have too much else to say to me, either. So I didn't have too much to say to him.

You see, I could watch both him and the ball at the same time because I didn't really have to watch the ball. As soon as a ball was hit I could tell where it was going to go, and I'd just take off and not look at it any more till I got there. So I'd take a quick glance at him while I was running.

Finally, one day Greasy came over and sat down beside me on the bench. "I want to end this, Roush," he says to me. "I guess you know I've been trying to run you down ever since you got here. I wanted that center field job for myself, and I didn't like it when Matty put you out there. But you can go get a ball better than I ever could. I want to shake hands and call it off. From now on, I'll holler."

And from then on Greasy and I got along just fine. Grew to be two of the best friends ever. In fact, I made a lot of good friends those years I played in Cincinnati, still my close friends to this day. I think that Cincinnati club from 1916 to 1926 was one of the nicest bunch of fellows ever gathered together.

We even had Jim Thorpe there one year, you know. By thunder, there was a man could outrun a deer. Beat anything I ever saw. I used to be pretty fast myself. Stole close to 300 bases in the Big Leagues. And I had a real long stride, for the simple reason that in the outfield if you don't take a long stride your head bobs up and down too much and makes it hard to follow the flight of the ball. But Jim Thorpe would take only two strides to my three. I'd run just as hard as I could, and he'd keep up with me just trotting along.

One day I asked him, "Jim, anybody in those Olympic games ever make you really run your best?"

"I never yet saw the man I couldn't look back at," he says to me. I believed him.

Well, sir, I really hit my own stride those years in Cincinnati. Led the league in batting twice, hit over .350 three years in a row—'21, '22, and '23—and generally had a ball. The lowest I ever hit while I was there was .321 in 1919, and that was good enough to lead the league that year. We won the pennant and the World Series in 1919, and finished either first, second, or third in seven of the 11 years I was there. Good teams—very much underrated. Like I say, *better* than the 1919 White Sox.

Of course, I hit very different from the way they hit today. I used a 48-ounce bat, heaviest anyone ever used. It was a shorter bat, with a big handle, and I tried to hit to all fields. Didn't swing my head off, just snapped at the ball. Until 1921, you know, they had a dead ball. Well, the only way you could get a home run was if the outfielder tripped and fell down. The ball wasn't wrapped tight and lots of times it'd get mashed on one side. I've caught many a ball in the outfield that was mashed flat on one side. Come bouncing out there like a jumping bean. They wouldn't throw it out of the game, though. Only used about three or four balls in a whole game. Now they use 60 or 70.

Another thing that's different now is the ball parks. Now they have smooth infields and outfields that aren't full of rocks, and they keep them nice. Back in the old days there were parks weren't much better than a cow pasture. Spring training was the worst. Some of those parks they'd want you to play exhibition games in had outfields like sand dunes, and others were hard as a cement sidewalk. The hell with that! I wouldn't go to spring training, that's all.

I used to hold out every year until the week before the season opened. That's the only time they ever had any trouble with me, contract time. Why should I go down there and fuss around in spring training? Twist an ankle, or break a leg. I did my *own* spring training, hunting quail and rabbits around Oakland City.

After 11 years with the Reds, they traded me to the Giants for George Kelly. That was after the 1926 season. Well, I figured that was it. I was around thirty-four, and I wasn't about to start taking abuse from McGraw that late in life. However, I figured I had one chance: maybe I could get McGraw to trade me.

So in January of '27, when the Giants sent me a contract for $19,000, same as I'd been getting with Cincinnati, I sent it right back and wrote them I wouldn't play in New York. A couple of weeks later another one arrived, calling for $20,000. I figured they hadn't gotten the point. So

Edd Roush in 1916

I wrote a letter telling them I wouldn't play with the Giants for *any* kind of money. And wouldn't you know it, two weeks after that another contract arrived, calling for $21,000. I didn't even bother to send that one back.

Since they didn't seem to get the point the way I was doing it, I finally wrote and said I wanted $30,000. I figured that would sink in and they'd get the idea. Send me to another club.

Well, spring training started—and ended—and the team began to move up north, playing exhibition games along the way. I was still busy hunting quail right here around Oakland City. Then one day I got a call from McGraw. Would I meet him in Chattanooga next week? After thinking it over, I decided I might as well.

I arrived at the hotel in Chattanooga at eight o'clock on a Thursday morning, and when I registered the clerk said to me, "Mr. McGraw left a message for you to come up to his room as soon as you arrive."

Well, it was eight o'clock, and I hadn't had any breakfast. So I went into the dining room and ordered a good meal. About nine o'clock a bellboy comes over and says, "Mr. McGraw would like to see you in room 305."

"All right," I says, "tell him I'll be there."

About that time the ballplayers started to drift in, so I visited with them awhile. One of them gave me a good cigar, so I sat down in a comfortable chair in the lobby and talked to some of the boys while I enjoyed it. About eleven o'clock one of the coaches came over. "McGraw wants to know why you're not up there yet?"

Finally, by about 12:30 or so, after I'd finished visiting with the ballplayers, completed a detailed reading of three newspapers, and had a haircut and a shoeshine, I decided to go upstairs and see Mr. John J. McGraw.

"What the devil's the matter with you, Roush?" he says, "Don't you want to play ball for me?"

"Hell, no," I said. "I don't want to play ball for you. Haven't you figured that out by now?"

"Why not?"

" 'Cause I don't like the way you treat your players, that's why. First time you call me a damn so-and-so, somebody's going to get hurt."

"Listen, we'll get along fine. Don't you worry," he says.

"Yeah. I've heard that one before."

"Sit down," he says, "and listen to me. You know this game as well as I do. You play your own game and I'll never say anything to you."

"That's another one I've heard before."

"Well," he says, "it's the truth."

"The first time something happens out there, and you start on me," I said, "I'm taking off for Oakland City, Indiana. Why don't we stop all this horsing around and you just send me to another ball club?"

"I won't do it," he says. "I've been trying to get you back ever since I traded you away a long time ago. Now you're either going to play for me or you're not going to play ball at all. I'm sure not going to let you go a second time."

"OK," I said, "if that's the way you feel about it. If you give me my salary, I'll try it. But I still say I'll be back in Oakland City, Indiana, in ten days."

"How much do you want?"

"$25,000."

"I can't pay it."

Well, I took my hat and started for the door. "Where do you think you're going?" he says.

"Back to Oakland City, Indiana. Why?"

"Now hold on," he says. "Come back and sit down. I'll tell you what I'll do. I'll give you a three-year contract for $70,000."

"All right," I said, "I'll take it."

I signed the contract, went out to the ball park, got into a uniform, and played six innings that afternoon. Got two hits out of three times up, too.

I played that three-year contract out, and after that I quit, and finally did come back to Oakland City, Indiana. McGraw kept to his word and never bothered me. But it wasn't like playing in Cincinnati. I missed my teammates, and I missed the Cincinnati fans.

I've read where as far as the Cincinnati fans are concerned I'm the most popular player ever wore a Reds' uniform. I don't know about that. It's not for me to say. But—assuming it's true—I'll tell you one thing: the feeling is mutual.

17 *Bill Wambsganss*

The dogs did bark, the children screamed,
Up flew the windows all,
And every soul bawled out: "Well Done!"
As loud as he could bawl.
—WILLIAM COWPER, *The History of John Gilpin*

FUNNY THING, I played in the Big Leagues for thirteen years—1914 through 1926—and the *only* thing anybody seems to remember is that once I made an unassisted triple play in a World Series. Many don't even remember the team I was on, or the position I played, or anything. Just Wambsganss—unassisted triple play.

Actually, more people probably know me as Bill Wamby than as Bill Wambsganss. Wamby fits in a box score easier, so that's how it usually was reported. But it doesn't matter. Same thing: Wamby—unassisted triple play. You'd think I was born the day before and died the day after.

Fact is I was born in 1894, 26 years before that play, and now it's 45 years after it and—knock on wood—far as I know I'm still bright-eyed and bushy-tailed. I was born right here in Cleveland, although I grew up in Fort Wayne, Indiana. You see, my Dad was a Lutheran clergyman, and in 1895, when I was only about a year and a half old, he was transferred from Cleveland to a church in Fort Wayne.

Naturally, it was assumed that I'd follow in his footsteps. That was just taken for granted, that some day I'd be a minister too, same as Dad. I even believed it myself for a long time. In those days, you know, the old-fashioned Lutherans thought that all you had to do was bring your boy up the right way and the Lord would take care of the rest. High Persuasion, you might say. Especially if you were a minister's son.

And, of course, I accepted this. Everything seemed like it was all sort of cut and dried as far as my future was concerned. Then it happened: I went to Concordia College in Fort Wayne, and played ball on the

231

college team, and that started me to thinking that maybe I'd better reconsider the whole thing.

In the first place, once I got to playing on the college team, all I did was sit in the classroom and look out the window, wishing that class was over so I could go out and play ball.

Then, in the second place, about becoming a minister—well—I just couldn't figure out how I could possibly do it. The trouble was I just couldn't talk in front of people, public speaking in front of a group of people I mean. I simply couldn't do it. I was a pretty bashful youngster and I stuttered a bit, and I still remember one day I got up to make a recitation in class and I couldn't get a word out, not a single word.

So I got to worrying about how to get out of the whole situation. There was my father, though, and what he expected of me. I just dreaded telling him I didn't want to be a minister. Even now, I get nervous when I think about it. So I just kept right on wading through the whole business.

I finished college, and after that you were supposed to go to the theological seminary down in St. Louis for a couple of years. So that's what I did, went to divinity school in St. Louis even though I still couldn't speak in front of people without working up a terrible case of stage fright every single time. Unfortunately, nobody there was willing to take the bull by the horns and say right out that this kid just wouldn't make a good minister. So I went on through. It's a joke, but I did.

What happened while I was there, though, was a pure stroke of luck. The good Lord must have really taken pity on me. One of the other seminary students had played some professional baseball, and by sheer chance the manager of the Cedar Rapids club wrote to him and asked him if he knew a good shortstop he could recommend. Well, he recommended me! So during the summer vacation from the seminary I went and played ball. That's how I got my start: 1913, Cedar Rapids, Central Association, professional baseball.

Of course, first I went home and talked to my father about it. I told him it was just for the summer, so he let me go, and I joined Cedar Rapids at the beginning of July and played there all summer.

Then I went back to the seminary that fall. They often have opportunities for the students to go and get practical experience in the ministry and related fields, you know. Well, it so happened there was an opening in North Dakota for a man to teach school until Easter. This was just exactly what I wanted. So I went up there and taught school

Bill Wambsganss in 1916

in North Dakota until Easter, after which I was free. And since that was just about the time the baseball season started, I went from North Dakota right back to Cedar Rapids to play ball again.

I had a very good season at Cedar Rapids in 1914, and before it was over they sold me to the Cleveland club for $1,250. Speaking of money, by the way, my salary with Cedar Rapids was $100 a month. It was more when I joined Cleveland, but not a heck of a lot more. There was no such thing as a minimum salary in the Big Leagues then, like there is now. In those days minimum was minimum, you might say.

Now, being sold to Cleveland, the moment of trial by fire had really arrived. I had to go back and straighten all this out with my father. Which I did. I took a deep breath and told him I did not want to become a minister, that I didn't think I was equal to the task, that I always had ambitions to become a professional ballplayer, and that I knew I had talent. At least it looked that way, because Cleveland had bought me.

Well, Dad really amazed me. The biggest surprise of my life. He agreed to let me do whatever I thought best, didn't argue much at all, and said whatever I wanted to do was fine with him. Which was a very big thing, when you think about it. I'll tell you one thing, it surely took a burden off my mind. I felt as though a thousand-ton load had been taken off my back. (Actually, fact is, I have a sneaking feeling that what really did it was that I was going to play for Cleveland. Dad had always

A 1906 advertisement

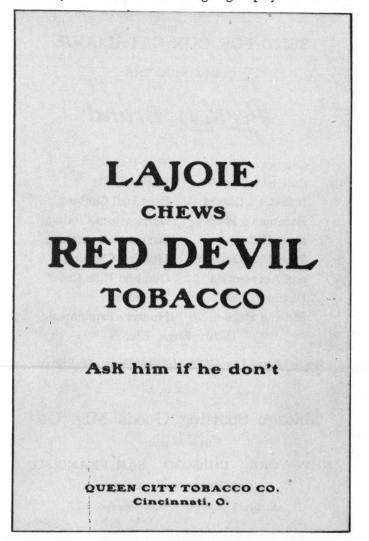

been a Cleveland fan, especially a Larry Lajoie fan. I'm still not sure
what he would have said if I'd been sold to the Detroit Tigers!)

So I joined the Cleveland Indians as a shortstop in August of that
year. That would be 1914, my second year in organized ball. Actually,
they were known as the Naps then, after Napoleon Lajoie. We became
the Indians the next year, after Lajoie left. We didn't have a very good
club that year—I think we ended last, to tell the truth—but we had
some awfully good players.

Shoeless Joe Jackson was there—he was traded to the White Sox the
next year—and Ray Chapman at shortstop, Jack Graney in left field,
Steve O'Neill catching, and Terry Turner at third base. Terry Turner
had been playing in the Cleveland infield since 1904. And, of course,
Lajoie was still there at second base. That was his last year with Cleveland. As it turned out, I was his successor at second.

As I mentioned, Ray Chapman was the regular shortstop when I got
there. A great one, too. Ring Lardner was writing sports in those days,
and he must have gotten intrigued by my name—he wasn't the first, nor
the last. I'd hardly joined the team before I read this limerick in the
newspaper:

> The Naps bought a shortstop named Wambsganss,
> Who is slated to fill Ray Chapman's pants.
> But when he saw Ray,
> And the way he could play,
> He muttered, "I haven't a clam's chance!"

It was true enough. Although I'd been a shortstop in the minors, they
tried experimenting with me at second and third. One of the first games
I got in was at Detroit. I was put in at third base. I hadn't been on the
club more than a week or so, and the Tigers tried to rattle me by yelling
insults of one sort or another at me. See, their bench was right next to
third base, maybe only 15 or 20 feet away. Well, all those guys yelling
at me while I'm in the field, I looked over at them to see what all the
excitement was about. And darned if Ty Cobb wasn't yelling louder
than all the rest of them put together.

"Gee," I thought to myself, "that's funny. A star like Cobb picking on
a raw rookie like me." So I yelled back at him, something like: "If you
think I'm such a busher, you ought to see yourself!"

It's a peculiar thing, I'd get so nervous I couldn't even talk in front
of people, but I was never a bit nervous out there on the ball field. Not

even with 50,000 people in the stands. All those guys did by yelling at me was make me mad.

In the first inning Cobb came up to bat. Well, before the game, Terry Turner, who'd been in the league a long time, had told me what to watch for. He said that Cobb was a very good bunter, and that I better be on the alert for a bunt down the third-base line whenever Cobb was up there at the plate.

"However," Turner said to me, "I'll give you a tip. If he's going to bunt, he'll grit his teeth. He'll grit his teeth like he's going to murder the ball, and *that's* when he'll bunt. He does that to throw you off, see."

So Cobb came up to bat and I'm watching him real close for this teeth-gritting business. Since he was a left-handed batter, I could see his face real good. By golly, darned if all of a sudden he didn't start gritting those teeth to beat the band, looking as fierce as Mephistopheles himself.

"Here it comes," I thought, "a bunt."

And I started creeping in, even before the pitcher let the ball go. By the time the pitch got to the plate I was halfway in. Crack! Cobb swung with all his might and slammed one down at me a mile a minute, so hard I thought it would take my head right off my shoulders. I threw up my hand to protect myself and by sheer accident the ball stuck right in my glove. Whew! After that I let Terry Turner keep his advice to himself.

Finally, after a lot of scuffling around, they settled on second base as my position. I played second alongside Ray Chapman at shortstop for six years. He was one of my best friends, and we got so we worked together like clockwork in the field. Ray always said he would never play shortstop next to anybody else. And, sadly enough, that was true. He was hit in the head by a pitched ball and killed in 1920.

That was a terrible thing to happen. Chappie was probably the most popular man on the team. As a matter of fact, he'd talked of retiring after that season. His wife was pregnant at the time and his father-in-law, a millionaire, was going to set him up in business. It was an awful tragedy. Such a sweet guy.

We slumped very badly after that. It happened in the middle of August, and we went into a tailspin for a while. But, as you know, we eventually recovered and went on to win the pennant and beat Brooklyn in the World Series. Tris Speaker was our manager and center fielder, Joe Sewell took Chappie's place, and we had real good pitching—Stan Coveleski, the great spitball pitcher, Jim Bagby, and Ray Caldwell. And, of course, that was the World Series where I made that unassisted triple play.

It happened this way. It was the fifth game of the Series, and we were tied with the Dodgers at two games apiece. The date was Sunday, October 10, 1920. We jumped out to an early lead when Elmer Smith hit the first grand-slam home run ever hit in a World Series, and at the end of the fourth inning we were way ahead, 7–0.

The first man up for Brooklyn in the top of the fifth inning was their second baseman, Pete Kilduff. He singled to left field. Otto Miller, their catcher, singled to center. So there were men on first and second, and none out. Clarence Mitchell, the Brooklyn pitcher, was the next batter. Well, in a situation like that, with them behind by seven runs, we didn't expect them to bunt or hit-and-run or anything. We figured they'd just hit away. Mitchell was a pretty good hitter. And being a left-handed batter, he generally pulled the ball to right field.

So with all that in mind I figured to play pretty deep for him, not especially caring whether we got a double play or not, not playing close for that. We didn't need a double play. Just stop the rally, that would be enough. So I played way back on the grass.

Well, Jim Bagby was pitching for us, and he served up a fast ball that Mitchell smacked on a rising line toward center field, a little over to my right—that is, to my second-base side. I made an instinctive running leap for the ball, and just barely managed to jump high enough to catch it in my glove hand. *One out.* The impetus of my run and leap carried me toward second base, and as I continued to second I saw Pete Kilduff still running toward third. He thought it was a sure hit, see, and was on his way. There I was with the ball in my glove, and him with his back to me, so I just kept right on going and touched second with my toe (*two out*) and looked to my left. Well, Otto Miller, from first base, was just standing there, with his mouth open, no more than a few feet away from me. I simply took a step or two over and touched him lightly on the right shoulder, and that was it. *Three out.* And I started running in to the dugout.

I knew exactly what had happened. The reason I did is that just a few years before I joined the club another Cleveland player, Neal Ball, had done the same thing in a regular league game against the Red Sox. He had made the first unassisted triple play in Big League history, and many of the fellows on the club knew Neal and talked about the play a lot. So it was familiar to me.

However, it took place so suddenly that most of the fans didn't know

Wambsganss tags Brooklyn's Otto Miller—standing a few feet on the first-base side of second base—for the grand finale of the most famous triple play in baseball history. Miller seems to be in a state of shock as Wamby puts the ball on him for the third out. Simultaneously Pete Kilduff, on his way around third base to score a run, looks back in astonishment to discover that he was the second out, and that the inning has ended. Hank O'Day is the second base umpire, starting to call Miller out, Bill Dinneen is the nonchalant third-base umpire, and Larry Gardner is the Cleveland third baseman.

what had happened. They had to stop and figure out just how many were out. So there was dead silence for a few seconds. Then, as I approached the dugout, it began to dawn on them what they had just seen, and the cheering started and quickly got louder and louder and louder. By the time I got to the bench it was bedlam, straw hats flying onto the field, people yelling themselves hoarse, my teammates pounding me on the back.

"How did it feel, Bill?" they all wanted to know.

Well, that's how it felt. Pretty exciting and pretty wonderful. I guess that's still the only unassisted triple play in World Series history. There have been a few since in regular league games. I think the last one was in 1927. The rarest play in baseball, they say. I'm still very proud of it.

That happened in 1920. But baseball is a game of ups and downs. Three years later, on Christmas Eve, 1923, I was traded to Boston. We had just bought this very house, and my wife was pregnant. We moved in here in December, and had no more than gotten settled before we got the news: traded to the Red Sox. I'd been with the Cleveland Indians for ten years and I liked the town. But you simply have to expect that in baseball, I guess. No choice. That's the way it is, that's all.

Being traded was a shock, but not near as much as when I started to realize that I was through. That was almost impossible to accept. My last year in the Big Leagues was 1926. I was only thirty-two. I just couldn't adjust to not playing ball, so I went back to the minors and played there. Managed some there, too.

My last year in professional ball was 1932. I was thirty-eight years old, it was the middle of the depression, opportunities for scouting and managing just ceased to exist, and other jobs were even scarcer. So I worked around at odds and ends, managed a girls softball team for four years, did this and that, until I finally got straightened out. Having to leave the game is a very difficult adjustment to make, and that goes for every single ballplayer. Don't let any one of them tell you different.

So there are highs and lows in a baseball career. It has its glories, and it also has its sorrows. You know, one day when I was playing with Cleveland we came to New York to play the Yankees. I was on the elevated train going up to the Polo Grounds—that was before Yankee Stadium was built—and I was reading the paper. On the way, I came across a poem in that paper and before I got to 155th Street I cut it out and put it in my wallet.

That poem stayed there in my wallet until it disintegrated. By then it didn't matter, because I'd memorized every line of it. I don't remember who wrote it, and I don't remember the name of the poem, but I do remember every word in every single line of it. It went like this:

> Now summer goes
> And tomorrow's snows
> Will soon be deep,
> And the sky of blue
> Which summer knew
> Sees shadows creep.
>
> As the gleam tonight
> Which is silver bright
> Spans ghostly forms,
> The winds rush by
> With a warning cry
> Of coming storms.
>
> So the laurel fades
> In the snow-swept glades
> Of flying years,
> And the dreams of youth
> Find the bitter truth
> Of pain and tears.
>
> Through the cheering mass
> Let the victors pass
> To find fate's thrust,
> As tomorrow's fame
> Writes another name
> On drifting dust.

18 Sam Jones

How dear to my heart was the old-fashioned hurler
   Who labored all day on the old village green.
He did not resemble the up-to-date twirler
   Who pitches four innings and ducks from the scene.
The up-to-date twirler I'm not very strong for;
   He has a queer habit of pulling up lame.
And that is the reason I hanker and long for
   The pitcher who started and finished the game.

The old-fashioned pitcher,
   The iron-armed pitcher,
The stout-hearted pitcher,
   Who finished the game.

            —GEORGE E. PHAIR

YOU KNOW, I think one reason I pitched so long is that I never wasted my arm throwing over to first to keep runners close to the base. There was a time there, for five years, I never *once* threw to first base to chase a runner back. Not once in five years. Ripley put that in "Believe It or Not."

"Take a good lead on Jones," they all said around the league. "He won't throw. He never does."

Well, I never did. Not for five years. And then one day I fooled 'em. I *threw*. Had the guy out by a mile, but the first baseman dropped the ball. Seems like I fooled him, too. He claimed the shock was too much for him! And me setting the situation up so carefully and all.

You don't have to throw over to first to keep a runner on. I once heard Eddie Plank say, "There are only so many pitches in this old arm, and I don't believe in wasting them throwing to first base." And he rarely did. Made sense to me. I was just a young punk, and I figured if it was good enough for Plank it should be good enough for me. What you do instead of throwing is look at the guy on first. Yeah, that's all, just stand there on the pitching rubber and *look* at him. No need to throw.

Sam Jones

If you stand there, like you're ready to pitch, and just stare at him long enough, it'll get to be too much for him and he'll lean back toward the base. *Then* you pitch. Or else the batter won't be able to stand it any more and *he'll* step out of the box and call time. That's all you have to do—just stand there and wait. Of course, some of them bear more watching than others. Like Cobb, for example. But all you need is patience.

I broke into the American League in 1914, with Cleveland. I'll never forget the fellows on that Cleveland club—Joe Jackson, Ray Chapman, Steve O'Neill, Terry Turner, Larry Lajoie, Willie Mitchell. I'll never, never, never forget how nice those fellows treated me when I first came up. They were just wonderful. Of course, wherever I was I always made friends easy. Every club I was ever on, everybody and me was friends. But this was different, being a rookie and all. Just a big country boy out of the hills here, and they made me feel right at home. You sure do remember that, someone being so nice to you when you're just starting out.

In 1916 Cleveland traded me and a fellow named Fred Thomas and $50,000 to Boston, for a fellow named Tris Speaker. I sure did hate to leave that Cleveland club, though. Those guys were like big brothers to me. However, I started moving pretty good with the Red Sox. And it turned out the fellows at Boston were just as nice—Harry Hooper and Babe Ruth and all. Won 16 games and lost only 5 in 1918, and started to figure I was cock-o'-the-walk, you know. Pitchers tend to get a bit that way when they're going good. Especially young ones. Goes to your head real quick.

I remember one day in 1918, I was playing checkers in the clubhouse before the game. I had pitched (and won) the day before, and was playing with the fellow who had just finished pitching batting practice. Walt Kinney was his name, a left-handed pitcher.

While we were in the middle of the checker game the bat boy comes in and says, "Mr. Barrow would like to see you out on the field. He wants you to have your picture taken."

"OK," I said, "I'll be right out." Ed Barrow was the manager of the Red Sox then.

About five minutes later the bat boy comes back in. "Mr. Barrow wants you out there right away."

"OK," I said, "tell him I'll be right there."

About five minutes after that a bit of commotion at the clubhouse entrance, and in comes Mr. Barrow himself. As you might know, he was a pretty rough talker. Huge man, with these fantastic bushy eyebrows. They always fascinated me. Couldn't take my eyes off them. Well, he gave me a good going over for sitting in the clubhouse playing checkers when he'd asked for me outside.

"And," he winds up with, "what the hell are you doing in here in the first place?"

"Well," I said—still sitting at the checkerboard—"I pitched yesterday, and Walt just finished pitching batting practice, so I didn't reckon either one of us had any business out there just now, necessarily."

"This newspaper photographer came all the way from Providence to take your picture," he says.

"Is that so?" I said. "Well, he can go all the way back to Providence without it."

Oh, did that get him! He turned on his heel and stormed out, then turned around and came all the way back in again. I thought he was going to take a sock at me. He'd been known to do that on occasion, you know.

"This will cost you $100," he shouts. His face was so red he could hardly talk. And you should have seen those eyebrows!

"Make it $200," I said, still sitting there.

"It's $200, all right."

"Make it $300," I said, "and then go straight to hell."

"It's $300," he roars, and slams the door.

Finally, I went out on the field and the photographer posed me and Mr. Barrow together. Arms around each other's shoulders, both smiling, best friends ever. But as soon as the shutter clicked we both walked real fast in opposite directions.

Cocky young pitchers! Yeah, I was one, till I learned a little better. Doesn't take many 9–5 losses to bring you back down.

After that simmered down, Ed Barrow and I got along just fine. I'd pitch for him any time he wanted me to, and he'd do anything for me. One day he was stuck and needed a relief pitcher real bad. I'd just pitched the day before, but after looking up and down the bench he said, "Sam, would you warm up and go in for us next inning?"

"Sure," I said, and went down to the bullpen to get loose.

When I was all warmed up I came back in. "I don't think I have too much today," I said, "but I'll try."

"Good," he said, "I know at least you'll *look* like a pitcher."

And later on, when Mr. Barrow became general manager of the Yankees, he brought me over there. I guess I liked playing with the Yankees best of all. I was there for five years, 1922 through '26. It was a good club to play for. They always had plenty of money, paid real well, and drew good crowds. And three of the five years I was there we won the pennant. What more could you ask for? The Yankees always did things in a big way. Why, when the season was over they'd even give each player three brand new baseballs. Just *give* them to us. No other club ever did that.

Not to mention the fact that we had a pretty fair-to-middlin' ball club—Lou Gehrig at first base, Tony Lazzeri at second, Everett Scott or Mark Koenig at shortstop, and Joe Dugan at third in the infield; Earl Combs, Bob Meusel, and a man named Ruth in the outfield; Wally Schang and Benny Bengough catching. Miller Huggins managing. Yes, a pretty fair ball club. And pitching! Herb Pennock, Urban Shocker, Bob Shawkey, Waite Hoyt, Joe Bush, Carl Mays, George Pipgras, myself —my goodness!

People forget that the Yankes in the twenties were more than a great offensive club. They were the best *defensive* team in both leagues, as well. That outfield, terrific pitching, a great infield. It was a well-balanced ball club, in every way. Everybody played in the shadow of George Herman Ruth, of course, so a lot of people don't even remember who else was on that team.

Oh, they remember Lou Gehrig, I guess. One of the nicest fellows ever lived, Lou was. He never really got the publicity he deserved. A very serious-minded fellow, very modest and easy to get along with, always every inch a gentleman. Lou was the kind of boy if you had a son he's the kind of person you'd like your son to be.

And they remember Tony Lazzeri at second base, maybe. Tony was an epileptic, you know. They say that's how he died a few years ago: had a seizure and fell down the cellar steps. He had one of those spells most every spring on the trip back north. But never during a game. Tony was a very witty guy, full of fun. Quiet, but always up to something. A real nice guy. And a great second baseman, too. How they can keep leaving him out of the Hall of Fame is beyond me.

And that was some outfield on that team. Bob Meusel had a fantastic arm. He had an arm as long as this room, know what I mean? Once he got his hands on a ball it was as good as wherever he wanted to fire it. It was as good as there already. I've seen him throw flatfooted from deep in the outfield all the way to home plate. On a low line, and very accurate, too. Combs didn't have that good an arm, but he could really go get 'em. He could cover the whole outfield all by himself. And Ruth: well, he was the champ, that's all you can say.

I guess I saw my share of Mr. George Herman Ruth. Not much doubt about that. I broke into the American League the same year he did,

1914, and left one year after him. The Babe's last year was '34, and mine was '35. I was his teammate on the Red Sox for four years, and on the Yankees for five. We won five pennants and three World Series together.

And the rest of the years, I faced him from a distance of 60 feet 6 inches. I'll tell you one thing, when Jidge was up at bat that pitching distance seemed to shrink somehow. Maybe it was still 60 feet, but it sure felt more like six.

Babe Ruth could hit a ball so hard, and so far, that it was sometimes impossible to believe your eyes. We used to absolutely marvel at his hits. Tremendous wallops. You can't imagine the balls he hit. And before that he was a great pitcher, too. Really great.

In fact, he was strictly a pitcher when I first played with him, on the Red Sox in 1916, after I'd come over from Cleveland. Of course, for a while there he did both. Like in 1917, he won 24 games for us as a pitcher, and also batted about .325. It was hard to believe the natural ability that man had.

Well, to give you an example: in 1920 he hit over 50 home runs all by himself, and everybody else in the whole rest of the league added together hit only about 300 homers. That's a fact. Look it up if you don't believe it. About one out of every seven home runs hit in the American League that year was hit by Babe Ruth.

My God, if he was playing today! Nowadays they hit about 1,500 home runs a season in the American League. If Babe was as good relative to everybody else today, like he used to be, he'd hit *over 200* homers a season. That'll give you an idea of how the big fellow dominated baseball back then. Take Mantle, Mays, Killebrew, and anybody else you want to name today, and *add them all up,* and they still won't match Ruth's home runs relative to the rest of the league!

I *should* say, of course, that when I pitched against him he never gave *me* much trouble. But it's not so. I always figured the best way to pitch to Ruth, especially in a pinch, was to walk him. Maybe that's why I stayed in the league so long. From 1914 through 1935—22 *consecutive* years of pitching in the American League. No one's ever done that before or since.

I was forty-three when I finally retired. Came back home to Woodsfield, Ohio, where I was born. Bill McGeehan of the *Herald Tribune* used to call me "Sad Sam, the Sorrowful Sage from Woodsfield." He said he used to watch me on the field and I always looked sort of downcast to him: so "Sad Sam." Actually, what it was, I would always wear

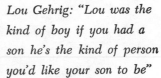

Lou Gehrig: "Lou was the kind of boy if you had a son he's the kind of person you'd like your son to be"

Tony Lazzeri: "How they can keep leaving him out of the Hall of Fame is beyond me"

"Babe Ruth could hit a ball so hard, and so far, that it was sometimes impossible to believe your eyes"

my cap down real low over my eyes. And the sportswriters were more used to fellows like Waite Hoyt, who'd always wear their caps way up so they wouldn't miss seeing any pretty girls.

Well, of course, I don't know about being any "sage." I would always ask for advice, and listen. Of course, you had to be a little careful about *who* you'd ask. My idea about getting a point of view is to feel your way along. I'd always sit there and observe everything that went on. Golly, I don't know why, but whenever anything went wrong they'd blame me. Heck, I was just watching things. But if someone's shoes were nailed down, or socks tied in knots, seemed like I'd always get the blame. Never could understand it.

I guess in all those years of pitching my biggest thrill came when I pitched a no-hitter for the Yankees on September 4, 1923. It was against the Philadelphia Athletics. I realized it as I was going along. Round about the fourth or fifth inning you begin to realize that nobody's got a hit yet, and then you start to get a little tense. But when I'd come back to the bench between innings no one would say a word to me about a no-hitter, or anything like that. The scoreboards then, they only gave the score. They didn't have things like hits and errors on the scoreboards in those days.

Along near the end of the game I started to get real tired, way more than usual. Chick Galloway, the A's shortstop, was the last man up in the bottom of the ninth. "I'm gonna break it up if I can," he yelled at me, and he bunted down the third-base line. I fielded it and threw him out and there it was: a no-hitter.

It was a terrific thrill as soon as it was over, the fans and all the players flocking down on the field to congratulate me. But I think the biggest kick of all came the next day, when I got telegrams from all over the country, from people all over the whole country who'd taken the time to send me a wire.

But baseball is a game where you feel great one day and down in the dumps the next. I pitched that no-hitter on September 4, and then only a few weeks later I lost a 1-0 World Series game to the Giants. That was the first World Series ever played in Yankee Stadium, 1923, and this game—the third of the Series—was played before the largest crowd ever to see a baseball game anywhere up to that time, about 65,000 people.

Art Nehf and I both pitched shutouts through six innings, but then in the seventh Casey Stengel hit one of my fast balls into the right-field stands. That was the only run of the game, and Nehf beat me, 1-0. Oh, that really hurt! But you know, that Art Nehf, he was an awfully nice fellow—awfully nice. And a wonderful pitcher, too.

Well, I managed to stay up there a good long time. Saw a lot of wonderful things. Twenty-two years in the American League—five World Series. You know something? In all that time I don't remember ever being nervous before a game. A bit impatient maybe, but not really nervous. I was a bit like those horses pawing the ground in the stocks at the rodeo, sort of eager to get started. I couldn't keep still before the game began, especially if it was my day to pitch. Didn't know what to do with myself. Back and forth, one place to the other, going to the bathroom (thought you had to go, but really didn't, you know), doing this and that. But I don't call that really nervous, do you? More like just awaitin' for to get in there.

Bob O'Farrell

19 *Bob O'Farrell*

The scene is instant, whole and wonderful. In its beauty and design that vision of the soaring stands, the pattern of forty thousand empetalled faces, the velvet and unalterable geometry of the playing field, and the small lean figures of the players, set there, lonely, tense and waiting in their places, bright, desperate solitary atoms encircled by that huge wall of nameless faces, is incredible. And more than anything it is the light, the miracle of light and shade and color— the crisp blue light that swiftly slants out from the soaring stands and, deepening to violet, begins to march across the velvet field and towards the pitcher's box, that gives the thing its single and incomparable beauty.

The batter stands swinging his bat and grimly waiting at the plate, crouched, tense, the catcher, crouched, the umpire, bent, hands clasped behind his back, and peering forward. All of them are set now in the cold blue of that slanting shadow, except the pitcher who stands out there all alone, calm, desperate, and forsaken in his isolation, with the gold-red swiftly fading light upon him, his figure legible with all the resolution, despair and lonely dignity which that slanting, somehow fatal light can give him.

—THOMAS WOLFE, *Of Time and the River*

I N 1924 a foul tip came back, crashed through my mask, and fractured my skull.

It was my own fault. It was an old mask and I knew I shouldn't have worn it. You know, a lot of times a catcher's mask gets so much banging around it gets dented here and there. If you try to bend it back the way it's supposed to be, it weakens it. Well, I put on an old mask that day and asked the clubhouse boy to go get me my regular one. Before he could get back with it, the ball had spun off the bat, smashed through the mask, and knocked me unconscious.

I had caught almost all the Cubs' games the two previous seasons, and hit a solid .320 both years. Gabby Hartnett had come up to the Cubs in '22, and he was sort of crowding me. But the catcher's job was mine until I got my skull fractured. I didn't play much the rest of that season, however, and the next year the Cubs traded me to the St. Louis Cardinals. A good break for me, I guess, now that I look back at it. At the time, though, I was brokenhearted. Still, it turned out for the best, because the Cardinals won the pennant in 1926, and I was even voted the league's Most Valuable Player that year. We won the World Series, too.

That was *the* World Series, the famous one against the Yankees, where old Grover Cleveland Alexander, at the tail end of his long career, came in late in the seventh game to strike out Tony Lazzeri and save the Series for the Cardinals. I guess that's maybe the most famous strikeout in the whole history of baseball, wouldn't you say?

I had caught Alex for years on the Cubs before we were both traded to the Cardinals. I think he was as good as or better than any pitcher who ever lived. He had perfect control, and a great screwball. He used to call it a fadeaway, same as Mathewson.

I don't believe Alex was much of a drinker before he went into the army. After he got back from the war, though, he had a real problem. When he struck out Lazzeri he'd been out on a drunk the night before and was still feeling the effects. See, Alex had pitched for us the day before and won. He had beaten the Yankees in the second game of the World Series, and *again* in the sixth game, pitching the complete game both times. He was thirty-nine years old then, and naturally wasn't expecting to see any more action.

However, after the sixth game was over, Rogers Hornsby, our manager, told Alex that if Jesse Haines got in any trouble the next day he would be the relief man. So he should take care of himself. Well, Alex didn't really intend to take a drink that night. But some of his "friends" got hold of him and thought they were doing him a favor by buying him a drink. Well, you weren't doing Alex any favor by buying him a drink, because he just couldn't stop.

So in the seventh inning of the seventh game, Alex is tight asleep in the bullpen, sleeping off the night before, when trouble comes. We had each won three games in the Series and now all the chips are down. The score is 3–2 in our favor going into the bottom of the seventh inning of the seventh game, Jesse Haines pitching for us against Herb Pennock for the Yankees. Suddenly Haines starts to tire. The Yankees get the bases loaded with two out, and the next batter up is Tony Lazzeri.

Rogers Hornsby and I gather around Haines at the pitching mound. Jesse's fingers are a mass of blisters from throwing so many knuckle balls, and so Hornsby decides to call in old Alex, even though we know he'd just pitched the day before and had been up most of the night. So in he comes, shuffling in slowly from the bullpen to the pitching mound.

"Can you do it?" asks Hornsby.

"I can try," says Alex.

We agree that Alex should pitch Lazzeri low and away, nothing up high. Well, the first pitch is a perfect low curve for strike one. But the second one comes in high, and Tony smacks a vicious line drive that lands in the left-field stands but just foul. Oh, it's foul by maybe ten feet. Actually, from home plate I can see it's going to be foul all the way, because it's curving from the time it got halfway out there. Of course, I'm giving it plenty of body english too, just to make sure.

The pitch had been high, so I run out to Alex. "I thought we were going to pitch him low and outside?"

"He'll never get another one like that!" Alex says.

And he didn't. The next pitch was a low outside curve and Tony Lazzeri struck out. Fanned him with three pitches.

Most people seem to remember that as happening in the ninth inning and ending the ball game. It didn't. It was only the seventh inning and we had two innings still to go. In the eighth Alex set down the Yankees in order, and the first two men in the ninth. But then, with two out in the bottom of the ninth, he walked Babe Ruth. Bob Meusel was next up, but on the first pitch to him the Babe took off for second. Alex pitched, and I fired the ball to Hornsby and caught Babe stealing, and *that* was the last play of the game and the Series.

You know, I wondered why Ruth tried to steal second then. A year or two later I went on a barnstorming trip with the Babe and I asked him. Ruth said he thought Alex had forgotten he was there. Also that the way Alex was pitching they'd never get two hits in a row off him, so he better get in position to score if they got one. Well, maybe that was good thinking and maybe not. In any case, I had him out a mile at second.

Then the most fantastic thing of all happened. That winter the Cardinals up and trade Rogers Hornsby to the Giants for Frankie Frisch and Jimmy Ring! They trade away the manager of the World's Champions, who also happens to be a guy who had hit *over .400* in three of his last five seasons! Boy, that really shook us up. Traded away a national hero. And to top it all off, who do they make the new St. Louis manager? Me!

What a position to be in, huh? Hornsby couldn't get along with the owner, Sam Breadon, and in a way I wound up as the goat. I didn't want to be the manager. I was in the prime of my career, only thirty years old, and managing always takes something away from your playing.

Nevertheless, we almost won the pennant again in 1927. Lost out to the Pirates by only 1½ games. But we *didn't* win it, so the following season I wasn't the manager any more, and I found myself traded to the Giants early in 1928.

Hornsby was a great manager as far as I'm concerned. That year in

St. Louis he was tops. He never bothered any of us. Just let you play your own game. He was fine. Of course, they say later on he couldn't get along with his players. Got a little bossy, they say. Seems like he changed. But as far as I'm concerned, he was great.

Now McGraw, he was rough as a manager. Very hard to play for. I

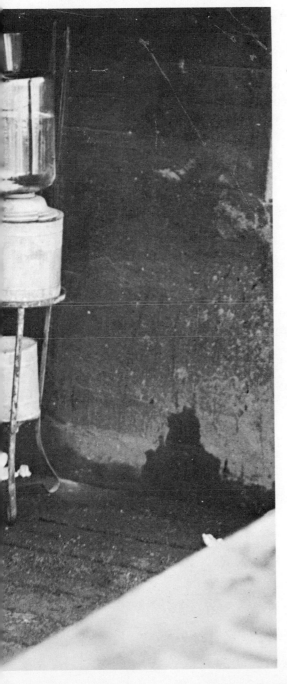

Manager John J. McGraw: "He was always so grouchy"

played for him from '28 to '32, when he retired, and I didn't like it. You couldn't seem to do anything right for him, ever. If something went wrong it was always your fault, not his. Maybe it was because he was getting old and was a sick man, but he was never any fun to play for. He was always so grouchy.

I remember one time Bill Terry was at bat with the count three balls and no strikes on him, and McGraw let him hit. Bill hit a home run. Right out of the park. As he came back to the dugout, McGraw said, "I'll take half of that one!" Meaning he should get some credit for letting Bill hit away with the count three and nothing.

"You can have it all!" Terry says.

No, McGraw was never a very cheerful man to be around. At least that's my opinion.

The greatest player I ever saw? Oh, I don't know, there were so many great ones. Guys like Paul Waner, Hornsby, Alex, Terry, Hubbell, Ruth, Vance, Mel Ott, Rixey, Roush. There were too many great ones to say any one is *the* greatest.

Although I'll say this: the greatest player I ever saw in any one season was Frankie Frisch in 1927. That was his first year with the Cardinals, when I was managing him. He'd been traded to St. Louis for the man of the hour, Rogers Hornsby, and he was on the spot. Frank did *everything* that year. Really an amazing ballplayer.

You know, I always thought it was pretty wonderful to be a ballplayer. I was a Chicago White Sox fan until one day in 1915. When I was a kid, about eight years old—that must have been about 1905—my Dad took me to see the White Sox play. They were *his* team. Billy Sullivan was their catcher, and I thought he was really something. I wanted to be another Billy Sullivan and catch for the White Sox. And naturally, like all good White Sox fans, the team I hated most was the Chicago Cubs.

In 1915, when I was finishing high school, I was just as rabid a White Sox fan as ever. I was catching for the local Waukegan semipro team then, and one day in the middle of the summer we played an exhibition game with the hated Chicago Cubs. Well, lo and behold, after the game the Cubs offered me a contract! I grabbed it up, and suddenly, after all those years of being a White Sox fan, there I was, of all things, a Cub fan!

The exact same magical transformation took place in Dad. Fact is, my Dad saw just about every Cub home game all the years I was with them. Which was until 1925, when, like I said, I was traded to the St. Louis Cardinals. And *then,* of course, we both became Cardinal fans.

Today I'm still a Cardinal fan, even though I never caught as many games for them as I did for the Cubs. Or later for the Giants, for that matter. I was in the Big Leagues an awfully long time, you know, I think longer than any other catcher. Twenty-one years, from 1915 through 1935.

Roger Bresnahan was the manager of the Cubs when I joined them in 1915. The old Giant catcher from way back—the guy who caught Mathewson and Marquard and all the rest of them, the man who invented shin guards back in 1908 or so. How about that? Hard to believe they ever caught without shin guards, isn't it? But he was the first to ever wear them. Mr. Bresnahan helped me a great deal. He more or less showed me the ropes and taught me how to catch. He was still catching then, though not too much. There actually were three catchers on that team: Bresnahan, Jimmy Archer, and Bubbles Hargrave. Four, I guess, if you include me.

Except for Bresnahan, nobody paid any attention to me. I didn't get in many games. I was straight out of high school, and mostly I just sat

Roger Bresnahan:
. . . the man who invented
shin guards back in 1908"

around and watched. Of course, aside from Bresnahan, nobody helped me any. They didn't want a rookie to come in and take one of their buddies' jobs. But they weren't *too* bad. They just more or less ignored me.

The next year I only got in one game before they shipped me out to Peoria, in the Three-I League. And the year after that I played with Peoria until the Cubs recalled me, near the end of the season. After that I stayed up. Those were the days when catching was really rough. There were so many off beat pitches then, you know. Like the spitball, the emory ball, the shine ball. You name it, somebody threw it.

The emory ball—the pitcher would hide an emory cloth inside his sleeve, or inside his glove, and rub the ball on it. That would make a slight rough spot, and boy, would that ball ever break. Some pitchers would raise an eyelet on their glove, you know, where the lacing goes through. Well, they'd raise one of those eyelets up and scratch the ball on it. Then it would act the same as an emory ball. Really take off. Those things weren't legal. You had to do them on the sly.

Eddie Cicotte had a great shine ball. He'd have some transparent paraffin on his trousers or somewhere, or some talcum powder, and every chance he'd get he'd rub the ball there. That would make the ball slide off his fingers and put a real break on it when it came up to the plate. Acted something like a spitter. A catcher's life wasn't easy.

I certainly enjoyed those years, though. I did get a little discouraged at times, but I guess you do in any job. Of course, when you play every day it gets to be sort of like work. But, somehow, way down deep, it's still play. Just like the umpire says: "Play Ball!" It *is*. It's *play*.

20 *Specs Toporcer*

I remember the Chillicothe ball players grappling the Rock Island ball players in a
    sixteen-inning game ended by darkness.

And the shoulders of the Chillicothe players were a red smoke against the sundown
    and the shoulders of the Rock Island players were a yellow smoke against the
    sundown.

And the umpire's voice was hoarse calling balls and strikes and outs, and the um-
    pire's throat fought in the dust for a song.
                                        —Carl Sandburg, "Hits and Runs"

A S FAR BACK as I can remember, baseball has been the passion of my
life. I don't think I'm exaggerating when I say that in the last 75 years
hardly a day has gone by when my thoughts haven't turned to baseball at
some time or other. Of course, when I was a youngster I never thought I'd
actually get to play in the Big Leagues myself. That was beyond my wildest
dreams. I was just a skinny kid with eyeglasses, most of the time the last to
be picked when we used to choose up sides. That I eventually played
seven and a half years in the majors is still a source of great wonderment
to me.

But I'm getting ahead of myself. To begin at the beginning, I was born in
New York City in 1899. We lived on 77th Street between 1st and 2nd
Avenues, above the shop where Dad made shoes and boots. Incidentally,
Jimmy Cagney lived a few blocks away, on 79th Street. Jimmy and I went
to grade school together and have been good friends ever since; we still
stay in touch and get together from time to time.

I guess it was the 1905 World Series that first hooked me on baseball. I
was only six then, so I couldn't really appreciate Christy Mathewson's
three shutouts over the Philadelphia Athletics in less than a week. But for
months afterwards my two older brothers, Rudy and Gus, talked about
little else. Both of them were red-hot Giant fans. Soon I was also, and
within a year or two I was living and dying with each Giant victory and
defeat. I still remember when the Cubs won the 1908 pennant by beating
the Giants in a play-off game that was needed after Fred Merkle forgot to
touch second base; I cried myself to sleep that night.

George Burns: "I loved them all, but my special favorite was George Burns, the unassuming left fielder."

When I was ten years old I started making frequent afternoon excursions up to the Polo Grounds, at 157th Street and 8th Avenue, to see the Giants play. This meant a five-mile walk each way from our home on 77th Street. It wasn't so bad. Only took me an hour and a half each way. Dad was able to give me a weekly allowance of only one cent—yes, one cent—so I didn't have enough money for street cars or subways, and of course I couldn't pay my way into the ball park either.

Fortunately, I was able to see my heroes from a perch on Coogan's Bluff, a hill situated behind the home-plate area of the grandstand. An open space below the roof of the stadium made it possible for me, and for others crowded together on the rocky hill, to peek at part of what was happening on the field.

The Giants were managed by the greatest manager of his time, John McGraw, and as I grew up I learned a lot by observing how he handled his teams. Even then, I was interested in strategy, tactics, in what used to be called "inside baseball." I admired McGraw, but of course it was the Giant players who thrilled me. I loved them all, but my special favorite was George Burns, the unassuming left fielder. I kept scrapbooks where I pasted everything written about my idol, and I probably fretted more than he did when he went hitless or failed to come through in the clutch.

Occasionally, I also went up to see the Yankees, then called the Highlanders, who at that time played at their Hilltop Park at 165th Street and Broadway. Although I had no real interest in the Highlanders, I en-joyed watching any ball game. Also, I wanted to see some of the American League stars in action—like Ty Cobb, Sam Crawford, Hal Chase, Tris Speaker, Eddie Collins, Joe Wood, and Walter Johnson.

Some years later, of course, the Yankees moved and Columbia Pres-byterian Medical Center was built on the site where Hilltop Park had been. Ironically, 40 years later I spent many months in that hospital under-going five unsuccessful operations to save my eyesight. While lying there, going blind, I often had vivid recollections of the games and players I had seen perform on that very site.

But again I'm getting ahead of myself. Back in 1912, when I was 13 years old, I got a job posting scores in an old-fashioned corner saloon at 85th Street and 1st Avenue. The scores would come in on a Western Union ticker tape, and I'd proudly write them on a large blackboard in the back room of the saloon. For this, I got 50 cents a week and the right to eat whatever free lunch was on the counter. Games started at four o'clock in the afternoon in those days, so even when school was in session it was easy for me to get there on time.

Naturally, this job made me the envy of all the kids in the neighborhood. Dozens of them crowded outside the saloon when I was posting the scores. The most agile would perch on a ledge outside a side window through which the blackboard could be seen. As I wrote the scores, those on the ledge would shout them down to the kids below. One of them always chalked the scores on the sidewalk for the benefit of people passing by.

During the regular season, the ticker tape provided only the inning-by-inning scores and the pitchers and catchers. At World Series time, though, a complete play-by-play came over the ticker, and instead of just writing the scores on the blackboard, the management had me stand on a platform and read the tape in a loud voice. This was 1912, remember, the Giants versus the Red Sox, and the saloon was jammed to overflowing with hundreds inside and out eagerly following each game's progress.

Unfortunately, that was the year Fred Snodgrass, one of my favorites, dropped a fly ball in the tenth inning of the last game, after which the Red Sox scored two unearned runs to come from behind and win the Series. I broke down and found it almost impossible to announce the tragic events to the hushed crowd. After it was all over, I sat on the platform silently reading and re-reading the doleful news on the tape, as though repeated reading would erase the awful words.

When I was in the seventh grade, our history teacher decided to organize a school baseball team. I was overjoyed and eagerly showed up for tryouts—only to be turned down because I was too frail and wore eyeglasses. I had worn glasses practically ever since I'd started school because I was so near-sighted I couldn't see the blackboard without them. In those days, however, nobody played ball with eyeglasses on.

I was heartbroken at being rejected, but I persisted in following the school team around from game to game anyway. One day I got a lucky break: only eight of our players showed up for a game and I was the only rooter from our school who was on hand to cheer the team on. So our history teacher-manager put me in center field, probably because it was the least desirable position. The playing field was under the Queensboro Bridge and had a basketball court near the center-field area. With two wooden standards and kids shooting baskets, center field posed hazards the other members of the team wanted no part of.

As things turned out, though, I had no accidents, was lucky enough to make a sparkling one-handed catch, and also contributed two hits. From then on, I was a regular!

As I mentioned before, Dad was a shoe and boot maker and a good one.

However, he had a tough time keeping his head above water financially. When I was in school he invented an arch support of the type now in general use. But without capital to exploit the invention, he continued to struggle financially until, when things appeared to be coming his way at last, he died.

That was in 1913, just after I'd graduated from grade school. My brother Rudy, who was 19, took over the arch-support business. There was no chance for me to go on to high school, because I was needed at the shop, too. In later years, I often regretted not having gone further in school. I was an avid reader and quite studious, especially when it came to subjects that interested me.

But maybe it was all for the best, because Rudy was sympathetic with my love for baseball. He devised a system where I worked at the shop for four hours each morning, then would make deliveries of our arch supports to shoe stores and chiropodists in the afternoon. Once my deliveries were completed, the rest of the day was mine. Naturally, I'd hurry over to a local playground to play ball or else wend my way up to the Polo Grounds and watch my beloved Giants.

My financial status improved at this time because Mom paid me a dollar a week for working with Rudy. In addition, I got another 50 cents a week for helping a tenant in our building with her English and a quarter every Friday night for being what is called a *Shabbes goy*—turning the lights on and off in a nearby Jewish synagogue. Now I was really in the chips, and for the first time in my life I didn't have to sit up on Coogan's Bluff to watch the Giants play. I could actually afford to pay my way into the ball park.

In those days, by the way, bleacher seats at the Polo Grounds cost only 50 cents. Better yet, for a time a section of the bleachers was roped off and could be occupied for only a quarter. Later on, the rope was removed, but the first 200 people through the turnstiles were still admitted for a quarter. Needless to say, I generally managed to be one of those 200!

As I grew up, I was determined to try my best to be a ballplayer myself. I practiced every aspect of the game hour after hour, day after day. I taught myself how to hit left-handed, although I'm a natural righty, and became a good enough fielder to play second or third base or shortstop on some of the best semipro teams in the New York area.

In 1920 I was playing second base with a top semipro team in Orange, New Jersey. Our manager was Billy Swanson, a veteran who had been up with the Boston Red Sox for a while. He helped to polish off a lot of my

Specs Toporcer warming up on Opening Day in 1921, before taking the field as second baseman for the St. Louis Cardinals. It was his first professional game.

rough edges, because up until then I'd been mostly self-taught. That was my last year as a sandlotter; shortly after the season ended, I signed a contract with the Syracuse Stars in the International League and looked forward to playing the next year as a full-time professional.

What actually happened, though, was beyond my wildest dreams. In December, just a couple of months after I'd signed my contract, Syracuse became a farm team of the St. Louis Cardinals. As a result, some of us were invited to go to spring training early with the Cardinals instead of waiting for the Syracuse training camp to open up a few weeks later. I had a sensational spring and in April, Branch Rickey, the Cardinals' manager, transferred my contract from Syracuse to the St. Louis Cardinals. So when the 1921 season opened, who do you think was the starting second baseman for the St. Louis Cardinals? Lo and behold, none other than the first bespectacled infielder in Big League history, yours truly!

This was quite a dramatic change, because the previous year the Cardinals' second baseman had been Rogers Hornsby, the league's leading hitter. Mr. Rickey put me at second base to open the season and switched Hornsby to left field. It didn't work out, though, because Hornsby was no outfielder. He had always been weak on fly balls, which is annoying when you're a second baseman but catastrophic when you're an outfielder. So Rickey soon moved Hornsby back to second base, and I became an all-around infield utility man, a role I played with the Cardinals for most of the 1920's. I don't know of anyone else, by the way, who jumped directly from sandlot ball to the Big Leagues without ever playing high school, college, or minor-league baseball.

Incidentally, can you possibly imagine how I felt every time we played McGraw's Giants at the Polo Grounds? I never walked through the players' entrance at the Polo Grounds without getting goose pimples. I'd think back to the countless hours I'd spent peeking at the field from Coogan's Bluff and wonder whether or not I was dreaming.

Most often I was at shortstop during my years with the Cardinals. I hit .324 in 1922 and .313 in 1926. I also led the National League in pinch-hitting in 1926. The most important hit of my life was a key pinch-hit double in the game that clinched the pennant for the Cardinals in 1926. But I wasn't a top-notch defensive shortstop. Unfortunately, second base was my natural and best position defensively. I say unfortunately because I had the bad luck to be on the same team as two of the greatest second basemen in the history of baseball—Rogers Hornsby and Frankie Frisch.

All Hornsby did was lead the league in hitting year after year. He hit over .400—yes, *over* .400—in 1922, '24, and '25. I'm competing for the second-base job with the man who is generally considered the greatest right-handed hitter of all time!

Hornsby replaced Branch Rickey as field manager in 1925 (Rickey stayed as general manager) and took us all the way to the pennant and the World Championship in 1926. That was the famous World Series where Grover

Cleveland Alexander came in to strike out the Yankees' Tony Lazzeri in the seventh game.

A couple of months later, we were astonished to learn that our manager and second baseman, Rogers Hornsby, the hero of St. Louis, had been traded to the New York Giants for Frankie Frisch. So who am I competing with now—just Frankie Frisch, the Fordham Flash, maybe the best all-around second baseman who ever lived!

Rogers Hornsby in 1926, the year he led the Cardinals to the World Championship

Nowadays, so many ballplayers wear glasses that no one pays any attention. But it wasn't like that in the old days. Lee Meadows, who came up in 1915, was the first Big-League pitcher to wear eyeglasses. I was the first infielder. Ballplayers with glasses were so unusual then that both of us were automatically nicknamed "Specs."

In fact, eyeglasses—or spectacles, as they were often called then—were rare among ballplayers until after World War II, when shatterproof and plastic lenses started to appear. Since there wasn't any such thing as shatterproof glass in my day, I wore regular glasses and never thought twice about it. Just ordinary gold-rimmed eyeglasses, hooked securely over my ears so they stayed put. I was never hit in the glasses, either at bat or in the field. Well, that's not completely true: once, in infield practice, the ball took a bad bounce and hit me between the eyes, on the bridge of the nose. Cut my nose and bent the bridge of my glasses a little, but the glass didn't break.

In 1928, after seven and a half years with the Cardinals, Branch Rickey sent me down to Rochester in the International League, the Cardinals' top farm club. I didn't mind, because I'd never liked being a utility man. I wanted to play every day, something I'd never been able to do with the Cardinals.

As it turned out, Rickey did me a favor sending me to Rochester. I had seven great years there, the last three as manager, and got to play second base every single day. In 1929 I successfully accepted 1,064 chances, still a record for second basemen in any league. We made 223 double plays that year, also a record. We won the International League pennant four years in a row—1928 through 1931—and in two of those years—1929 and 1930—I was named the league's Most Valuable Player.

After managing Rochester from 1932 through 1934, I got into a financial dispute with Mr. Rickey and left the Cardinal organization. I managed elsewhere in the minors for the rest of the thirties and the early forties, and then became farm director for the Boston Red Sox in 1943. I was still holding down that job in 1948 when I had my first serious eye trouble.

I don't know what caused it, but one day I was working in my office at Fenway Park in Boston and I got dots in front of my eyes and couldn't see very well. I went across the hall to Eddie Collins, who was general manager of the Red Sox then, and asked him if he knew a good eye doctor. Eddie sent me to a Boston specialist, who examined me at great length and finally told me that I had a detached retina in my left eye. I had to have an operation immediately to re-attach the retina, although he thought the chances were only fifty-fifty the sight in that eye could be saved.

There were two doctors in New York who specialized in such operations, so I contacted one immediately and the operation was scheduled for a couple of days later at Columbia Presbyterian Medical Center. This doctor was of the opinion that after the operation you should lie on your back without moving your head for thirty days, to make sure the retina wasn't jarred loose again. The other doctor had patients on their feet in a week or so, but my doctor was much more conservative.

The operation took place in February of 1948, and I lay on my back in my hospital bed, my eye bandaged, not moving my head, for a month afterwards. I wasn't allowed out of bed for any reason, and to make sure I didn't turn on my side at night, they placed the equivalent of sandbags alongside me so I couldn't even turn my head. After thirty days the doctor removed the bandages and we discovered, unfortunately, that the operation had been a failure. I had become totally blind in my left eye.

The doctor recommended that we try again, so after a couple of days on my feet I was wheeled back into the operating room and did it all over again. I lay there on my back, sandbagged in, my head still, my eyes bandaged, for another thirty days. When he finally removed the bandages, nothing had changed. The second operation was a failure, too.

Now I'm blind in one eye. "How about the other one?" I asked the doctor.

"Well," he said, "I don't think you're likely to have any problems. Don't strain it too much and things will probably be all right."

So I went back to work and tried not to worry about it too much. In 1951, however, my other eye developed the same problem. I returned to the same doctor at Columbia Presbyterian, this time for an operation on my right eye. After all, he was a highly respected eye surgeon with an outstanding reputation. It was the same routine again. Confined to bed for thirty days after the operation, on my back the whole time, not moving my head, my eye bandaged, waiting for the verdict.

This was a lot more frightening than 1948, though, because this time, as I lay on my back, I couldn't see anything at all. My left eye was blind and my right eye was bandaged. For the first time, I started thinking about what life would be like if I could never see again. As I lay there, I often daydreamed about the games I'd seen right in that very location many years ago, when the Yankees—or rather the Highlanders, as they used to be called—played in their old Hilltop Park on that exact site. I replayed those games over and over in my mind's eye, and once again saw Ty Cobb and Walter Johnson and Joe Wood as vividly as though forty years hadn't intervened. Naturally, I wondered whether I'd ever get to see another baseball game again.

With those fears to keep me company, thirty days on my back took a lot longer to pass than they had in 1948. Seemed more like a year than a month. While I was lying there, by the way, I heard Bobby Thomson hit his historic home run off Ralph Branca and heard the Yankees beat the Giants in the World Series a few days later. Anyway, the operation was a failure. We tried two more times, both of which were also failures. All in all, I lay in that same position for three solid months, all to no avail. After the third try—which was my fifth operation altogether, counting both eyes—it finally sunk in that I'd never see again.

It took a while for me to adjust to that reality. But I never believed in feeling sorry for myself, and I tried to make the best of it. I became a writer and a public speaker and have pursued those vocations ever since I lost my sight, which is now over thirty years ago. I've written two books and lots of magazine articles and spoken hundreds of times, usually before high-school audiences.

Mabel and George Toporcer on their 25th wedding anniversary in 1947

Of course, I never could have done it without my wife, Mabel. We've been married for more than sixty years now, sixty wonderful years, and for the past three decades she's been my eyes as well as my companion. Obviously, any success I've had is due largely to her.

The theme that I emphasize in a lot of my writing and public speaking is that the ballplayers of today are *better* than the ballplayers of yesterday. This shocks a lot of people, who expect me to say just the opposite. They're so used to hearing old-timers like me talk about how today's ballplayers can't hold a candle to yesterday's that they only half listen. Then when I say that baseball players are *better than ever*, they almost swallow their teeth!

Old-timers often get quite upset when they hear that. They say, "What does that old geezer know, anyway? He hasn't even seen a game in thirty years."

Well, in a sense they're right, of course. It's true that I haven't seen a game since 1951. But I listen to games on the radio all the time—mostly the Mets, Yankees, and Red Sox. Many's the day I listen to two games, sometimes three. And I read a lot. I was always a big reader all my life, and now I read more than ever. That is, Mabel reads to me. I may have lost my sight, but I still have Mabel and a brain and I can think, can't I?

I spend a lot of time thinking about baseball in the "good old days" and baseball today. I love the good old days. They were great: Coogan's Bluff . . . Hilltop Park . . . Mathewson . . . my idol, George Burns. But let's face reality. Baseball was in its infancy then. Today athletes are bigger, stronger, faster, and smarter than they used to be. Everybody admits it in football, basketball, and track. What makes baseball so different?

21 Lefty O'Doul

How dear to my heart was the old-fashioned batter
　　Who scattered line drives from the spring to the fall.
He did not resemble the up-to-date batter
　　Who swings from his heels and then misses the ball.
The up-to-date batter I'm not very strong for;
　　He shatters the ozone with all of his might.
And that is the reason I hanker and long for
　　Those who doubled to left, and tripled to right.

　　The old-fashioned batter,
　　　The eagle-eyed batter,
　　The thinking-man's batter,
　　　Who tripled to right.

—George E. Phair

I PLAYED FOR A LOT OF MANAGERS in my day. Miller Huggins, Frank Chance, John McGraw, Miss Rosie Stultz. Most successful of all was Rosie Stultz. She was our seventh-grade teacher at Bay View Grammar School, and she managed the school team. Won the grade-school championship of San Francisco in 1912, we did, with Miss Rosie Stultz managing.

A manager can only do so much, you know that. The rest is up to the players. It's the players make the manager, not the other way around. I managed for 24 years myself, in the Pacific Coast League. In 1935 I had Joe DiMaggio in right field and won the pennant. He hit .398. Sold him to the Yankees over the winter, and the next year I finished next to last.

Take Frank Chance. One of the greatest, right? Won all those pennants with the Cubs. He was my manager on the Red Sox in 1923. Well, in 1923 we ended dead last. Just proves if you haven't got the horses you haven't got a Chance!

I signed my first professional contract with San Francisco in 1917, and they farmed me out to Des Moines in the Western League. Des Moines in the Western League in 1917. What a life! You'd get on a

Frank Chance,
the Peerless Leader

coal-burning train with the old wicker seats, carrying your own uniform and your own bats and everything, and ride from Des Moines, Iowa, to Wichita, Kansas. All night and part of the next day. If you opened the window you'd be eating soot and cinders all night long. If you closed the window you'd roast to death. Get off in the morning either filthy or without a wink of sleep. Usually both.

In the Pacific Coast League, later on, I used to play Sunday morning at Stockton, grab an egg sandwich, ride 60 or 70 miles on the bus, put the wet uniform back on, and play an afternoon game in Sacramento. Play in Oakland on a Sunday morning, wolf down a bean sandwich and rush over on the ferry boat, carrying your own equipment, to play an afternoon game in San Francisco. Same clammy uniform again. That wasn't semipro ball. That was professional baseball. The San Francisco Seals in the Pacific Coast League. And you know what? I loved every minute of it.

I was a pitcher at first. Spent seven years at it, but never got very far. Was up with the Yankees and the Red Sox, but hurt my arm and never did much. In 1924 the Red Sox sold me to Salt Lake City, and you know the high altitude there. Cripes, you could hit a ball with one hand and it would fly out of the park.

So I said to the manager, "I am now an outfielder."

"You don't know how to play the outfield," he says.

"Well," I said, "I'll learn."

And you know the rest of it. I played the outfield that year and led the Coast League in hitting with .392. Hit .398 with the Phillies five years later, closest any man ever came to hitting .400 in the Big Leagues without making it. Only eight fellows in the history of baseball ever hit .400

Eleven years in the Big Leagues and a lifetime batting average of .349. That's *lifetime* average, .349. Only guys ever did better are Cobb, Hornsby, and Joe Jackson. So you might say I have the highest batting average of any man living. Yeah—rest of the guys are dead.

So that's it. Story of my life. Think we could make a movie of that? Well, maybe not. Too many things happened on the sidelines we couldn't put in. Right?

If I had it to do all over I'd be a ballplayer again without pay. Yeah, without pay. I loved it. That's why I never squawked when I didn't get big salaries. I liked to play too much.

Of course, if I were playing now and they gave some kid one of those big bonuses to sign a contract, why I'd be kind of disappointed in the whole setup. I led the National League in batting in 1929 with a .398 average, got 254 hits that season—still the record—and I got a $500 raise. That's right, $500.

Was I making about $20,000 then? Are you kidding? I was lucky to get as much as eight. In 1932 I led the National League in hitting again, with .368, and they *cut* me a thousand dollars. That's the truth!

How can they give these kids, without knowing what's inside their bodies, what kind of heart they have, what kind of intestinal fortitude, give them $100,000 to sign a contract? I can't understand it. Imagine if the Bank of America here would go to say Stanford University, and give the honor student there $100,000. And tell him that some day he'll be one of the big shots in the bank. Same idea. They wouldn't dare do that, would they?

When a man proves himself, has shown that he's a Big Leaguer, why I think those are the fellows should get the dough. Not some youngster who doesn't know his way into the ball park yet. I can't understand it. It doesn't help morale on a ball club, I'll tell you that.

Of course, a lot of things are different today. When I was playing, it was an unwritten law that if a batter ever hit a pitch when the count was three balls and no strikes, the next time he came up there, boy, he was knocked down four consecutive times. They're always yelling about the "bean ball" nowadays. Be better off if they forgot about it. Hell, they've got an iron helmet on their head, haven't they? They look like steel workers. If I was pitching today I'd see if I couldn't skip a few off their noggins.

We didn't wear an iron helmet. We wore a felt hat. I saw many a ball coming right at my head. When I pitched for San Francisco in 1921 I hit 19 men. *On purpose.* No way to say how many I missed! Then when I became an outfielder the shoe was on the other foot. Shoe was on the other foot, see? They hit me in the legs, hit me in the back, broke my elbow, broke my rib. That's all right. Let the ballplayers fight themselves out of it. Drag the ball and spike the pitcher.

Why are the general managers and the managers always hollering about bean balls? They don't have to go up there and hit, do they? What are they screaming about? And the umpires, going out and warning a pitcher about throwing bean balls. *Fining* him. How does the umpire know? The ball could have slipped, couldn't it? A pitcher is a human being. Not a lathe. Not a piece of machinery. The ball could slip, right?

When I hit .398 they were knocking me down all day long. The catchers used to say, "Well, here you go, Frank," and I'd duck. Nobody interfered. They left us alone. We worked our way out of it by ourselves.

When I was playing ball in the Big Leagues my bats would be jumping up and down in the trunk. Couldn't wait to get to the ball park and grab that bat. Big crowd, sock a triple, nothing like it! Maybe I was a ham. What's the use of doing something when nobody's looking? But a packed ball park, crowd roaring, the guy throws you a great breaking curve, you hit it on the nose and drive it over the outfielder's head. What a thrill!

I marvel at how some of those guys used to hit the ball, back when

I first started. The pitchers would use dirt and tobacco juice and licorice and make the ball as black as your hat. Why, just imagine Ty Cobb, hitting the emery ball, the shine ball, the spitball, the coffee ball—they used to chew coffee beans and spit it in the seams—just imagine him hitting .367 lifetime for more than 20 years.

I was at a dinner a few years ago, about 1960, and Leo Durocher spoke about the great Willie Mays and all. After he was finished I got up and said that evidently Mr. Durocher never saw Mr. Cobb or Mr. Ruth or several others, like Mr. Joe Jackson or Mr. Harry Heilmann, saying that Mays was the greatest baseball player who ever lived. He's a

Mr. and Mrs. Babe Ruth and daughter Dorothy in 1921.

great fielder and he can run the bases pretty good, but he couldn't carry the bat of many a player. Not a chance. And I talked about Cobb hitting all those pitches, .367 lifetime.

After I'd finished, one of the kids in the audience asked me, "What do you think Cobb would hit today, with this white ball and all?"

"Oh," I said, "about the same as Mays, maybe .340, something like that."

"Then why do you say Cobb was so great," the kid says to me, "if he could only hit .340 or so with this lively ball?"

"Well," I said, "you have to take into consideration the man is now seventy-three years old!"

Nowadays the ballplayers don't want to talk baseball. They think the old-timer is living in the past. They'd rather talk about stocks, bonds, real estate, their commercials. They don't care to discuss baseball.

Of course, when I was playing there wasn't much else to do. Wasn't any television or any of that malarky. We'd sit around hotel lobbies and talk baseball. In St. Louis there was a fountain at the old Buckingham Hotel, and on hot nights we'd sit around that fountain and talk about how to beat the guys the next day. Talked baseball all day and night. So if we did that, you *know* it must have been better baseball. Had to be.

St. Louis, boy did it ever get hot there. Jeez, you'd roast out on that field, and the nights were just as bad. Try to sleep and before you knew it you were lying in a pool of water. Get up in the morning and grope your way out to the ball park. Now everything's air conditioned. They're even air-conditioning the stadiums. What next?

Yes, that's true, I started professional baseball in Japan. How did that happen? Well, see, years ago—I think it was 1931—I went to Japan on an American All-Star team. Interesting country, interesting people. I liked them, and they liked me. So the next year I went back and coached at the Six Universities. I kept going back and finally went to work organizing a professional setup, like we have here. I'm the one who named the Tokyo Giants. I was on the New York Giants at the time.

See, I like people who you're not wasting your time trying to help. Teaching Americans and teaching Japanese is just like the difference between night and day. The American kid, he knows more than the coach. But not the Japanese kid. They want to learn. They don't think they know everything. Entirely opposite psychology.

Take when we blow an automobile horn. We want the pedestrian to get out of the way, right? Horn blows: Get out of the way. We're com-

Lefty O'Doul

ing through. Honk, honk: Get out of the way. Well, when *they* blow the horn they're telling the pedestrian it's OK: we see you. Horn blows: We see you. Honk, honk: We see you. So when the horn blows they don't jump or anything. They know they won't get hit. The driver's told them he sees them. Get it? Just the opposite from us.

Jesus, so many of my friends in Japan got killed in the war. So many. Awful. Right after the war I went back. I wanted to, because I knew if we brought a baseball team over there it would help cement friendship between them and us.

When I arrived it was terrible. The people were so depressed. When I had been in Japan before the war their cry had been "Banzai, Banzai." But when I got there this time they were so depressed that when I hollered "Banzai" they didn't respond at all. No reaction at all. Nothing. But when I left there, a few months later, all Japan was cheering and shouting "Banzai" again!

So that's it. It's been a lot of fun, beginning to end. As I told you, I played in my first professional ball game with Des Moines in the Western League in 1917. I was twenty years old then. I played in my last game forty years later, Vancouver in the Pacific Coast League, 1956. Was fifty-nine then. I was the manager and put myself in to pinch-hit. Mostly a gag, you know. But I hit a ball between the outfielders and staggered all the way around to third.

A triple. Fifty-nine years old. How about that? Right there—forty years too late—I learned the secret of successful hitting. It consists of two things. The first is clean living, and the second is to bat against a pitcher who's laughing so hard he can hardly throw the ball.

22 *Goose Goslin*

More than a quarter of a century has elapsed since Goose Goslin retired, but one question remains persistently unanswered.

That question does not deal with Leon Allen Goslin's playing career. For that is plainly stated in the record books for all to see:

18 years in the major leagues with a lifetime batting average of .316 (higher than Fred Clarke's or Bill Dickey's)

Over 2700 hits (more than Lou Gehrig or Joe DiMaggio)

Over 900 extra-base hits, 12th on the all time list (ahead of Napoleon Lajoie and Charlie Gehringer)

500 doubles (more than Jimmy Foxx or Mel Ott)

Over 170 triples (more than Harry Heilmann or Al Simmons)

A slugging percentage of .500 (better than that of Honus Wagner or Heinie Manush)

Over 1600 runs batted in, 10th on the all-time list (ahead of Tris Speaker and Rogers Hornsby)

No, the unanswered question does not deal with Goose Goslin's playing career. It relates to the fact that 14 names are mentioned above, in addition to Leon Allen Goslin, and all 14 of them are in the Baseball Hall of Fame.

The question is, very simply: Why not the Goose?

H ECK, LET'S FACE IT, I was just a big ol' country boy havin' the time of his life. It was all a lark to me, just a joy ride. Never feared a thing, never got nervous, just a big country kid from South Jersey, too dumb to know better. In those days I'd go out and fight a bull without a sword and never know the difference.

Why, I never even realized it was supposed to be big doin's. It was just a game, that's all it was. They didn't have to pay me. I'd have paid *them* to let me play. Listen, the truth is it was *more* than fun. It was heaven.

Of course, finally, after about 20 years, I figured I'd had it. Forty years old, it starts to get a little too much like work. The old bones stiffen up and get a little frickle, you know, and then it's about time to stop. Anyway, you can't live out of a grip *forever* . . . hotel . . . taxi . . . train . . .

taxi . . . hotel . . . train . . . and then all over again. Could just about fit into those pullmans in the first place. Poor Schoolboy Rowe, six foot four, how he ever slept in them I'll never know. Myself, I never was prone to trains to begin with.

So finally I up and said, "Goose, ol' boy, it's time to go fishin'." And that's pure and simple what I did, and been doing ever since. I used to have a big billboard down there at the fork in the road: GOOSE GOSLIN—FISHING—BOATS AND TACKLE FOR RENT.

But they bothered me so much about it I took the darn thing down. Sent me letters every week telling me I had to pay a tax on it. Well, when the bill finally came it turned out to be for sixty cents. Oh, boy! Five dollars, OK, but *sixty cents!* How the devil do you make out a check for sixty *cents?* Made me so mad I took the billboard down and just put my name up there on a little stick. Did you see it? Hard to, 'cause the weeds have grown higher than the stick by now. Who cares? No more billboards for me. Sixty *cents!* Think of it.

Everybody knows me here, anyway. I was born and raised near Salem, 18 miles from here. I always played ball around the sandlots here when I was a kid. I'd ride 10 miles on my bike to play ball, play all day long, and then get a spanking when I got back 'cause I'd get home too late to milk the cows. And without anything to eat all day! Then I got in semipro ball around here and one day this umpire saw me. Bill McGowan it was, later he became an American League umpire for about 20 years.

"I can get you a professional job with Rochester, kid," he says.

"Great," I said, "I'm ready to go."

Well, turned out he couldn't. Rochester had all the pitchers they needed that season. I was a pitcher then, see.

So then he says, "Well, I can get you a job down in Columbia, South Carolina, in the Sally League. How about that?"

"Great," I said, "I'm ready to go." Didn't matter to me. I'd have played anywhere!

And that's where I went. To Columbia, South Carolina. That was 1920 and I was twenty years old. Well, it turned out that professional ball was a little different from sandlot ball. Around here I used to be quite a pitcher. That's what *I* thought, anyway. Used to strike 'em out one after the other. But down there it seemed like the harder I threw the ball the harder they hit it.

One of the first games I pitched at Columbia our manager, Zinn Beck, came over to me from third base, where he was playing.

"Listen, young man," he says, "I've been in baseball a long time, but the fact is I'm not thirty-one yet. Won't be till the season ends. If you keep this up I'll never make it, 'cause the way they're hitting you I'll get killed out here for sure."

Goose Goslin in February: "I never could wait for spring to come so I could get out there and swat those baseballs"

I guess he wasn't kidding, because a little later he made me into an outfielder. The next year I hit .390 and before the season was over Clark Griffith, the owner of the Washington Senators, bought me.

"My-oh-my," I thought, "isn't this something. Me in the Big Leagues!" I couldn't wait to get there.

You know, baseball always came so easy to me. I was lucky, being raised on a farm, I guess. Always worked hard, hefty work, and it made me pretty strong. I could always swing that bat real quick, just natural.

Never had to train or practice a whole lot. Good eyes, quick reflexes, strong arms—oh, did I ever love to get up there and hit! And most of all I truly loved those fast balls. They were right down my alley. Zip they'd come in, and whack—right back out they'd go. I never could wait for spring to come so I could get out there and swat those baseballs!

Of course, I had my bad days, too. Like April 28, 1934. How can I ever forget that day? I got up to bat four times, hit the ball good each time, and hit into *four consecutive double plays*. Think of that! I mowed those guys off the bases like shooting blackbirds off a bush. After the fourth time I didn't know whether to laugh or cry. That's still a record. What makes me mad, though, it was tied by a boy name of Mike Kree-vich. He did the same thing about five years later. Tied my record. I didn't like that one bit. I wanted to be *undisputed* double-play champ!

One year I was hitting way out in front of everybody else in the league by 20 or 30 points all season. That was 1928. But in September Heinie Manush kept gaining and gaining and gaining on me, and by the last day of the season he was only a fraction of a point behind me. We played the St. Louis Browns on that last day, and Heinie played left field for the Browns. I was in left field for the Senators. So Heinie and I were playing against each other, with the batting title on the line.

Well, do you know that battle went right down to my very last time at bat. It came to my turn at bat in the ninth inning of last game of the season, and if I make an out I lose the batting championship, and if I get a hit I win it—his average is .378 and mine is .378 and a fraction. If I get up and don't get a hit I'll drop below him. I had that informa-tion before I went to bat. One of the sportswriters sent it down to me, with a note that said: "If you go to bat and make an out Manush will win the batting title. Best thing to do is don't get up to bat at all, and then you've got it made."

Gee, I didn't know what to do. Bucky Harris left it up to me. He was the manager.

"What do you want to do, Goose?" he asked me. "It's up to you. I'll send in a pinch hitter if you want me to."

"Well," I said, 'I've never won a batting title and I sure would love to, just for once in my life. So I think I'll stay right here on the bench, if it's OK with you."

Of course, everybody gathered around, wanting to be in on what's going on.

"You better watch out," Joe Judge says, "or they'll call you yellow."

"What are you talking about?"

"Well," he says, "there's Manush right out there in left field. What do you think he'll figure if you win the title by sitting on the bench?"

So this starts a big argument in the dugout: should I go up or shouldn't I? Finally, I got disgusted with the whole thing. "All right, all right," I said, "stop all this noise. I'm going up there."

And doggone if that pitcher didn't get two quick strikes on me before I could even get set in the batter's box. I never took my bat off my shoulder, and already the count was two strikes and no balls. So I turned around and stepped out of the box and sort of had a discussion with myself, while I put some dirt on my hands. I wasn't too much afraid of striking out, but a pop-up or a roller to the infield and I was a dead duck. Or a gone Goose, you might say.

Well, I didn't know what to do. And then it came to me—get thrown out of the ball game! That way I wouldn't be charged with a time at bat, and it was in the bag. The umpire was a big-necked guy by the name of Bill Guthrie, so I turned on him.

"Why, those pitches weren't even close," I said.

"Listen, wise guy," he says, "there's no such thing as close or not close. It's either *dis* or *dat.*"

Oh, did that ever get me mad (I acted like). I called him every name in the book, I stepped on his toes, I pushed him, I did everything.

"OK," he said, after about five minutes of this, "are you ready to bat now? You're not going to get thrown out of this ball game no matter *what* you do, so you might as well get up to that plate. If I wanted to throw you out, I'd throw you clear over to Oshkosh. But you're going to bat, and you better be in there *swinging* too. No bases on balls, you hear me?"

I heard him. And gee, you know—I got a lucky hit. Saved me. I guess that hit was the biggest thrill I ever got. Even bigger than that single that won the World Series in 1935. Another lucky hit.

Well, it was a great honor to win a batting title in those days. It wasn't an easy thing to do. I hit .344 in 1924 and didn't even come close; Babe Ruth won it with .378. In 1926 I hit .354, but that year Manush hit .378. The next year Harry Heilmann hit .398. The first year I came up George Sisler hit .420. Jeez, you had to be a wizard to come anywhere close to the top in those days. A guy who hit .350 was considered just an average hitter. These days he'd lead both leagues by 20 points every year.

Funny thing, two years after that, in 1930, I was traded to the St. Louis Browns for, of all people, Heinie Manush. Heinie went to Washington and I went to the Browns. That wasn't a very happy day for me. First time I ever got traded. I'd been with the Senators for ten years, and it came as a mighty unpleasant surprise. Happened while we were in St. Louis, too.

We'd played in Chicago the day before, and got into St. Louis about eight o'clock in the morning. We went to the hotel and had breakfast, and then I had a few hours with nothing to do. So I thought I'd go over to the zoo. They had a nice zoo in St. Louis, not far from the hotel. Had bears over there, and monkeys, and I'd give them peanuts and things like that. So I spent a couple of hours at the zoo, and when I got back to the hotel there's Sam Rice, my roomate, sitting there in the lobby waiting for me.

"Hey, you're in the wrong hotel," he says, as soon as he sees me.

I didn't get it.

"I tell you, you're in the wrong hotel," he says again.

"What are you talking about?"

"Well," he says, "you'll find out."

I smelled a mouse somewhere.

"Don't you know that they traded you to the St. Louis Browns?" he says.

"No!" I said. "Did they really?"

Well, it broke my heart. It really did. That afternoon I had to go to the other clubhouse, and I played that day against all my old teammates, all my best friends.

A couple of years later, though, the Browns traded me back to Washington, and then Manush and I played together in the same outfield for one season. That was 1933, and we won the pennant in Washington that year. The Senators have won only three pennants—1924, '25, and '33—and I was there each time. Come to think of it, they've never played a World Series game I didn't play every single inning of.

Talk about excitement, that 1924 World Series beats them all. In the seventh game of the Series—each of us had won three games—we were two runs behind the Giants going into the bottom of the eighth inning, and it looked like the end was awfully close. But in the last of the eighth we got the bases loaded and then, with two out, Buck Harris hit a grounder down to Freddy Lindstrom that hit a pebble and bounced over his head and tied the score.

Walter Johnson then went in to pitch for us, with the score tied 3–3, and two more breaks gave us the Series a few innings later. In the twelfth, Hank Gowdy, who was catching for the Giants, tripped over his own mask trying to catch a foul pop-up by Muddy Ruel, and then Ruel went and doubled to left field. After that, Earl McNeely hit another grounder to Lindstrom at third which *also* hit a pebble and bounced over his head, just like in the eighth inning, and Muddy Ruel scored and won the Series for us.

A flukey win. Clark Griffith said, "That mask up and *bit* Gowdy. He was going to catch that pop foul and it *grabbed* him away from it." Griff always said God was on our side in that one. Else how did those pebbles get in front of Lindstrom not once, but *twice?*

Well, if so, the good Lord took it back the next year. We were ahead of Pittsburgh three games to one in the '25 Series, and we never did win that fourth game. We were ahead in the seventh game, too, 4–0, as late as the third inning. Oh, that was ridiculous. That seventh game of the 1925 World Series was played in a terrific rainstorm. I'm not kidding, it was pouring like mad from the third inning on, and by the seventh inning the fog was so thick I could just about make out what was going on in the infield from out there in the outfield.

In the bottom of the eighth we were still ahead, 7–6, when Kiki Cuyler hit a ball down the right-field line that they called fair, and that won the game for Pittsburgh. It wasn't fair at all. It was foul by two feet. I know it was foul because the ball hit in the mud and *stuck* there. The umpires couldn't see it. It was too dark and foggy.

Well, what the heck—I guess it all evens out in the long run. Too late to do anything about it now, anyway. I never saw an umpire change a decision he made 40 seconds ago, much less 40 years ago. Might as well leave it stand, huh? Maybe if we raise these matters they'll take away some of *my* hits, too. I got 19 hits in those two Series, six of them home runs, and drove in 13 runs. In the 1924 Series I got six hits in a row. Still a record, I reckon.

Roger Peckinpaugh made eight errors in that Series. In the '25 one, I mean. Eight errors. He was jinxed. Before the Series started he was named the Most Valuable Player in the American League. He was a great shortstop. Made miraculous plays for us all season, hit about .300, and then they put the old hex on him by giving him that award *before* the Series instead of after it.

We won the pennant again in 1933, but it was bad times that year.

Goose Goslin: "I truly loved those fast balls. Zip they'd come in, and whack—right
armband Goose is wearing is in memory of Christy Mathewson, who had died a few

back out they'd go." (This picture was taken during the 1925 World Series. The black days before.)

The banks were shut down that year, you know. Bad depression. After the season was over, Clark Griffith told me he couldn't afford to keep me. We won the pennant, all right, but we didn't make any money. So he sold me to Detroit, and I walked right into two more pennants there, in '34 and '35. The '35 Series was where I got that single in the ninth inning of the last game to win it for Detroit. First time the Tigers had ever won a World Series.

Lucky hit, that's all it was. I mean at least you're lucky to get up to bat at just the right time. I hadn't had a hit all day in that game, and when I came up to bat there in the ninth, with the score tied, two out, and Mickey Cochrane on second, I said to the umpire, "If they pitch that ball over this plate, you can go take that monkey suit off."

And sure enough, the first ball Larry French threw in there—zoom! Oh, did those Tiger fans ever go wild. I'll never forget it. You know, I played with the Senators for 12 years, the Browns for two, and the Tigers for four, and the best baseball town I ever played in and for was Detroit. The fans there were great.

I *always* had a rooting section behind me in those left-field stands in Detroit. Mostly school kids, they'd have whole sections of the upper stands roped off for them. When I came up they'd all yell, "Yeah, Goose!" I loved it. We weren't allowed to throw balls into the stands, you know, but I'd always take four balls out with me, in my back pockets, when I went out for fielding practice. And just before I went back in, after I'd taken my throws, I'd sail them up to the kids.

Yeah, I always got a big kick out of the fans. Gee, I used to love to play in Philadelphia. Real close to home, you know, and would they ever razz me.

"Hey, farm boy! Get back to that Jersey farm where you belong!" Oh, I used to love that. I ate it up.

They used to razz me a lot in St. Louis, too. One day there in St. Louis—I think it was in 1930—I had hit two consecutive home runs, and when I came up the next time they really gave it to me. And darned if I didn't hit a third one, right over that right-field fence. I laughed all the way around the bases, and by golly they stopped booing and gave me a big hand as I went around.

Best of all, though, I loved to play against the Yankees, especially in Yankee Stadium. Boy, did I get a kick out of beating those guys. They were so great, you know, it was a thrill to beat them. Babe Ruth was my hero. He was my idol. He was a picture up there at the plate. What a ballplayer. And such a sweet guy, too. I tried to copy everything he did. But I still loved to beat him.

My last year was 1938. The Tigers released me in May, and Clark Griffith heard about it and called me up. He was a wonderful man, always helpful and kind. He wasn't like a boss, more like a father. He was *more* than a father to me, that man. He called me up after Detroit released me.

"You started with me 18 years ago," he said, "why don't you come back to Washington and finish up with me?"

So I did. I went back to the Senators for the rest of that season. Didn't play too much, though. Couldn't gallop around in that pasture like I used to 20 years before. Fact is, I didn't even complete my last time at bat. Lefty Grove was pitching against us—he wasn't any spring chicken any more, either—and I swung at a low outside pitch and wrenched my back.

Bucky Harris was back managing Washington again—Bucky had been my manager there from 1924 to 1928, the best manager I ever played for, and I played for quite a few. So Bucky had to send in a pinch hitter to finish out my turn at bat.

"Come on out, Goose," he said, "and rest up a bit."

That was the last time I ever picked up a bat in the Big Leagues. It was also the first and only time a pinch hitter was ever put in for the ol' Goose.

Note: Goose Goslin was elected to the Baseball Hall of Fame in 1968.

23   *Willie Kamm*

Now Mister Willie Kamm, you don't know who I am,
But that needn't make a bit of diff to you,
For I'm just a common fan, tho' I do the best I can,
And I always root for everything you do.

I like to see you play, in that easy graceful way,
Which doesn't seem to bother you at all,
If a batter pops a fly, way up high into the sky,
It's a cinch that batter's out, and that is all.

When you swing that ashen stick, very hard and very quick,
And the ball lands in the bleachers for a tally,
Or when it's hit-and-run, right there begins the fun,
For I know it's gonna start a winning rally.

Now it's no make-believe that we hate to see you leave,
For we'll miss you, yes we'll miss you every day,
For we like you, Willie boy, and it takes away our joy,
Just to think that we'll no longer see you play.

It's hard to say good-bye, and I feel as tho' I'll cry,
Notwithstanding that the best of friends must part,
So wherever you do play, in that easy graceful way,
You will always have a warm place in my heart.
                    —JUST AN ORDINARY FAN (84 years old)*

I PLAYED THIRD BASE for the White Sox for nine years. Led the league
in fielding time after time, and hit a solid .280 or .290. Hardly ever
missed a game. And then, bang! I was traded to Cleveland.

You know, nobody from the White Sox ever notified me that I'd been
traded. Nobody. After nine years with the club. I read it in the newspapers! Actually, a telephone operator was really the one who told me.
She'd been listening in, I presume. About a week before the trade the
phone rang one night and it's this operator. I didn't know her from
the man in the moon.

* Letter received by Willie Kamm in 1922 after being sold by the San Francisco
Seals to the Chicago White Sox for $100,000.

"You know something, you're going to be traded to Cleveland," she says.

"Oh, yeah," I said, "what's the difference?" I thought she was just some nut.

A couple of days later she calls again. "It's getting closer and closer," she says.

And then on Saturday night the phone rings again. "The deal went through," she says, "you're traded to Cleveland." And I got up the next morning and got the Sunday papers and read where, sure enough, I'd been traded to Cleveland for Lew Fonseca, my old buddy.

"What am I supposed to do now?" I wondered. "It has to be official. It's in the papers."

There was still no word from the ball club. So instead of going to the ball park at the usual time, I waited until the game had started and then went out. Nobody was in the clubhouse then, see. I should have said good-bye to everyone, but somehow—I don't know—I just didn't want to see anybody. Nine years there and contented and all, doing a good job, I thought; I just couldn't understand why I'd been traded.

After I got all my baseball duds packed I went to the club office to see about transportation. All they could say to me was, "Yeah, you've been traded." That's all.

What the heck! It was all worth it, anyway. I was always nuts about baseball. I couldn't play enough. It was always that way, far back as I can remember. There were three cemeteries near our house when I was a kid, and I remember throwing balls, or stones, up against the walls of those cemeteries for hour after hour. All by myself, hour after hour.

When I got bigger I had a paper route, and as soon as I threw my last paper I'd hustle over to Golden Gate Park, where there were always lots of kids playing ball. Before long I got to playing semipro around San Francisco here. There was an old gentleman name of Spike Hennessy, he took a liking to me. Rough and ready man, very poor, he just barely existed, but he devoted his whole life to kids. He was a trainer, just one year, with the Sacramento club, and that year he talked them into signing me. That was 1918, and I'd just turned eighteen years old.

The Sacramento club released me after a month and then Mr. Hennessy got me a job up in Oregon in the Shipyard League. Worked in the shipyards during the week and played ball on weekends. After that I came back home and worked at the Union Iron Works, where they had a company team called the Timekeepers. And from there the San Francisco Seals signed me up. Pacific Coast League. That was in 1919.

Willie Kamm

In the beginning I was a real shy, bashful kid. In fact, when the Seals first signed me, Charlie Graham, the manager, said to me, "You're going to be our regular third baseman."

"Oh no," I told him, "I'm not that good. I just hope that when we get to spring training I'll be good enough so you'll farm me out for a couple of years."

Charlie strung along with me, though. Jeez, was I ever lousy that first year. Must have made 40 million errors. Well, I was only a kid, nineteen years old, skinny, couldn't have weighed over 140. Later on I had my tonsils out and then I started to put some weight on, but that first year

I was just a gangling, awkward kid. Still, Charlie Graham stuck with
me, and I'm thankful to him for it.

Of course, Mom and Pop, they didn't know what to make of all this.
They were old-fashioned German people, and they didn't know baseball
from shmaseball. First game they ever saw they were dumbfounded.
What's going on?

Mom got to be quite a rabid fan, though. She never really understood
the game, but that didn't stop her. Not one bit. She had lots of life and
zip, and boy, she'd root like nobody's business. Everything I did was
sensational as far as she was concerned. Now my father, as far as *he* was
concerned I never got a hit. If I got a single, my mother would scream,
"Willie's hit a triple." And Pop would say "Ach, the guy should have
caught it."

That's just the way he was. All this didn't make any difference to him.
Or if it did, he wouldn't let on. He was a little bitty fellow, less than
five feet tall. An old-fashioned German father.

If you had a turkey for Sunday dinner, you'd ask, "How's the turkey,
Pop?"

"Ach, turkey's turkey."

He was that way with everything. You know, turkey's supposed to be
what it's supposed to be, that's all. My mother, she was the enthusiastic
one. She got a kick out of everything. Mom picked up the game pretty
well, because she used to go fairly regular. But Pop, he only went about
once a week or so.

Mom went to the ball park so much she used to hear a lot of stories
about me. She'd listen to the folks around her, you know. When I first
started with the Seals she went out one day and two guys were sitting
in back of her.

"See that skinny kid out there throwing the ball?" one of them says.

"Yeah."

"That's Willie Kamm."

Well, my mother's all ears, because she'd never seen anything like a
ball park this big before, with so many people in it, and here they're
talking about her son.

So the guy continues, "Yeah, that's Willie Kamm. They're going to try
to make a ballplayer out of him."

"Is that so?" the other guy says. "How come?"

"Oh," says the first guy, "his father's a millionaire, owns half of Market
Street. You know the Kamm Building there." And on and on they went.
Owns this and owns that.

When I got home that night my mother looked at me and said, "Willie, I don't think you should go to that place any more. The people there, they talk very peculiar."

I played third base with the San Francisco club for four years. After the second year was when I had my tonsils out, and that winter I put on a good 20 or 25 pounds. The next season I felt real strong and my batting average went up 50 points. That would be 1921. In 1922 it went up another 50 points, to about .340, and that's when the White Sox bought me for $100,000.

I was only twenty-two years old then, more than 40 years ago, but I still remember that day like it was yesterday. It was June of 1922. The San Francisco club had to make a trip to Los Angeles that week, but I had a bad charley horse so they decided to leave me home to rest up. I didn't have anything in particular to do that evening, so I thought I might as well take a little walk and get some fresh air.

I'm walking up Market Street, at Powell, when suddenly I hear the newsboys yelling, "Willie Kamm sold to White Sox for a hundred thousand dollars! Willie Kamm sold to White Sox for a hundred thousand dollars!"

So I stop dead in my tracks. What are they saying? Can this be true? Me? I walk over to get one of the papers, and one of the kids looks at me and shouts, "Hey, there he is, it's Willie Kamm. Hey, it's Willie Kamm."

Well, I don't know what got into me, but I panicked. Completely. I started running as fast as I could go up Market Street, charley horse and

all, with that pack of newsboys at my heels. "Hey, it's Willie Kamm. Hey, it's Willie Kamm."

Oh, Lord! I ran up two blocks and around a corner and quick ducked in a theater, and there I sat, panting and sweating. I must have sat there for hours. The longer I sat there and thought about it, the more frightened I got. It *can't* be true. I'm not that good. But suppose it is true. It *must* be. What'll I do? I won't go, I'm no Big League player. I won't go, that's all! I don't know how long I sat there. Finally I looked up at the movie. I'd seen the exact same picture the night before, and hadn't even realized it.

Well, then all the hullabaloo started. Record price for a ballplayer. Hundred Thousand Dollar Beauty. All that. And, of course, I went. I always forced myself to do things. Here's the original check, by the way. The Chicago White Sox gave it to me years later. A hundred thousand dollars for me! What do you think of that?

You know, I don't ever remember a ball game where I wasn't nervous before it began. But it seemed like once the first pitch went in, my mind would go completely on the game and I'd lose my nervousness. But it never left me before a game, not in all the years I played.

Yes, you can hear the fans when they yell something to you. Or more likely *at* you. Especially if you're playing third base, you hear them all the time. After all, the box seats are only a few feet away. At least they used to be in the ball parks we played in. But a ballplayer never lets it bother him. Never bothered me, anyway. Just rolls right off your back, like water off a duck.

Willie Kamm's mother and father,
better known as "Babe" and the "Kid"

The worst day I ever had being razzed was one day in Chicago when we were playing the Yankees. It was in 1923 and there had just been all this publicity about the White Sox paying $100,000 for me. I was so terrible that day it was unbelievable. If there was a man on third I struck out, and if there was a man on first I hit into a double play. I did that, and worse, all day long.

Finally, the last time I was up they walked the man ahead of me to get to me, and on the first ball pitched I hit into *another* double play. Well, there must have been about 25,000 people there that day, and I think about 24,999 of them stood up as I walked back to the dugout and told me what a bum I was and that I could go right back to California. Of course, you try to be nonchalant about it. You want to hurry up and get back inside that dugout in the worst way. But you don't want to show them that—so you've got to take your time, yet still hurry, see. Oh, it's a hell of a feeling.

I remember another day, too. We were playing Cleveland a double-

Not all of the mementos of a baseball career consist of balls and gloves. Below: A rather utilitarian notification of being traded, softened somewhat by the letter on the facing page. Also, on the opposite page: The front and back of the record $100,000 check with which nine years earlier the White Sox had bought Willie Kamm from the San Francisco Seals.

Charles A. Comiskey, President
J. Louis Comiskey, Treasurer
Harry M. Grabiner, Secretary
Owen J. Bush, Manager

Comiskey Park
35th and Shields Avenue
Chicago

Chicago

May 18th. 1931

Mr. Wm. Kamm
℅ Cleveland Baseball Club
Cleveland, Ohio

My dear young man:

I am sorry I did not get to
see you before you left Chicago as I wanted
to personally wish you all the luck and a very
successful future in Baseball.

I wish to thank you most
sincerely for the splendid efforts and services
you have given the Chicago Club while a member
not only on the Baseball field but for the
splendid manner in which you conducted yourself
off the ball field.

It is a pleasure to me to have
young men of your class and character and I
trust you will have many, many years of success
in the major leagues.

Sincerely yours

Chas a Comiskey

Pay to the
San Francisco Base
Ball Club

Charles H. Strub
President

John H. Farrell Secy
Natl Assn.

THE AMERICAN LEAGUE BASE BALL CLUB OF CHICAGO   No A 465
CHAS. A. COMISKEY, PRES.
Chicago, June 6 1922
Pay to the order of John H. Farrell Secy Natl Assn $ 100,000
One hundred thousand Dollars #   Dollars
TO FIRST NATIONAL BANK,   THE AMERICAN LEAGUE BASE BALL CLUB OF CHICAGO
2-1   CHICAGO, ILL.   Chas. a. Comiskey

header at Chicago. Well, a guy in the third-base boxes started in on me early in the first game. He had a foghorn for a voice.

"You bum, why don't you go back to California? You never could play ball and you're getting worse. You're all thumbs. You never hit in the clutch. How stupid can you get? What a fathead!"

He was practically right on top of me in that small park, and with that bellow of his I heard every word loud and clear. He kept it up all during the first game and was still going strong well into the second. It wasn't that he'd let loose a blast once in a while. This guy kept screaming without a stop. He'd hardly stop to take a breath. George Moriarty, the old Detroit infielder, was umpiring at third base, and about the middle of the second game he says, "Lord, how long can this guy keep it up?"

Well, about the sixth inning of the second game he finally started losing steam. His voice got hoarser and hoarser, and pretty soon I almost had to strain to catch the words. I'm watching him out of the corner of my eye, see, and in the top of the eighth inning he finally gets up and makes his way through the stands toward the exit behind home plate. By this time he can hardly even whisper any more.

"Thank God!" I say to myself.

But just as he gets to the exit he turns around one last time and bellows, louder than he had all day long, "YOU PUNK, YOU!"

He sure had lungs, that guy. But no, as far as I was concerned the fans never did bother me very much. Hardly heard them.

24 *Heinie Groh*

Strange, that some great sculptor has not seized upon little Heinie Groh as the inspiration for a wondrous modeling. There have been statues, some almost classic in their perfection, showing ballplayers in action. But the famous third baseman and captain of the Cincinnati Reds would give a matchless verve and breathless interest to the conception.

A tiny man, yet faultless as the Pythian Apollo; a small figure, bent half forward like a crouching runner waiting for the starter's gun; an eager face, with glowing eyes and parted lips; the hands swinging free, waiting for instantaneous demands.

The bat crashes . . . a spurt of dust as the little man goes to the ground in one steel-muscled diving leap . . . up again, ball firm-gripped against the black and battered glove . . . the arm crooks . . . the shoulder swings forward . . . and the thud of the ball spatting into the first baseman's glove. That is Heinie Groh!   —Editorial in the Cinicinnati *Times-Star,* 1919

T HERE WAS A PERIOD of about 15 years there, where it seemed like if anything real big happened I was right on the spot. Like a guardian angel, you might say. Or a lead nickel, maybe. Take your choice.

Like when Fred Snodgrass muffed that fly ball in the World Series in 1912, when Fred Toney and Jim Vaughn both pitched no-hitters in the same game in 1917, when the Black Sox threw the World Series in 1919, when that ball hit a pebble and bounced over Freddy Lindstrom's head in the World Series in 1924—you name it and I was there. Some writer once called me the ambiguous Mr. Groh, 'cause it seemed like regardless of what was going on, or where, I'd be somewhere around the premises. Or was it the ubiquitous Mr. Groh? I don't remember. But you get the idea.

Take that double no-hitter, for instance. It happened in Chicago in 1917. I was leading off and playing third base for Cincinnati that day. Both Fred Toney and Jim Vaughn pitched nine no-hit innings, and at the end of the ninth the score was 0–0. Not a single person on either team had gotten a hit. Amazing. Actually, Vaughn had walked me twice, so I was on first base a couple of times during the game, but each time the next man up hit into a double play.

Do you know who won that game for us in the tenth inning? It was big Jim Thorpe, the great Indian athlete. He was playing right field for us that day. Larry Kopf, our shortstop, got the first hit of the game, a single to right field, in the tenth inning. Then he went to third when Hal Chase a hit a line drive that the center fielder dropped. Then, with two out, Jim Thorpe got the second hit of the game, a dinky infield single that the pitcher couldn't handle, and Larry scored on it. Fred Toney kept the Cubs hitless in the last half of the tenth and so we won, 1–0.

I don't think that's ever happened before or since, both pitchers in a game pitching no-hitters. So it's a big thing when you look back at it. But that day, when it happened, most of us didn't realize what was going on until it was all over. In a game where the score is 0–0 everybody gets so tense worrying about their own jobs that they don't have time to keep checking on does the pitcher have a no-hitter going or not. We have our own problems to worry about. That was the way it was with me, anyway. I had enough to do at third base to keep me busy, so I didn't realize what had happened until after the game had ended. And even then I thought, "Well, that's interesting," and that was that. Now, though, it's a big thing.

And Lindstrom in that 1924 World Series. Gee, we should have won that one. The seventh game of the Series and all, and not once but *twice* the ball hits a pebble and bounces over his head. I guess the good Lord just didn't want us to win that game, that's all there was to it.

By that time, you see, I was back on the Giants, where I'd started out in 1912. Well, of course, I didn't really start out with them. What I mean is that the Giants were the first club I played with in the Big Leagues. I actually began with Oshkosh, which was in the Wisconsin-Illinois League. That was back in 1908, when I was only eighteen years old.

I was planning to start at the University of Rochester that year. But one day a fellow from this Oshkosh club came along and asked me if I'd like to play ball with them.

"Well, I believe I will," I said.

We didn't have much money, and this looked like a good way to pay my own way for a change. My father and mother didn't think too much of the idea, but they didn't try to stop me. Dad said, "Let him go. He'll be back."

But I didn't come back; I stayed the whole season with Oshkosh. In fact, I played there three full years. I was a shortstop in those days, and I've got to admit that if it hadn't been for my fielding I'd have been back in Rochester before they'd have even known I was gone. I think—

no, I don't think, I *know*—I hit .161 that first season, which didn't exactly lead the league.

But I kept practicing and practicing at it, and the next year I hit about .285, and the year after that I made it to .300. That was in 1910. Then in 1911, after three years with Oshkosh, the New York Giants bought me and farmed me out to Buffalo in the Eastern League. I did pretty well there, so in 1912 McGraw brought me up the big city.

That's how come I was there in 1912 when Snodgrass dropped that fly ball and the Red Sox beat us in that Series. I never got into any of those games, but I was a Giant that season, sitting on the bench most of the time. They had a crackerjack infield, you know, with Fred Merkle, Larry Doyle, Art Fletcher, and Buck Herzog, and I just couldn't break into that lineup to save my life.

The next year, though, McGraw traded me to Cincinnati and that's where I started playing regular, in 1913. I was a second baseman for the first few seasons I was with the Reds, and then they made me into a third baseman. We had a darned good club those years in Cincinnati, during the 'teens and early 'twenties: Hal Chase and then Jake Daubert at first base, Maury Rath at second, Larry Kopf at short, myself at third, and Eddie Roush, Greasy Neale, Rube Bressler, and Pat Duncan in the outfield. With Ivy Wingo catching and a whole slew of terrific pitchers, like Eppa Jeptha Rixey, Dutch Ruether, Dolph Luque, Slim Sallee, Jimmy Ring, and Hod Eller. Old Hod had what we called a shine ball. What it was, he had a file in his belt and every once in a while he'd rub the ball against that file.

That was a good team, a real good team, and I still don't see why the White Sox were supposed to be such favorites to beat us in the 1919 World Series. I know how good Joe Jackson and Happy Felsch were in the outfield, but they weren't any better than Eddie Roush. Why Eddie used to take care of the whole outfield, not just center field. He was far and away the best outfielder I ever saw. And our pitching was just as good as theirs, for sure.

Well, maybe the White Sox did throw it. I don't know. Maybe they did and maybe they didn't. It's hard to say. I didn't see anything that looked suspicious. But I think we'd have beaten them either way; that's what I thought then and I still think so today.

I played with Cincinnati from 1913 through 1921, and then they traded me back to the Giants, and I stayed there until 1926. So that's how come I played in so many World Series—in 1919 with Cincinnati, in '22, '23, and '24 with the Giants, and then in 1927—my last year—

I caught on with Pittsburgh and got in the Series with them. So between 1919 and 1927 I played in five World Series with three different clubs. And if you count 1912 I was in six World Series altogether.

I figure that's probably a record for anybody who never played with the Yankees. You know how they're so record happy these days: most errors by a left-handed right fielder on Saturdays where the date is an odd number, and all that. Well, there's one record I hold: most World Series on the most different teams for a right-handed third baseman who didn't switch-hit and who never played for the Yankees. If I didn't add that switch-hitting in there I think maybe my old roommate, Frankie Frisch, would take the cake.

As a matter of fact, though, I think I still do hold the record for the highest season's fielding average for a third baseman. I got that because I have a strong chest. I'd get in front of that ball one way or the other, and if I couldn't catch it I'd let it hit me and then I'd grab it on the bounce and throw to first.

McGraw's the one who taught me that when I first came up. "Get in front of those balls," he'd say, "you won't get hurt. That's what you've got a chest for, young man."

McGraw's also the one who started me using my bottle bat. When I first came up he didn't like the bat I had, and he told me to try to get one with a larger barrel. But the large-barreled bats had large handles, and my hands were too small to grip a bat like that very well. See, I'm not too big. I'm 5 feet 7, and I weigh about 160. That isn't real small, but it's not real big either. So I went to Spalding's in New York and we went down in the basement and right there we whittled on a bat until it was just what I needed.

What I wanted was a bat with a big butt end but with a skinny handle, so I could get a good grip and swing it. We whittled down the handle of a standard bat, and then we built up the barrel, and when we were finished it looked like a crazy sort of milk bottle or a round paddle—real wide at one end and then suddenly tapering real quick to a thin handle. The handle part had to be longer than on most bats, because I choked up quite a bit and kept my hands a little apart, too. But I wanted it big starting right above my hands, so if I hit an inside pitch near my hands it would have some power. That bat weighed about 46 ounces, and all the weight was in the barrel, where it counted.

You couldn't hold that bottle bat down at the knob end, 'cause the way the weight was distributed the ball would knock it right out of your hands. But I always choked up and chopped at the ball. I didn't swing from the heels. I'd chop at the ball and drive it over the in-field, see.

I had good luck with that bat, stuck with it from 1912 on and never changed. And for a guy who hit .161 his first season at Oshkosh, you see what it did: I had a lifetime average of over .290 for all the while I was in the Big Leagues, and one period there, 1917 through 1921, I hit about .315. And in the 1922 World Series, you know, when we beat the Yankees four straight, I hit .474. I still carry 474 as my license plate on my car. Have every single year since 1922, as a matter of fact.

I had the Yankees' signs in that 1922 World Series. Not their pitching signs, their hitting signs. I knew when they were going to bunt and when they were going to hit away. Which is something it's very nice for a third baseman to know. I figured them out in the very first game from what Miller Huggins was doing, and had them the whole Series.

That was also the Series where Babe Ruth crashed into me at third base and almost started a real donnybrook. Whew! The Babe wasn't doing very well—I think he only got two hits in the whole Series—and the Yankees were getting beat and I was hitting like nobody's business. So in the third game the Babe got on base, and when the next man up singled, Babe came tearing around into third and as he came in he gave me the shoulder and sent me flying. I didn't complain. That's baseball. But the fans really got on him and gave him a terrific going over.

When I finally got on my feet the Babe said to me, "Kid, you know we're both entitled to part of that base path."

"OK," I said, "you take your side and I'll take mine. And if I ever find you on my side, you better watch out!"

Hell, I couldn't have budged that big guy if I'd have hit him with a locomotive, and he knew it, too. But you got to let them know who's boss, right?

Babe Ruth was a nice guy, though, there's no doubt about that. I never held it against him. A ballplayer can't carry a grudge off the field, anyway. Never! As soon as that gate's closed out there, it's all over. You just forget it. Tomorrow's another day. You can't take the game home with you every night, or you'll go crazy before the season's half over.

So much of baseball is mental, you know, up there in the old head. You always have to be careful not to let it get you. Do you know that I was scared to death every time I went into a World Series? Every single one, even after I'd been in so many. It's a terrific strain. But once I'd fielded that first ball, it was just another ball game. Well, almost. Not quite, of course.

People used to ask me, before a World Series started, "Well, how do you feel?"

"I'll let you know after I handle that first ball," I'd say.

If you handle that first ball clean, then you relax. It's when you mess up that first one that things go from bad to worse. You start worrying, and once you do that you've had it.

Didn't I start to tell you about Freddy Lindstrom's tough luck in that 1924 Series? Yeah, I thought I did. That was McGraw's fourth pennant in a row, and as it turned out it was to be his last. He was a fine man, Mr. McGraw was. I really liked him. I was the Giants' regular third baseman that year, but late in the season I tore my knee and couldn't play, so Freddy Lindstrom—who was only eighteen years old then—was put in.

The Series was tied at three games apiece, and in the seventh game we were ahead 3–1 in the eighth inning. Then the Senators loaded the bases with two out. Bucky Harris slammed a sharp grounder to third and,

Heinie Groh and his famous bottle bat

President and Mrs. Coolidge applauding the victorious Washington team as the winning run scores in the twelfth inning of the seventh game of the 1924 World Series. Mrs. Coolidge was a particularly rabid Washington fan.

just as Freddy was about to field it, it took a wicked hop right over his head and two runs scored to tie the game. And then in the twelfth inning the exact same thing happened—a grounder to third hit a pebble again, bounced way over the kid's head, and we lost the game and the Series, 4–3. It wasn't Freddy's fault. It could have happened to anybody. He never had a chance to get the ball. It was Fate, that's all. Fate and a pebble.

I stayed with the Giants two more years, but I didn't play very much after 1924 because my knee never got well again, and they let me go after the 1926 season. I was thirty-seven then, and you don't play very much third base at that age, anyway. I was lucky, though, and good old Donie Bush picked me up as a utility infielder for the Pittsburgh Pirates in 1927. So I got to see another World Series for free when Pittsburgh won the pennant that year.

That was the first year both the Waner boys were in the outfield for Pittsburgh, and it sure was a delight to watch those two play baseball. Criminy sakes, could they ever hit! No bloopers, either. All line drives. And both of them fast as antelopes.

That was my last season. I knew it would be. So I just sat back on the bench and watched the Waners go to it. Boy, that's the way for an old guy to pass the time of day. Watching two beautiful ballplayers like Paul and Lloyd starting out on what you just *know* are going to be real great careers. That was such a treat that I actually enjoyed that last season just as much as I did my first. Maybe even more.

25 *Hank Greenberg*

When Jackie Robinson first broke in with the Brooklyn Dodgers in 1947, a barrage of racial insults was directed at him from fans in the stands and from opposing players. One team even threatened to go on strike rather than play against Brooklyn if Robinson were in the lineup.

But there were encouraging signs as well. In a game against Pittsburgh early in the season, Jackie and Pittsburgh first baseman Hank Greenberg accidentally collided in a close play at first base. No words were exchanged. A couple of minutes later, though, Greenberg said, "I'm sorry. I should have asked you if you were hurt."

"Thanks," said Jackie. "I'm OK."

"Don't let them get to you," said Greenberg. "You're doing fine. Keep it up."

Asked about the incident by reporters after the game, Jackie said, "Hank Greenberg has class. It stands out all over him."

—Newspaper reports, 1947

L OTS OF PEOPLE were surprised when they heard I'd signed up to play professional baseball. Most people never considered me that good a ballplayer. A few friends thought I had some talent, but I was generally thought of as a big, awkward, gawky kid who was always stumbling over his own two feet. When I was thirteen, I was already 6 feet 3 inches tall, and by the time I was sixteen I weighed close to 200 pounds. I had flat feet— really flat—so I couldn't run very fast and I wasn't too well coordinated, either, to put it mildly.

Under the circumstances, the chances of me getting to the Big Leagues didn't look too good; most people who'd seen me play didn't think I'd make it. For instance in 1928, my last year in high school, when I was seventeen, I was chosen the best high-school first baseman in the New York metropolitan area. Based on that, my Dad asked a friend of his to see if he could get me into the Polo Grounds. Dad was in the textile business—inspecting and shrinking cloth—and one of his customers was close to some people in the New York Giants' organization.

The Giants played all afternoon games then, of course, and at ten in the morning, the substitutes would take batting practice. They needed people in the outfield to shag balls—to catch fly balls and grounders and throw them back to the infield—and that's all I wanted an opportunity to do. We figured it might be a foot in the door.

Hank Greenberg

But word came back through my Dad's friend that the Giants didn't want me to shag balls; they said they'd seen me play for James Monroe High School and didn't think I had any future.

Back then I always thought of myself as a Giant fan. The first major-league game I'd ever gone to had been at the Polo Grounds. My Dad took me to a Sunday double-header between the Giants and the Phillies when I was about thirteen. I still remember that Frankie Frisch, the Fordham Flash, a New York boy, got seven hits for the Giants in the double-header.

Also John McGraw, the Giants' manager, had always made a big thing of looking for a Jewish ballplayer. He figured a Jewish player would be a good gate attraction in New York. Well, here I was, and the city's best high-school first baseman in the bargain—and they wouldn't even let me into the Polo Grounds to shag balls at ten in the morning!

Looking back, I have mixed feelings about that rejection by the Giants. It wouldn't have cost them anything to let me shag balls. On the other hand, I've got to admit that they were in the majority—in those days, most people simply didn't take my baseball talents very seriously. What they didn't count on, though, was my determination.

I wasn't a "natural" ballplayer, like Babe Ruth or Willie Mays. In fact, as a teenager I was better at basketball and soccer than at baseball. I played center on the James Monroe basketball team and fullback on the soccer team. Believe it or not, while I was there we won city championships in all *three* sports. I also played on the football team my senior year, but I didn't like it. When I had some free time, I was on the swimming team and threw the shot put. The wonder of it is that I ever graduated, because when I look back on high school I can't figure out when I ever had any time to study. I used to get up at five in the morning to cram for exams.

Actually, basketball was my first love and if pro basketball had existed back then, I would probably have chosen it over baseball. But I loved baseball, too, and was determined to make good at it.

We lived in the East Tremont section of the Bronx on Crotona Park North, which is another name for East 174th Street, just across the street from Crotona Park and only a block from the park's baseball field. That's where I spent most of my time, practicing, practicing, practicing. Someone once said I didn't *play* ball when I was a kid, I *worked* at it, and I guess they were right. I'd play pepper by the hour, for example, to improve my fielding. Guys would hit or bunt the ball to me and I'd catch it. Over and over again. I'd count how many balls I'd fielded without an error, and then after I missed one I'd start counting all over again.

To improve my hitting, I'd get friends and kids hanging around the park to pitch to me and to shag balls for me. Usually there would be three or four of them—one pitching and two or three shagging in the outfield. Sometimes I'd have a couple of infielders, too. There was no backstop in Crotona Park, which meant I had to hit the ball, because if it got past me I was the one who had to chase it. The idea was to hit fly balls to the guys shagging and get a fly ball to each of them often enough so they didn't get bored and quit. But you couldn't hit the ball too far away from them so they had to do too much running, because then they'd quit not because they were bored, but because they were tired. You also had to be careful not to hit the ball hard straight back at the pitcher, because if he got hit with a batted ball, he'd quit and go home, too.

I got so I was able to hit fly balls within 10 or 15 feet of where I wanted in the outfield, or hit ground balls within a few feet of where I was aiming for in the infield, and whenever a bad pitch came in, I could successfully throw my bat at it and stop it from getting by me. You do this all day long, every day, day after day, and sooner or later you're bound to get pretty good.

I know I spent a lot of time in Crotona Park because I wanted to make myself a better ballplayer, but in all frankness I suspect it was also more complicated than that. I'm no psychologist, but I think one reason I spent so much time there was related to the fact that I was 6 feet 3 inches tall when I was only thirteen. I was awkward and clumsy and had a bad case of adolescent acne and felt out of place. At school, I'd squeeze behind one of those tiny desks, and if I had to go to the blackboard it would be the event of the day: all the kids would titter 'cause I'd tower way above the teacher. Everybody always teased me. "How's the air up there?" I heard that a dozen times a day. At home, if company was at the house they'd be astounded: "My God, look how much he's grown! He's grown two feet in a week!"

I began to think I was a freak. I felt that everybody was laughing at me. It was embarrassing. I was always slouching around, more or less hiding, never standing up straight.

Sports was my escape from all that. Many of the very things that were liabilities socially were assets in sports. I felt more comfortable with athletics, and I think that had a lot to do with why I spent most of my time in Crotona Park.

In any event, whatever the motivation, it paid off. Paul Krichell, a Yankee scout, came to one of our high-school games in 1928 to see one of our pitchers. He didn't care much for the pitcher, but I had a good day at bat and at first base, and he got interested in me.

I graduated from James Monroe in February of 1929 and, because my folks wanted me to, I enrolled at New York University starting in September. Mom and Dad had immigrated here from Rumania around the turn of the century. They were only kids then, and they had to go to work when they were very young. They wanted us to have the college education they'd never had.

Meanwhile, I kept on with my usual routines in Crotona Park, and I also played on a few sandlot and semipro teams while waiting for college to start in the fall. Wherever I played, there would be Mr. Krichell, watching me and taking notes.

That summer, 1929, Mr. Krichell invited me to go with him to a game at Yankee Stadium. It was only the second time I'd ever been to a major-league game; the first time had been when my Dad took me five years earlier and Frankie Frisch got those seven hits for the Giants.

We sat in a first-row box right next to the Yankee dugout. When Lou Gehrig came out and took his place in the on-deck circle in the bottom half of the first inning, Krichell leaned over and whispered to me, "He's all washed up. In a few years you'll be the Yankees' first baseman."

I heard what Krichell was saying, but it made no impression on me because I was so awed at the sight of Gehrig kneeling in the on-deck circle only a few feet away. His shoulders were a yard wide and his legs looked like mighty oak trees. I'd never seen such sheer brute strength. "No way I'm going to sign with this team," I said to myself. "Not with *him* playing first base."

The Yankees made me a very good offer—a $10,000 bonus for signing. That was a fortune in those days. But I'd made up my mind that I'd be a fool to sign with them. And as you are well aware, Gehrig played first base every single day for the Yankees until 1939. There was a long line of first basemen owned by the Yankee organization who spent their whole careers in the minors waiting for him to leave. I'm just glad I escaped being one of them.

Detroit was also interested in me, as well as Washington and Pittsburgh. I liked the Detroit scout better than the others. His name was Jean Dubuc and he'd been a pitcher with Detroit before becoming a scout. He'd gone to college at Holy Cross and Notre Dame and was a very nice person, soft-spoken, low-key, in my opinion a cut above the others. He understood how much my parents wanted me to go to college, and he took that into account. Detroit offered me a $9,000 bonus, a thousand less than the Yankees, but it was drawn up with my mother and father in mind. I was to receive $3,000 immediately on signing and the other $6,000 when I reported to the ball club after college. That pleased my parents, so I signed with Detroit.

I entered New York University that September, as planned, but after one semester I got bored. I wanted to play ball. I finally convinced my folks to let me try it, so in the spring of 1930, at the age of nineteen, I quit school and went to spring training with the Detroit Tigers.

For three years the Tigers farmed me out to the minor leagues. In 1930 I played with Raleigh in the Piedmont League, and in 1931 with Evansville in the Three-I League. And then in 1932 it all came together, and I hit 39 home runs and drove in 131 runs with Beaumont in the Texas League. Del Baker was our manager at Beaumont and Schoolboy Rowe and Pete Fox were also on that team; we won the Texas League pennant and I was voted the league's Most Valuable Player.

In many of the small southern towns where I played during those years, I think I was the first Jew they'd ever seen. They seemed surprised I didn't have horns and a long beard. I encountered some hostility, but I'd say much more curiosity than hostility.

In the minor leagues, I did what I'd always done. I got out to the ball park early, whether it was a game-day or an off-day, and practiced hitting and fielding. It wasn't hard to talk some of the other guys into doing the same thing. What else was there to do in most of those minor-league towns anyway besides play ball? We were all young, in our teens or early twenties, hardly any of us married, so we'd hustle out to the ball park at ten in the morning and have fun while waiting for the game to start.

I did the same thing when I was in the major leagues, too, for that matter. Got out to the ball park early for extra batting practice and often for some extra fielding practice. I did it not only at home in Detroit but also on the road everywhere except in New York. The Yankees wouldn't let me into Yankee Stadium early, to take extra batting practice, but no other club objected. In Boston I remember climbing up on top of that left-field wall in Fenway Park to retrieve baseballs I'd hit up there.

For a short while I had a problem in Shibe Park in Philadelphia. After about half an hour of batting practice one day, the groundskeeper came over and said we had to leave. As usual, I had a whole crew with me—a pitcher and several guys to shag balls in the outfield. We were getting our gear together, preparing to leave, when an elderly gentleman none of us had noticed, sitting about 20 rows up in the grandstand, called to me. I went up to see what he wanted and he said, "I very much admire what you are doing, young man. You tell that groundskeeper to assist you in every way possible. Tell him that those are John Shibe's instructions. And if he doesn't like it, send him right up here to see me." Needless to say, I never had any trouble in Shibe park afterwards.

After that fine year with Beaumont in 1932, MVP and all, I counted on being Detroit's first baseman in 1933. However, the first thing Tiger manager Bucky Harris greeted me with when he saw me in spring training was, "Kid, I'm glad to see you. You're gonna be my third baseman."

Who, me? I'd never played third base in my life, never even had a finger glove on my hand. Detroit had a smooth-fielding first baseman named Harry Davis who they'd bought for $75,000—big money in those days—on Bucky Harris's recommendation. There were a lot of flashy-fielding left-handed first basemen with no power around then—like Lu Blue, Joe Judge, and Joe Kuhel—and Harry Davis was a carbon copy of that type except he wasn't quite as good a hitter. But he'd had a pretty fair year in 1932, hit around .270, and the Tigers felt they needed a third baseman more than a first baseman.

"I don't know how to play third base," I told Harris. "I've played first base since I was in grade school."

"Oh, there's nothing to it," Bucky Harris says. "You get out there and practice and you'll do a great job."

So they put me on third base in spring training. I got myself a fielder's glove and worked like a dog. We started north to open up the '33 season and played the usual exhibition games along the way. In one of them, I remember, there was a man on first and somebody hit a ground ball to me at third. I fired it to second base so hard, trying for a double play, that the ball was out in right field before Charlie Gehringer could get to the bag. A couple of plays later I booted one by cutting in front of Billy Rogell at shortstop when he had the play practically made. I really made a mess of it.

The next day I wasn't in the lineup. No one said a word to me. The following day I'm not in the lineup again, and furthermore I'm not listed to take batting practice with the regulars. Still, nobody's said a thing to me. However, I was starting to get the message. After a couple more days of this, I came to the park one morning and took that third baseman's glove and buried it way in the back of my locker. I found my old first baseman's mitt, put it on my left hand, and walked out onto the field.

Harry Davis was the regular first baseman, but I stood nearby, in short right field or in foul territory, and whenever he left I took over at first base and practiced ground balls. When the time came for pre-game infield practice, I'd wait until he was through and then I'd go out and take his place. No one said a word to me and I didn't say anything to anyone. It was pretty clear from my actions where I thought I was playing, but nobody seemed to care one way or another.

The season opened with me still sitting on the bench. After the game ended one day, I couldn't contain myself any longer. I showered, dressed, and marched straight up to the front office and asked the switchboard operator if I could see Mr. Navin, the owner. She didn't know who I was. I told her: "I'm Hank Greenberg. I'm on the team."

Mr. Navin said to come in to his office, and as I walked in I was trembling. "Mr. Navin," I blurted out, "I can't sit on the bench anymore. I want to play. I'd rather play in Detroit, but if Detroit doesn't want me then let me go someplace where they *do* want me."

"Now, young man," he said, "I appreciate how you feel. It's very understandable. But why don't you sit on the bench for a while and observe what is happening on the field. You can learn a great deal, you know, by watching these major-league pitchers."

"But Mr. Navin," I said, "I'll get fat just sitting on the bench." Here I was, skinny as a rail.

"Have patience, young man," he said. "You'll be playing before you know it, don't worry."

So I sat there on the bench for about two more weeks, very unhappy. I'll never forget what happened next: one day we were just about ready to go out and start the ball game, when the phone rang in the manager's cubbyhole in the locker room. Bucky Harris answered it. Then he came out and went over to this big slate board, with the lineup on it, and erased Harry Davis's name and put mine in its place.

I played that day, it was against a left-handed pitcher. The next time I played was about a week later against another left-hander. The third time I got in the lineup, I hit a home run and a double, and the next thing you know I was in there every day. I played in about 120 games that season; I didn't hit many home runs, but I drove in about 90 runs.

That was the middle of the Depression, 1933. Most everyone was broke. We used to sit around in the hotel lobby waiting for someone to drop a newspaper. No kidding. We'd all sit in the lobby until someone got up and left their newspaper and then five guys would make a dash for it. No one ever thought of going to the newsstand to buy a paper for three cents, which is what they cost then.

And tipping—in those days a nickel was considered a pretty good tip. We'd hardly ever tip more than that. We used to tease Schoolboy Rowe for leaving a two-cent tip one time at dinner. That's right, a two-cent tip! We never let him forget it.

My salary was $3,300 in 1933, and I asked for $5,500 for 1934, figuring I'd had a pretty good year. They only wanted to give me $5,000, though, and that $500 difference led to my first holdout. Mr. Navin wrote me a letter in which he said something like "I've had many better ballplayers than you on my team. Ty Cobb once thought he was bigger than the game and I told him if he didn't want to play he could stay home. The same thing goes for you. If you don't want to play with us, you can stay home."

I was scared, but I didn't budge.

A couple of months passed, and then in late February I got a phone call from Detroit. It was Mr. Navin. "Listen, young man," he says, "if you don't want to play for us you can just hang up your uniform and stay out of baseball." And he went on and on like that for ten minutes. Then he said, "However, I'll tell you what I'll do. I'll give you $5,000 guaranteed, but if we finish one-two-three I'll give you a $500 bonus."

One-two-three! What a joke! We hadn't finished higher than fifth in ten years. But it's only a week before spring training begins and I'm ready to jump at anything provided I can save face.

So I said, "Thank you very much, Mr. Navin. I really appreciate that. I'll be there for spring training on March 1st, sir."

Funny thing, we'd been a fifth-place ball club in 1933, lost about as many games as we won. Over the winter, however, Bucky Harris was released, and Mr. Navin bought Mickey Cochrane from Philadelphia and made him playing manager. He also acquired Goose Goslin from Washington. As a result of these and other changes, we won the American League pennant in 1934, the first pennant for Detroit in 25 years, and I actually *got* that $500 bonus!

That was an outstanding team, the 1934 and '35 Tigers. We won the pennant both years and the World Series in 1935. The infield—with Charlie Gehringer at second, Billy Rogell at short, and Marv Owen at third—was superb both defensively and offensively. In 1934 that infield alone batted in a record 462 runs: 139 for me, 127 for Gehringer, 100 for Rogell, and 96 for Owen. The next year we batted in over 400 runs again—including 170 for me and over 100 for Gehringer.

The infield that batted in 462 runs in 1934 and 420 in 1935: Hank Greenberg,
Charlie Gehringer, Billy Rogell, and Marv Owen. The 462 runs batted in in 1934 is
still a record for an infield.

Mickey Cochrane: "We needed somebody
to take charge and show us how to win
and that's what Mickey did."

In the outfield Goose Goslin batted in about 100 runs each year, and Jo-Jo White, Pete Fox, and Gee Walker did their share, too. With Schoolboy Rowe, Tommy Bridges, Eldon Auker, Firpo Marberry, and General Crowder pitching, and Mickey Cochrane catching, I think it's one of the all-time great teams.

We had four future Hall of Famers on that team, by the way—myself, Gehringer, Goose, and Cochrane. Charlie Gehringer was possibly the best second baseman who ever lived, a marvelous player, and Mickey Cochrane was maybe the best all-around catcher.

Cochrane was the spark that ignited us. He was an inspirational leader. We needed somebody to take charge and show us how to win and that's what Mickey did. He'd been on three pennant winners with Philadelphia—in 1929, '30, and '31—and winning was a way of life with him. There was an intangible something about him, a winning spirit, that was really infectious.

We would have won the pennant in 1936 too, I think, if I hadn't been hurt. I'd been voted the American League's Most Valuable Player in 1935, when I hit .328, 36 home runs, and led the league with 170 runs batted in. In 1936, though, the season had hardly begun when Jake Powell ran into me at first base and broke my left wrist. I was out for the whole year and we wound up in second place.

The following year Mickey got beaned and we were never the same after that tragedy. Cochrane was hit on the head by a pitched ball in May of 1937 and he never played again.

In 1937, the year after I was out with the broken wrist, the Tigers sent me a $1-a-year contract. And I signed it. I had to go through spring training and prove I was healthy before they'd replace it with a regular contract. Imagine any ballplayer signing a $1-a-year contract today!

It turned out that 1937 was the best year I ever had. Most people would say 1938 was my best year—when I hit 58 home runs—but I don't think so. I'd pick 1937, when I hit .337, 40 homers, and batted in 183 runs.

I've always believed that the most important aspect of hitting is driving in runs. Runs batted in are more important than batting average, more important than home runs, more important than anything. That's what wins ball games: driving runs across the plate.

Charlie Gehringer used to bat ahead of me, and if we had a man on first base and Charlie was up, I'd yell, "Get him to third, Charlie, just get him to third. I'll get him in."

That was my goal: get that man in. It got to be a standing joke. Once

Charlie said to me, "I suppose if I hit a double with a man on first, you'd probably trip him if he tried to go past third base."

In 1930 Hack Wilson had set the major-league record for runs batted in: 190. A year later, in 1931, Lou Gehrig had set the American League record: 184. I'm third on the all-time list, with 183 in 1937. I was much more disappointed when I failed to break Gehrig's runs-batted-in record in 1937 than I was when I didn't break Babe Ruth's home-run record in 1938. Runs batted in were my obsession, not home runs.

Of course, it's true that in 1938 I almost broke Babe Ruth's record of 60 home runs in a season. I fell two short, with 58. That's become so closely associated with my name that by now they usually go together in the same breath: Hank Greenberg—58 home runs. Naturally, I was disappointed. I already had 58 and there were five games still to play, so it looked like I had a good shot at the record. But in one of the five remaining games, I was walked four times. In another, Bob Feller set a new strikeout record by striking out 18 men in one game, including me twice. It was one thing after another, and then the final game of the season was called on account of darkness in the sixth inning, and that was that.

Some people still have it fixed in their minds that the reason I didn't break Ruth's record was, because I was Jewish, the ballplayers did everything they could to stop me. That's pure baloney. The fact of the matter is quite the opposite: so far as I could tell, the players were mostly rooting *for* me, aside from the pitchers. I remember one game Bill Dickey was catching for the Yankees, he was even telling me what was coming up. The reason I didn't hit 60 or 61 homers is because I ran out of gas; it had nothing to do with being Jewish.

Anyway, it really doesn't matter too much as far as I'm concerned. Roger Maris and Hank Aaron broke Ruth's home-run records, but nobody pays much attention and rightfully so. Babe Ruth was the ultimate home-run hitter of his time and of all time. He was the greatest player in the history of the game, and whether someone breaks this home-run record or that one can't change that fundamental truth.

Speaking of Bob Feller, by the way, the first time I ever batted against him was in 1937, when he was only eighteen years old. He had such blinding speed and was so wild that everybody was afraid to go up to bat, including me. He had a very deceptive motion. You never knew where the ball was coming from or where it was going, and neither did he.

I saw him throw a ball *behind* Billy Rogell when Rogell was batting left-handed. Rogell almost dropped his bat and started out to the mound.

Bob Feller

Gives you an idea of how wild Feller was, a right-handed pitcher throwing behind a left-handed batter. Later he developed a terrific curve and then he was just unhittable. You couldn't hit the curve so you'd wait for the fastball, but that would be by you before you knew what happened!

Talking about Bob Feller reminds me of Joe DiMaggio, probably because they both came up at the same time. Everybody remembers Willie Mays's catch off Vic Wertz in the 1954 World Series, but very few people remember an even greater catch Joe made off me in 1939. I hit a tremendous line drive one day in Yankee Stadium that went at least 450 feet to deepest center field. Joe turned and raced toward the bleachers with his back to the plate; still running full speed, without turning around or looking back, he stuck his glove up and the ball landed right in it. Mays had time to turn his head to see where the ball was coming down, but Joe never even had time to turn. If he had turned his head, he would have lost it. So he just stuck up his glove. Sheer instinct.

There are great ballplayers nowadays, of course. But you know, I played in an era of super-great ballplayers, especially first basemen. Just think of the competition I had at first base in the American League: Hal Trosky, Zeke Bonura, Jimmie Foxx, Lou Gehrig, and Rudy York.

Most people have forgotten about Hal Trosky. A marvelous first baseman for Cleveland all through the thirties. The man batted in 162 runs one year! Zeke Bonura of the White Sox was another good hitter with power. Jimmie Foxx, maybe the greatest right-handed power hitter of all time. When I first came up, I used to talk about hitting with Jimmie whenever I had a chance. He was a friendly, warm person, always very helpful to everybody.

And of course Lou Gehrig, the best of all. He wasn't very friendly, though. I was in the league a year and a half before he said a word to me. I remember the first time he spoke to me, it was in the middle of the 1934 season just after we passed the Yankees and went into first place. I got a single and was standing on first base. He turned to me and said, sort of gruffly, "Aren't you even gonna say hello?"

"Hello, Lou," I said. That's all. I couldn't think of anything else to say. I think I was scared of him. From then on it was just "hello" and that was it. We never chatted.

Rudy York was special 'cause he was on my own team and he was also a close friend. Rudy was a great human being. In a sense, you might say that he took my job away from me. Rudy joined the Tigers in 1937 and hit 35 home runs. The next year he hit 33 homers and drove in 127 runs, and

Rudy York: "What a hitter!"

then he had another great year in 1939. What a hitter! Rudy's bat was too powerful to keep him out of the lineup, but the problem was where to play him. They tried him at third base, in the outfield, and as a catcher, but at each position he was losing as many games defensively as he was winning with his bat.

Well, in January of 1940 Jack Zeller, who had recently been made general manager, asked me to take a $5,000 cut in salary. Mr. Navin had died in 1935 and Walter Briggs became the Tigers' owner. He delegated a lot more authority than Mr. Navin had. Jack Zeller had the nerve to argue that I had a poor season in 1939 because I didn't hit 58 home runs again. I'd made $40,000 in 1939 and he wanted to cut me to $35,000.

"No way, Jack," I said. "I'm not taking any salary cut. I had a pretty good year last year. You can't expect me to hit 58 home runs *every* year. I should get at least $40,000 again, the same as last year."

"Well," he said, "I'll tell you what I'll do. If you go out to the outfield and play left field, and let Rudy York play first base, then I'll keep your salary at $40,000."

That $5,000 salary cut was just a ploy to get me to move to the outfield so they could put Rudy on first base. First base was probably his best position, and in fact he eventually developed into a fine defensive first baseman. But as far as I was concerned, it was no deal. "What are you talking about?" I said. "I'm not going to the outfield. If Rudy can beat me out of first base, then the job is his. No one gave me the job. Let him earn it, just like I did."

"Come on, Hank," Zeller said, "you know that with Rudy on first and you in the outfield we'll be a better team than last year."

I thought it over for a few days and then went back to him. "To begin with," I said, "I want the same salary as last year, $40,000. But if you want me to go to the outfield, I'll buy a fielder's glove and go down to spring training and work my tail off and give you all spring to make up your mind what you want to do. I won't even put on a first baseman's mitt. I'll practice in the outfield as hard as I can. Then on Opening Day, if you want me to stay in the outfield, you have to give me a $10,000 bonus. I'm taking all the risk in this experiment, I have the most to lose, so I deserve some compensation for it."

And that's what happened. On Opening Day I was in left field, I walked up to the front office, and Jack Zeller gave me a check for $10,000. And I could have kissed him. Because playing the outfield was sheer joy. I loved it out there.

It was a lot easier than playing first base, as far as I was concerned. For one thing, I didn't have to take as much riding from the opposing players. In Detroit first base is next to the *visiting* team's bench, so I was always fielding my position close to the opposition's yelling. I didn't have to take as much riding from the fans, either. I guess I had rabbit ears, because I often let what I heard bother me. In the outfield I was relaxed all the time. I was never tired. All I had to worry about was hitting. I think if I'd played in the outfield my whole career, I'd have hit 30 or 40 points higher.

I thought I got to be a pretty good outfielder. I had a strong and accurate arm and I knew where to throw the ball. I also knew the characteristics of the hitters, having been in the league a long time. A lot of outfielding is knowing where to play the hitters. If you do that properly, pretty soon the ball is hit to you instead of you chasing after it.

It all worked out just fine, because we won the American League pennant in 1940, the first time since 1935. I hit .340 with about 40 homers and drove in around 150 runs. Rudy York also hit well over .300 with about 30 homers and he drove in around 130 runs. And I was voted the league's Most Valuable Player again, I think the only time someone has won the MVP award at two different positions.

Del Baker was our manager that year. Cochrane had been let go in 1938. Baker, remember, had been my manager with Beaumont in the Texas League back in 1932. Del's claim to fame was that he was an expert sign stealer. I mean he could stand on the third-base coaching lines and read a catcher's signs or pick up on a pitcher's mannerisms and let you know in advance what kind of pitch was coming: fastball or curve or what have you.

I loved that. I was the greatest hitter in the world when I knew what kind of pitch was coming up. Baker chattered all the time while coaching at third base, and if he said "All right" when I was at bat it meant the next pitch was going to be a fastball. If he said "Come on," it meant a curve. Like, "All right, Hank, you can do it" would tell me a fastball was on its way. "Come on, Hank, you can do it" meant a curve was coming.

Some guys didn't want to know the signs. They preferred to figure out the pitch by themselves. Gehringer would never take the signs, nor Goslin. But Rudy York and I, we *thrived* on them, which is one reason we murdered the ball in 1940.

The only pitcher where I wouldn't take the signs was Bob Feller. With his speed I was afraid of risking the chance of a mistake. If Baker told me a curve was coming up and he was wrong—if it was really a fastball—I could be in big trouble. Feller had such a great curve that it would look like it was going to hit you, but then it would break over the plate at the last second. If I hung in there expecting it to break, but it was really a fastball and didn't break, I could get killed.

Rudy and I were having such a terrific year in 1940 that Del Baker started taking credit for our hitting. At one point it seemed as though if he called a pitch correctly and I hit a home run, he thought it was *his* home run. Baker was a real good sign stealer, no question about it, but there's a big difference between *knowing* what's coming and *hitting* it. Getting the signs doesn't guarantee that you'll hit the ball.

In fact, we had the signs of the Cincinnati Reds in the World Series that year and we still lost it. Ernie Lombardi, the regular Cincinnati catcher, was hurt, so Jimmie Wilson did most of their catching. We could read his signs from our bench and we flashed them to our batters, but it didn't help. Bobo Newsom pitched and won two games for us but then he lost the seventh game to Paul Derringer by a score of 2–1.

World War II came along the next year and that was the end of my baseball career for four and a half years. Hugh Mulcahy was the first and I was the second major-league ballplayer to go into the armed forces. I was drafted into the Army on May 7, 1941, and didn't get back into baseball until July of 1945. I was 30 years old and at the peak of my career when I left, and 34 years old and a bit shopworn when I got back.

I spent most of the war overseas in India and China with the Air Force. I hardly played any ball at all during that time. One game I do remember, though. When I was stationed at Fort Custer near Battle Creek, Michigan, shortly after I was inducted, a sergeant friend of mine told me he had a brother who was in the state prison at Jackson, about 50 miles away. He said that the prison warden was a great baseball fan, and it would do his brother a world of good if I could be talked into playing with the Fort Custer team when they played their annual game at the prison. I said OK, I'd do it, I'd play on the Fort Custer team for that one game only.

Sergeant Hank Greenberg in 1942. Greenberg joined the Armed Forces as a Private in 1941 and was discharged in 1945 as an Army Air Force Captain.

We traveled to the prison in an Army bus, and when we got there it turned out that the Army team didn't have a baseball uniform that would fit me. The prison team did, though, so I put on the prison uniform. Then I said, "Well, as long as I've got this uniform on, I might as well play with you guys." So I played on the prison team.

I found out that it was customary for the prisoners to root for the *visiting* team and ride the hell out of their fellow prisoners. And ride the umpire, too, who was also a prisoner: "You crook, you thief," they'd yell at him.

But now I'm playing first base for the prison team, and suddenly they're all rooting for me and for their own team. I hit a double, two singles, and a home run over the wall, the first time the ball had ever been hit out of the prison yard. And, of course, all the prisoners in the grandstand yelled, "I'll get it, I'll get it."

I rejoined the Tigers on July 1, 1945, and I had the two biggest thrills of my whole career that season. One was on my first day back, July 1st: 50,000 people came to the ball park to welcome me home and I hit a home run that day to help win the game. I was playing from memory. I'd hardly had a bat in my hands since I'd left in 1941, and after I hit that home run they gave me an unbelievable standing ovation.

The second thrill was on the last day of the season, when I hit a home run with the bases loaded in the ninth inning to win the pennant. There were two men on base and one out, and the opposing pitcher, Nelson Potter, walked Doc Cramer to load the bases and get to me. I hit his second pitch on a line into the left-field bleachers. I guess that was my biggest thrill of all: what was going through my mind as I was rounding the bases is that only a few months before, I was in India, wondering if the war would ever end, and now the war was actually over and not only that but I'd just hit a pennant-winning grand-slam home run. I wasn't sure whether I was awake or dreaming.

I had a pretty good year the following year, 1946. I hit under .300 for the first time since I'd been with the Tigers, but I still led the league in both home runs and runs batted in.

After the season ended, though, I got one of the biggest shocks of my whole life. In January of 1947, I heard on the radio that I'd been sold to the Pittsburgh Pirates. I wasn't even sold, really. Given away would describe it better. I was waived out of the American League and picked up by Pittsburgh for practically nothing. Evidentally nobody else felt they could afford my $75,000 salary.

I couldn't believe it. Detroit was my team. I identified 100 percent with the Tigers. I'd been in the Detroit organization for seventeen years. Only a little over a year ago I'd hit that pennant-winning home run on the last day of the season. And here I was being dumped without even the courtesy of a phone call. I did get a telegram: YOUR CONTRACT HAS BEEN ASSIGNED TO PITTSBURGH IN THE NATIONAL LEAGUE. That's all it said.

I never understood it. Still don't to this day. I've had a sour attitude toward Mr. Briggs ever since. He's the man who must have been responsible. I still remember Mrs. Briggs kissing me good-bye when I went into the Army in 1941. But now the war was over. It's an old story: what have you done for me *lately*? In my case it was just lead the league in home runs and runs batted in!

I was so shocked and hurt I quit baseball. Simply quit. I told the press I was retiring and that was that.

John Galbreath, Frank McKinney, and Bing Crosby had just bought the Pittsburgh Pirates. They announced that they had acquired Hank Greenberg—the American League's home-run and runs-batted-in leader—and in a week their advance sale picked up $200,000. So they were very eager for me to play. When I said I was retiring, they were quite unhappy.

Mr. Galbreath came to New York and phoned me to have lunch with him. I said, "Mr. Galbreath, I'm not going to play anymore. I've announced my retirement and I mean it."

"I don't want to talk you into playing," he said. "I just want to have lunch with you."

So we had lunch and while we were eating, he said, "Tell me what your objections are to playing in Pittsburgh."

"I don't have my heart in it," I said. "I've played all my career with Detroit and that's home to me. Not to mention things like the fences in your ball park. Pittsburgh has a big ball park. I'm used to a park that's 340 feet down the left-field line. Yours is 380 feet. I don't want to disappoint everybody."

"Don't worry about that," he said. "How far is it in Detroit? 340? Well, we'll make Pittsburgh 340, too. We'll bring the fences in so it'll be 340."

"That's not so important," I said. "There are a lot of things. For instance, I can't ride those trains anymore. The berths are too small. Every time I go in them I get a crick in my back."

"You don't have to go by train," he said. "You can go by plane."

"I can't stand a roommate anymore," I said. "At my age, I don't want to have to deal with roommates."

"Fine," he said. "Don't worry about roommates. We'll give you a suite by yourself on the road."

"Well," I said, "if I ever did play for anybody, they'd have to give me my outright release at the end of the season. I never want to hear on the radio again that I've been traded or sold."

"OK," he said, "we'll give you your outright release at the end of the season."

Everything I mentioned, he said, "Don't worry, we'll take care of it. We'll work it out."

So finally I said, "Well, you wouldn't pay me enough, anyhow."

"We'll pay you whatever you want. What did you get last year?"

"$75,000."

"What do you want for this year?"

"I'd say $100,000."

"Fine," he said, "you got it."

When he got through offering me all this, what could I do? He talked me into playing, so I went and played one more year.

I doubt if I really earned my salary on the field that year, even though I hit 25 home runs and drove in about 75 runs. I brought in a lot of money at the gate, however, and I think I earned my pay by training my own successor, so to speak. I worked a lot with Ralph Kiner, who was still a baby then, and helped him become the great home-run hitter he eventually became. I still feel as close to Ralph as if he were my own son.

Ralph had a natural home-run swing. All he needed was somebody to teach him the value of hard work and self-discipline. Early in the morning, on off-days, every chance we got, we worked on hitting.

"Let me ask you something," I said to him. "In a 150-game season, let's say you go to bat four times a game. That's 600 times at bat. Let's say you get two decent swings each time at bat. That's 1,200 swings. If you stand here at home plate and you make the pitcher throw strikes, don't you think that with 1,200 swings you'll hit 35 balls out of the park?"

"Sure," he said.

"Well," I said, "that's all there is to it. You know you're going to get 1,200 swings. Now the secret is to make the pitcher throw strikes. If you learn the strike zone, you're automatically going to have 35 home runs a season. It's as simple as that."

He learned the strike zone and instead of hitting 35 home runs, he hit over 50 twice and led the league seven straight years. Except for Babe Ruth, no one has ever hit as many home runs per time at bat as Ralph Kiner.

At the end of the '47 season, the Pirates kept their word and gave me my release, and then I really did quit playing. The passage of time and changes

Ralph Kiner: "He learned the strike zone and instead of hitting 35 home runs, he hit over 50 twice and led the league seven straight years."

in the game have pushed me way down in terms of number of home runs hit, but when I retired in 1947, my 331 lifetime home runs were *fifth* on the all-time list; the only ones who had hit more home runs than me were Babe Ruth, Jimmie Foxx, Mel Ott, and Lou Gehrig, in that order.

You have to realize that I lost four and a half seasons to World War II and another year because of that broken wrist in 1936. So I actually played only nine and a half years. During that time I hit 331 home runs and drove in 1,276 runs, which averages out at 35 home runs and 134 runs batted in a season. All together, I played in almost 1,400 games and batted in close to 1,300 runs, nearly one a game; the only one in baseball history who ever did as well driving runs across the plate is Lou Gehrig.

After I finished playing, I had a whole second career on the management level. I met Bill Veeck at the 1947 World Series, found a kindred spirit, and joined him in the Cleveland Indians' front office in 1948. In my opinion, Bill Veeck is the smartest and most innovative baseball executive of all time. Except for Branch Rickey, he doesn't even have any competition.

Veeck converted me. I was a ballplayer, you see, and the game was everything. What happened aside from the game was irrelevant to me. Bill taught me that baseball was more than just balls and strikes, hits and errors. You have to get people into the ball park, and to do that you have to attract them with a good time as well as a good team. I finally recognized that baseball is part entertainment and show business. I think that Veeck's genius of drawing more than two and a half million fans in Cleveland in 1948, a town that typically drew less than a million, was as big an accomplishment in its own way as Ted Williams hitting .406.

First I was farm director and then general manager at Cleveland, and afterwards vice-president of the White Sox when Veeck took over that club. I was part owner of each franchise as well, I guess one of the few who went from the sandlots through the players' ranks to the front office and eventually an ownership position.

When Veeck became ill and had to sell the White Sox in 1961, I had an opportunity to increase my stock ownership and acquire a majority interest in the club. After a lot of thought, I finally decided against it. What tipped the scales against buying was the other owners: I recognized then that there was a lot of prejudice against me. I'd have had my life savings tied up in the club, and I realized that if I ever needed any help, I sure wouldn't get it from my fellow owners. It would be closed ranks against me.

Strangely enough, that was the first time anti-Semitism really affected me adversely in baseball. As a player, I often had fans and opposing players taunting me, calling me names. For at least ten years I hardly played in a ball park where there wasn't some loud-mouthed fan popping off with anti-Jewish remarks. In the minors—the Piedmont League, the Texas League—and for many years in the majors, too, my religion was seen as an appropriate topic for ridicule.

However, I think that *helped* me more than it hurt. I was a very sensitive, fired-up ballplayer, and when they got on me that way, it brought out the best in me. I played all the harder.

In my mind, by the way, players belong in a different category than fans. It was considered fair game to try to probe for a guy's weak spot so you could catch his attention and destroy his concentration. Joe McCarthy used to have two third-stringers on the Yankee bench—we called them bench jockeys—whose main job was to ride the opposition and try to get their goat.

When opposing bench jockeys taunted me, was it really anti-Semitism or just a psychological ploy to distract me? Probably some of both, but in my opinion it was mostly a psychological ploy. After all, Al Simmons heard similar insults about his Polish ancestry and Joe DiMaggio about his Italian heritage. Babe Ruth was called a "big baboon," and much worse, and Zeke Bonura "banana nose." In all honesty, I couldn't then and I can't now single out the insults aimed at me as any different from all the others. I think they were all the same kind of thing.

You want to talk about real bigotry, that was what Jackie Robinson had to contend with in 1947. Teammates asking to be traded rather than play with him, opponents threatening to strike rather than play against him; in many places he couldn't eat or sleep with the rest of the team. I never encountered anything like that.

I was with Pittsburgh in the National League that year, so I saw it close up. Brooklyn was leading the league and we were in last place, they were beating our brains out, and here's some of our guys having a good time yelling insults at Jackie! I had to put up with little more than a mild hazing compared with what he went through.

Sometimes it could get pretty bad for me too, of course. The Chicago Cubs were especially vicious in the 1935 World Series. They got on me from the first pitch with some really rough stuff. George Moriarty was

Jackie Robinson

umpiring behind home plate, and it bothered him so much he went over to quiet them down. They told Moriarty to mind his own business: they weren't getting on him, they were getting on me. I broke my wrist in the second game of the Series and couldn't play anymore, so that ended that. They had a rough crew, but we had the last laugh: we won the Series.

I realize now, more than I used to, how important a part I played in the lives of a generation of Jewish kids who grew up in the thirties. I never thought about it then. But in recent years, men I meet often tell me how much I meant to them when they were growing up. It's almost the first thing a lot of them say to me. It still surprises me to hear it, but I think I'm finally starting to believe it.

They all remember that I didn't play on Yom Kippur, the Jewish holiday. They remember it as every year, but in fact the situation arose only once, in 1934. Both Rosh Hashanah and Yom Kippur came in September that year, and since we were in the thick of the pennant race, the first for Detroit in many years, it became a national issue whether or not I should play on those days. The press made a big thing out of it.

The question was put before Detroit's leading rabbi, Rabbi Leo Franklin. He consulted the Talmud, a basic source for Jewish morality, and announced that I could play on Rosh Hashanah, the Jewish New Year, because that was a happy occasion on which Jews used to play ball in the streets long ago. However, I could not play on Yom Kippur, the Day of Atonement, because that day should be spent in prayer.

So I played on Rosh Hashanah and, believe it or not, I hit two home runs off Boston's Dusty Rhodes. We beat the Red Sox, 2–1, with my second homer winning the game in the tenth inning. Just like in the movies, right?

Edgar A. Guest, whose poems used to be nationally syndicated, wrote a poem at about that time which he called "Speaking of Greenberg." I think I still have a copy around here someplace.

It's a strange thing. When I was playing, I used to resent being singled out as a Jewish ballplayer. I wanted to be known as a great ballplayer, period. I'm not sure why or when I changed, because I'm still not a particularly religious person. Lately, though, I find myself wanting to be remembered not only as a great ballplayer, but even more as a great *Jewish* ballplayer.

Probably Bill Veeck's fault, right? After all, he's the one started me thinking maybe there are other things in life besides balls and strikes. Back in good old Crotona Park, I never would have believed a word of it!

Speaking of Greenberg

By Edgar A. Guest

The Irish didn't like it when they heard of Greenberg's fame
For they thought a good first baseman should possess an Irish name;
And the Murphys and Mulrooneys said they never dreamed they'd see
A Jewish boy from Bronxville out where Casey used to be.
In the early days of April not a Dugan tipped his hat
Or prayed to see a "double" when Hank Greenberg came to bat.

In July the Irish wondered where he'd ever learned to play.
"He makes me think of Casey!" Old Man Murphy dared to say;
And with fifty-seven doubles and a score of homers made
The respect they had for Greenberg was being openly displayed.
But on the Jewish New Year when Hank Greenberg came to bat
And made two home runs off Pitcher Rhodes—they cheered like mad for that.

Came Yom Kippur—holy feast day world wide over to the Jew—
And Hank Greenberg to his teaching and the old tradition true
Spent the day among his people and he didn't come to play.
Said Murphy to Mulrooney, "We shall lose the game today!
We shall miss him on the infield and shall miss him at the bat,
But he's true to his religion—and I honor him for that!"

Hank Greenberg

26 *Paul Waner*

The year 1903 began auspiciously for the growing young game of baseball. The two-year feud between the established National League and the infant American League came to an end in January, and the upcoming season promised to be the best yet.

The idols of the day were Honus Wagner and Napoleon Lajoie, Cy Young and Ed Delahanty. The season before, in the new American League, Cy Young had won 32 games for the Boston Pilgrims and Big Ed Delahanty had led both leagues in batting. Over in the National League, Honus Wagner had led the league in doubles, Sam Crawford in triples, and the pacesetter in home runs—with six—had been Pittsburgh's Wee Tommy Leach.

And on April 16, practically opening day of the 1903 season, a son was born to the Waner family at their ranch near Harrah, Oklahoma. He was named Paul Glee. Two years and eleven months later, to the day, he was joined by brother Lloyd James. To become better known as Big Poison and Little Poison a little over two decades later, their very names were, in the clichés of the sports pages, sufficient to strike terror into the hearts of opposing pitchers.

Seldom have such clichés been more accurate. The Waner boys played in the Big Leagues for almost 20 years, 14 of them side by side in the Pittsburgh outfield. After it was all over, Paul had amassed the astounding total of over 3,100 hits, a figure exceeded by very few men in the entire history of baseball. Only eight men in history managed to better his output of doubles, and only nine were able to hit more triples. Yet Paul Waner stood only 5 feet 8 inches tall, and weighed less than 150 pounds.

For his part, Lloyd, who was even smaller, accumulated 2,500 hits and still holds the National League record for the most one-base hits in a season.

Simply put, the two Waners are far and away the best hitting brothers who ever played in the Big Leagues. Their 5,600 major league hits exceeds by almost 1,000 the total collected by all *five* Delahanty brothers, and is over 500 more than the total hits of all *three* DiMaggio brothers.

I COME FROM A LITTLE TOWN right outside of Oklahoma City, a town by the name of Harrah. You can spell that backwards or forwards. From there I went to State Teachers' College at Ada. And you can spell that backwards or forwards, too. Which just naturally explains why I've always been a fuddle-dee-dud!

I went to State Teachers' College at Ada for three years, although I didn't really intend to be a teacher. Maybe for a little while, but not forever. What I wanted to be was a lawyer, and I figured sooner or later I'd go to law school. Eventually I was going to go to Harvard Law School, I reckon. That was my ambition, anyway.

But all at once baseball came up, and that changed everything all around. Of course, I was playing ball on amateur and semipro teams all the while I was in high school and college. In those days, you know, every town that had a thousand people in it had a baseball team. That's not true any more. But in those days there were so many teams along there in the Middle States, and so few scouts, that the chances of a good player being "discovered" and getting a chance to go into organized ball were one in a million. Good young players were a dime a dozen all over the country then.

How did they find me? Well, they found me because a scout went on a drunk. Yes, that's right, because a scout went on a bender. He was a scout for the San Francisco Seals of the Pacific Coast League, and he was in Muskogee looking over a player by the name of Flaskamper that Frisco wanted to buy. He looked him over, and sent in a recommendation—that was late in the summer of 1922—and then he went out on a drunk for about ten days. They never heard a thing from him all this while, didn't know anything about him or where the heck he was.

He finally got in shape to go back to the Coast, but on the way back a train conductor by the name of Burns—you know how they used to stop and talk with you and pass the time of day—found out that this fellow was a baseball scout. Well, it so happened that I went with this conductor's daughter—Lady Burns—at school. So naturally—me going with his daughter and all—what the heck—he couldn't wait to tell this scout how great I was. How I could pitch and hit and run and do just about everything. He was such a convincing talker, and this scout needed an excuse so bad for where he'd been those ten days, that the scout—Dick Williams was his name—decided, "Doggone it, I've got something here."

When he got back to San Francisco, of course they wanted to know where the heck he'd been and what had happened. "Well," he said, "I've been looking over a ballplayer at Ada, Oklahoma. His name is Paul Waner and he's only nineteen years old, and I think he's really going to make it big. I've watched him for ten days and I don't see how he can miss."

Then Dick quickly wrote me a letter. He said, "I've just talked to the Frisco ball club about you. I heard about you through this conductor,

Burns. I told them that I saw you and all that, and I want you to write me a letter and send it to my home. Don't send it to the ball club, send it to my home. Tell me all about yourself: your height, your weight, whether you're left-handed or right-handed, how fast you can run the hundred, and all that. So I'll know, see, really know."

So I wrote him the letter he wanted, and sent it to his home, not really thinking too much about it at the time. But the next spring, darned if they didn't send me a contract. However, I sent it right back, 'cause my Dad always wanted me to go to school. He didn't want me to quit college. My father was a farmer and he wanted his sons to get a good education.

But they sent the contract right back to me, and even upped the ante some. So I said, "Dad, I'll ask them for $500 a month, and if they give it to me will you let me go?"

He thought about it awhile, and finally said, "Well, if they'll give you $500 a month starting off, and if you'll promise me that if you don't make good you'll come right back and finish college, then it's OK with me."

"Why surely, I'll do that," I said.

So I told the Frisco club about those conditions. But it didn't make any difference to them. Because they could offer you any salary at all and look you over, and if you weren't really good they could just let you go and they'd only be out expenses. They had nothing to lose.

So out I went to San Francisco for spring training. That was in 1923. I was only nineteen years old, almost twenty, just an ol' country boy. I didn't even know, when I got there, that they had a boat going across to San Francisco. My ticket didn't call for any boat trip. But after the train got into Oakland you got on a ferry and went across San Francisco Bay. Boy, as far as I was concerned that was a huge ocean liner!

I had hardly arrived out there before I met Willie Kamm, Lew Fonseca, and Jimmy O'Connell. Those three used to pal around together a lot, because they all came from the Bay Area. I was anxious to be friendly and all, so I said to them, real solicitous-like, "Well, do you fellows think you'll make good up here?" (All the while thinking to myself, you know, "Gee, you sure don't look like it to me.")

How was I to know that all three of them *already* were established Big Leaguers? It turned out that they were just working out with the Frisco club until their own training camps opened. But I didn't know that. That was a big joke they never let me forget—a kid like me asking them did they think they'd make good!

Anyway, there I was, a rookie who'd never played a game in organized ball, at spring training with the San Francisco club in the Coast League, which was the highest minor league classification there was. I was a pitcher then, a left-handed pitcher. At Ada I'd played first base and the outfield when I wasn't pitching, but the Frisco club signed me as a pitcher.

The first or second day of spring training we had a little game, the Regulars against the Yannigans—that's what they called the rookies— and I was pitching for the Yannigans. The umpire was a coach by the name of Spider Baum. Along about the sixth inning my arm started to tighten up, so I shouted in, "Spider, my arm is tying up and getting sore on me."

"Make it or break it!" he says.

They don't say those things to youngsters nowadays. No, sir! And maybe it's just as well they don't, because what happened was that, sure enough, I *broke* it! And the next day, gee, I could hardly lift it.

I figured that was the end of my career, and in a few weeks I'd be back in Ada. I was supposed to be a pitcher, and I couldn't throw the ball ten feet. But just to keep busy, and look like I was doing something, I fooled around in the outfield and shagged balls for the rest of them. I'd toss the ball back underhanded, because I couldn't throw any other way. I did that day after day, but my arm didn't get any better.

After the regular day's practice was over, the three Big Leaguers —Willie Kamm, Lew Fonseca, and Jimmy O'Connell—would stay out an extra hour or so and practice hitting, and I shagged balls for them, too. I figured I'd better make myself useful in any way I could, or I'd be on my way back to Oklahoma.

I don't know which one of them mentioned it to the others, but after about a week or so of this they decided that maybe I'd like a turn at hitting. Especially since if I quit shagging for them, they'd have to go chase all those balls themselves. And they didn't relish the idea of doing that.

So they yelled, "Hey, kid! You want to hit some?"

"Sure I do," I said.

So they threw, and I hit. They just let me hit and hit and hit, and I really belted that ball. There was a carpenter building a house out just beyond the right-field fence, about 360 or 370 feet from home plate. He was pounding shingles on the roof, and he had his back to us. Well, I hit one, and it landed on the roof, pretty close to him. He looked around, wondering what the devil was going on. The first thing you

Paul Waner

know, I slammed another one out there and it darned near hit him. So
he just put his hammer down, and sat there and watched. And I kept
right on crashing line drives out there all around where he was sitting.
Of course, they were lobbing the ball in just right, and heck—I just
swished and away it went.

When we were finished, we went into the clubhouse and nobody said
a word to me. Not a word. And there was only dead silence all the while
we showered, and got dressed, and walked back to the hotel. We sat
down to dinner, and still not a single one of them had said "You looked
good," or "You did well," or anything like that.

But when we were almost through eating dinner the manager, Dots
Miller, came over to my table. He said, "Okie, tomorrow you fool around
in the outfield. Don't throw hard, just toss 'em in underhanded. And
you *hit* with the regulars."

Well, boy, that was something! I gulped, and felt like the cat that just ate the canary. And from then on I was with the regulars, and I started playing.

Luckily, my arm came back a month or two later, a few weeks after the season started. We went into Salt Lake City, and was it ever hot. Suddenly, during fielding practice, my arm felt like it stretched out at least a foot longer, and it felt real supple and good. It caught me by surprise, and I was afraid to really throw hard. But I did, a little more each time, and it felt fine!

Duffy Lewis was managing Salt Lake City and he knew about my bad arm, so he'd told his players, "Run on Waner. Anytime the ball goes to him, just duck your head and start running, because he can't throw."

There was a pretty short right-field wall at Salt Lake City, and in the first or second inning one of their players hit one off the wall. I took it on the rebound and threw him out at second by 15 feet. Someone tried to score from second on a single to right, and I threw him out at home. Gee whiz, I could throw all the way from the outfield to home plate! I threw about four men out in nothing flat, and after that they stopped running on me. I never had any trouble with my arm after that. It never bothered me again.

I had a good year in the Coast League that first season; hit about .370. Then the next season I did the same thing, got over 200 hits, and batted in about 100 runs. I was figuring by then that maybe I should be moving up to the Big Leagues. Joe Devine, a Pittsburgh scout, was trying to get the Pirates to buy me, but the San Francisco club wanted $100,000 for me, and the Pittsburgh higher-ups thought that that was a little too much for a small fellow like me. I only weighed 135 pounds then. I never weighed over 148 pounds ever, in all the years I played.

So Joe said to me, "Paul, it looks like you'll have to hit .400 to get up to the majors."

"Well, then," I said, "that's just exactly what I'll do."

I was kidding, you know. But darned if I didn't hit .401 in 1925. I got 280 hits that season, and at the end of the year the Pirates paid the $100,000 for me. San Francisco sold Willie Kamm to the Big Leagues for $100,000 in 1922, and then did the same thing with me three years later.

After I got to Pittsburgh early in 1926, I told Mr. Dreyfuss, the president of the club, that I had a younger brother who was a better ballplayer than I was. So the Pirates signed Lloyd and sent him to Columbia in the Sally League to see how he'd do. Well, Lloyd hit about .350 and was chosen the league's Most Valuable Player.

The Pirates took Lloyd along to spring training in 1927, mostly just to look at him a little closer. They never thought he could possibly make the team, 'cause Lloyd only weighed about 130 pounds then. He was only twenty years old, and was even smaller than me.

Our outfield that season was supposed to be Kiki Cuyler, Clyde Barnhart, and myself. But Barnhart reported that spring weighing about 260 or 270 pounds. He was just a butterball. They took him and did everything they could think of to get his weight down. They gave him steam baths, and exercised him, and ran him, and ran him, and ran him. Well, they got the weight off, all right, but as a result the poor fellow was so weak he could hardly lift a bat.

So on the trip back to Pittsburgh from spring training, Donie Bush came to me and said, "Paul, I'm putting your little brother out there in left field, and he's going to open the season for us."

"Well, you won't regret it," I said. "Lloyd will do the job in first-rate style."

And he did, too, as you know. We won the pennant that year, with Lloyd hitting .355. I hit .380 myself, and between the two of us we got 460 base hits that season: 223 hits for Lloyd and 237 for me. It's an interesting thing that of those 460 hits only 11 were home runs. They were mostly line drives: singles, doubles, and a lot of triples, because both of us were very fast.

Don't get the idea that we won the pennant for Pittsburgh all by ourselves that year, though, because that sure wasn't so. We had Pie Traynor at third base, you know, and Pie hit about .340 that season. Pie was a great ballplayer, I think the greatest third baseman who ever lived. A terrific hitter and a great fielder. Gosh, how he could dive for those line drives down the third base line and knock the ball down and throw the man out at first! It was remarkable. Those two Boyer brothers who are playing now are both great fielding third basemen, but Pie could do all they can and more. In addition to his hitting and fielding, Pie was a good base runner, too. Most people don't remember that.

It's a funny thing, but Pie always said that I was the best first baseman he ever threw to. I played first once in a while, not too much, but every so often. I didn't know very much about how to play first base

at the beginning, but one of the greatest fielding first basemen of all
time practiced and practiced with me, until I knew my way around the
bag well enough to make do. That was Stuffy McInnes, the great first
baseman of the Philadelphia Athletics' "$100,000 infield" back in 1911
and 1912 and around there.

When I joined the Pirates in 1926, Stuffy was there as a substitute
first baseman. He must have been close to forty at the time, and I think
that was his last year in baseball. He'd been in the Big Leagues since
1910 or so. But he could still field that position like nobody's business,
and he tried to teach me all he knew. I was his roommate in 1926, before
Lloyd came up the next year, and Stuffy would spend hours with me in
the room showing me how to play first base, using a pillow as a base.
Gee, even at that age he was just a flow of motion out there on the field,
just everywhere at once and making everything look so easy.

Actually, I was a little too small to make a good first baseman. On
the other hand, I was almost as tall as Stuffy McInnes and George
Sisler. Neither of them were six-footers. They were a lot bigger than
I was, of course. They must have weighed at least 170 or 180. But
neither of them was real tall, like most first basemen are.

They say Hal Chase was the greatest fielding first baseman of all time.
I never saw him, so I don't know about that. But I did see Stuffy
McInnes and George Sisler, and I don't see how he could have been
better than them. They were the best I ever saw. I guess every generation
has its own, and it's hard to compare between generations.

Although I did see Honus Wagner play, I really did. Honus came
back as a coach with the Pirates during the 'thirties. He must have been
sixty years old easy, but goldarned if that old boy didn't get out there
at shortstop every once in a while during fielding practice and play
that position. When he did that, a hush would come over the whole ball
park, and every player on both teams would just stand there, like a
bunch of little kids, and watch every move he made. I'll never forget it.

Honus was a wonderful fellow, so good-natured and friendly to everyone. Gee, we loved that guy. And the fans were crazy about him.
Yeah, everybody loved that old Dutchman! If anyone told a good joke
or a funny story, Honus would slap his knee and let out a loud roar
and say, "What about *that!*"

So whenever I'd see him, the first thing I'd say would be, "What about
that, Honus," and both of us would laugh. I guess there's no doubt at

all that Honus was the most popular player who ever put on a Pittsburgh uniform. Those Pittsburgh fans were always fine fans, did you know that? They sure were. And I presume they still are, for that matter.

I remember soon after I came up, Pie Traynor said to me, "Paul, you're going to be a very popular ballplayer. The people like to pull for a little fellow."

And that's the way it turned out. In all the 15 years I played with Pittsburgh, I was never booed at home. Not even once. The same with Lloyd. No matter how bad we were, no booing. We never knew what it was like to be booed at home. I don't imagine it would help a fellow any.

Now on the road, I *liked* to be booed. I really did. Because if they boo you on the road, it's either 'cause you're a sorehead or 'cause you're hurting them. Either one or the other. In my first year in the Big Leagues, the players all told me to watch out for the right-field fans in St. Louis. "That right-field stand is tough," they said. "They ride everybody." And, of course, the fellows didn't know whether I could take a riding in the majors or not.

So the first time we went into St. Louis, I figured if they jumped on me I'd have a little fun. And sure enough, as soon as I showed up in right field they started in and gave me a terrible roasting. I turned around and yelled, "They told me for years about all you fans in St. Louis, that all the drunken bums in the city come here. And now that I'm here, I see it's true." I said it real serious and madlike, you know, never cracked a smile.

Oh, did they scream! Well, such as that went on back and forth between us for two or three months. Then one day in the middle of the summer we were giving them an awful licking. I bounced a triple out to right center and drove in two or three runs, and after the inning was over and I came running out to my position they stood up and gave me the very devil. And then, for the first time, I laughed and waved to them.

It so happened that on the very last out of that game a fly ball was hit out to me. I caught it, and then ran over to the stands and handed it to some old fellow that I'd noticed out there every time we played in St. Louis. Well, by golly, they started to clap, and soon all of them were cheering, and do you know that from then on all of them were for me. And that old fellow, any time I got the last ball after that I'd run over and give it to him.

Stuffy McInnis:
"The great first baseman of
the Philadelphia Athletics'
$100,000 infield"

Anyway, like I was saying, we won the pennant in 1927, the first year Lloyd and I played together in the Pittsburgh outfield. That was a great thrill for us, naturally. We even brought Mother and Dad and our sister to the World Series. But then the Yankees beat us four straight, so we weren't very happy about Mother and Dad seeing *that*.

The one thing I remember best about that Series is that I didn't seem to actually realize I was really playing in a World Series until it was all over. The first time we came to bat in the first game, Lloyd singled and I doubled, and from then on the two of us just kept on hitting like it was an ordinary series during the regular season. Neither of us was a bit nervous.

Finally, we came into the bottom of the ninth of the fourth game, with the score tied, 3–3. We were playing at Yankee Stadium, and the Yankees had already beaten us three times in a row. Before I knew what had happened, the Yankees had loaded the bases: Babe Ruth was on first base, Mark Koenig on second, and Earle Combs on third. And there were none out. But then Johnny Miljus, who was pitching for us, struck out Lou Gehrig and Bob Meusel, and it looked like we'd get out of it. While he was working on Tony Lazzeri, though, Johnny suddenly let loose a wild pitch that sailed over catcher Johnny Gooch's shoulder, and in came Combs with the run that won the game, and the Series, for the Yankees.

Out in right field, I was stunned. And that instant, as the run that beat us crossed the plate, it suddenly struck me that I'd actually played in a World Series. It's an odd thing, isn't it? I didn't think, "It's all over and we lost."

What I thought was, "Gee, I've just played in a World Series!"

And you know, I think that's the first time I really realized it. It's funny how much your frame of mind has to do with your ability to play ball. I guess I forced myself not to think about playing in a World Series, so I wouldn't get nervous.

It's the same way with superstitions. Most ballplayers know that such things are silly. But if it gives you a feeling of confidence in yourself, then it'll work. You figure, "If it helps, why not? What have I got to lose?"

Like the time I got six straight hits in a game. That was in 1926, my first year up. I used six different bats, and swung six different times, and came up with six different hits. You just know there has to be a lot of luck in a thing like that. It so happened that Bill McKechnie, who was our manager that year, changed our batting order a little that day, and I was put hitting second instead of third, where I usually hit. So I was in the corner of the dugout, smoking a cigarette, not figuring it was my turn yet, when somebody yelled, "Hey, Paul, hurry up, you're holding up the parade. Get up to bat."

I hustled out to the plate and just grabbed a bat on the way, any bat, I didn't even look. And I got a hit. So I thought, well, maybe that's not such a bad way to do. The next time up I did the same thing, just grabbed a bat blind, not looking, and off came another hit. So I did that all day. Six bats and six hits. (However, that system stopped working the next day, unfortunately.)

After that disastrous World Series, Mom and Dad and Lloyd and I went back home to Oklahoma, and darned if they didn't have a parade and all for us in our home town. Everybody was so happy that I was hard put to figure it out. After all, we hadn't won the Series, we'd lost it, and in four straight games to boot.

Well, it turned out that there had been a lot of money bet there, but it hadn't been bet on the Pirates against the Yankees. It had been bet on the Waner brothers against Ruth and Gehrig. And our combined batting average for the Series had been .367, against .357 for Ruth and Gehrig. So that's why everybody was so happy.

Well, after that 1927 pennant we never won another one, not one single one, all the years Lloyd and I played in Pittsburgh. Gee, that was tough to take. We ended second about four times, but never could get back on top again. We had good teams, too. You know, Pie, Arky Vaughan, Gus Suhr, Bill Swift, Mace Brown, Ray Kremer, all good boys. But we never quite made it.

It'd just tear you apart. We'd make a good start, but before the season was over they'd always catch up with us. And when you're not in the race any more, it gets to be a long season, really long.

The closest we came was in 1938. God, that was awful! That's the year Gabby Hartnett hit that home run. We thought we had that pennant sewed up. A good lead in the middle of September, it looked like it was ours for sure. Then the Cubs crept up and finally went ahead of us on that home run, and that was it.

It was on September 28, 1938. I remember it like it just happened. We were playing in Chicago, at Wrigley Field, and the score was tied, 5–5, in the bottom of the ninth inning. There were two out, and it was getting dark. If Mace Brown had been able to get Hartnett out, the umpires would have had to call the game on account of darkness, it would have ended in a tie, and we would have kept our one-half-game lead in first place. In fact, Brown had two strikes on Hartnett. All he needed was one more strike.

But he didn't get it. Hartnett swung, and the damn ball landed in the left-field seats. I could hardly believe my eyes. The game was over, and I should have run into the clubhouse. But I didn't. I just stood out there in right field and watched Hartnett circle the bases, and take the lousy pennant with him. I just watched and wondered, sort of objectively, you know, how the devil he could ever get all the way around to touch home plate.

You see, the crowd was in an uproar, absolutely gone wild. They ran onto the field like a bunch of maniacs, and his teammates and the crowd and all were mobbing Hartnett, and piling on top of him, and throwing him up in the air, and everything you could think of. I've never seen anything like it before or since. So I just stood there in the outfield and stared, like I was sort of somebody else, and wondered what the chances were that he could actually make it all the way around the bases.

When I finally did turn and go into the clubhouse, it was just like a funeral. It was terrible. Mace Brown was sitting in front of his locker, crying like a baby. I stayed with him all that night, I was so afraid he was going to commit suicide. I guess technically we still could have won the pennant. There were still a couple of days left to the season. But that home run took all the fight out of us. It broke our hearts.

I still see Mace every once in a while, when he comes down this way on a scouting trip. He's a scout for the Boston Red Sox. Heck of a nice guy, too. He can laugh about it now, practically 30 years later. Well,

The Waner family at the 1927 World Series: Lloyd, mother, sister, father, Paul

he can almost laugh about it, anyway. When he stops laughing, he kind of shudders a bit, you know, like it's a bad dream that he can't quite get out of his mind.

Well, there's a lot of happiness and a lot of sadness in playing baseball. The last full season that Lloyd and I played together on the Pirates was 1940. That was my fifteenth year with Pittsburgh, and Lloyd's fourteenth. Heck, I was thirty-seven by then, and Lloyd was thirty-four. Of course, we hung on in the Big Leagues with various teams for about five more years, but that was only on account of the war. With the war and all, they couldn't get young players, so I played until I was forty-two, and then my legs just wouldn't carry me any more.

I remember one day when I was with the Boston Braves in 1942. Casey Stengel was the manager. I was supposed to be just a pinch hitter, but in the middle of the summer, with a whole string of double-headers coming up, all the extra outfielders got hurt and I had to go in and play center field every day. Oh, was that ever rough! One double-header after the other.

Well, that day—I think we were in Pittsburgh, of all places—in about the middle of the second game, one of the Pittsburgh players hit a long triple to right center. I chased it down, and came back with my tongue hanging out. I hardly got settled before the next guy hit a long triple to left center, and off I went after *it*. Boy, after that I could hardly stand up.

And then the next guy popped a little blooper over second into real short center field. In I went, as fast as my legs would carry me. Which wasn't very fast, I'll tell you. At the last minute I dove for the ball, but I didn't quite make it, and the ball landed about two feet in front of me and just *stuck* in the ground there. And do you know, I just lay there. I *couldn't* get up to reach that ball to save my life! Finally, one of the other outfielders came over and threw it in.

That's like in 1944, when I was playing with the Yankees. I finished up my career with them. Some fan in the bleachers yelled at me, "Hey Paul, how come you're in the outfield for the Yankees?"

"Because," I said, "Joe DiMaggio's in the army."

Of course, in a sense, I've never really left baseball, because I've been a batting coach most of the years since I quit playing. I coached two years with the Phillies, two with the Cardinals, six with Milwaukee, and some with the Red Sox. I took the whole organization, not just the Big League club. When the parent team was at home, I'd usually be there. Then, when they went on the road, I'd start flying to all their minor-league clubs.

Even as a batting coach, you know, my small size has helped me. Because the youngsters figure that, me being small and all, I must know *something* about how to hit. It's obvious I can't strong-back the ball, and yet they know I got over 3,000 hits, over 600 doubles, and all that. So they say to themselves, "Gee, he must know the secret." And they listen.

So that's the way it was. Those 24 years that I played baseball—from 1923 to 1946—somehow, it doesn't seem like I played even a month. It went *so fast*. The first four or five years, I felt like I'd been in baseball a long time. Then, suddenly, I'd been in the Big Leagues for ten years. And then, all at once, it was twenty.

You know . . . sitting here like this . . . it's hard to believe it's more than a quarter of a century since Lloyd and I played together. Some-how . . . I don't know . . . it seems like it all happened only yesterday.

John J. McGraw and Honus Wagner: "It seems like it all happened only yesterday."

Acknowledgments

So many people have gone out of their way to help me with this book that it would be impossible to express here my appreciation to each and every one of them. But I would be woefully remiss if I did not take this opportunity to record my gratitude to Herman Krooss and Bob Kavesh, for thinking that this was worth doing in the first place; to Bill Veeck, for his encouragement very early in the game; to Eliot Asinof and Bob McKenzie, for their enthusiasm in a later inning; to Roslyn Purcell, for her cheerful and efficient secretarial assistance; to Larry Grossberg, of Sonocraft, who was never quite sure what this was all about, but who was always more than willing to take time out to render first aid anyway; and to Fred Lieb, who has forgotten more about baseball in the early days than I will ever know, for his hospitality and his help.

Finally, this whole endeavor, from beginning to end, has been the collective effort of two others besides myself. It could never have gotten off the ground without our first-base coach, Stephen Ritter, who either operated the tape recorder himself or, when there was no alternative, patiently showed me (a number of times) what levers to push to make a tape recorder record on tape. And it could never have been carried through to completion without our third-base coach, Barbara Neuwirth, who did a thousand and one things, including the proferring of much very good advice, most of which was taken and the rest of which should have been.

For the new enlarged edition, special thanks are due to Harvey Ginsberg, Donald Honig, Rolf Preuss, and Joan Raines. Each made a unique contribution toward launching this edition; without them, it never would have gotten off the ground.

Picture Credits

Many of the pictures in this book were obtained from the personal albums of the players themselves. The sources of the others are as follows:

BETTMANN ARCHIVE   *pages 61, 133*

BOSTON PUBLIC LIBRARY   *31*

BROWN BROTHERS   *11, 32, 44, 50, 102, 115, 134–35, 177, 190, 272, 346–47*

CULVER PICTURES   *17, 22, 64, 90, 93, 98, 181, 193*

EUROPEAN PICTURE SERVICE   *37, 104, 112–13, 119* (top), *120, 122, 182, 188, 220–21, 247* (bottom), *248, 341*

FREDERIC LEWIS, INC.   *247* (top)

FREELANCE PHOTOGRAPHERS GUILD   *255, 275, 281, 304*

HAYWARD BINNEY   *143, 146, 148* (top)

ILLINOIS CENTRAL RAILROAD   *4–5*

NEW YORK DAILY NEWS   *207, 277*

NEW YORK PUBLIC LIBRARY   *88, 234*

PHOTOWORLD   *275*

THE SPORTING NEWS   *130, 197*

UNDERWOOD AND UNDERWOOD   *238, 344*

UNITED PRESS INTERNATIONAL   *257, 286–87, 318, 323*

WIDE WORLD PHOTOS   *29, 58, 205*

Index*

*Numbers in italics indicate that a photograph appears on that page.

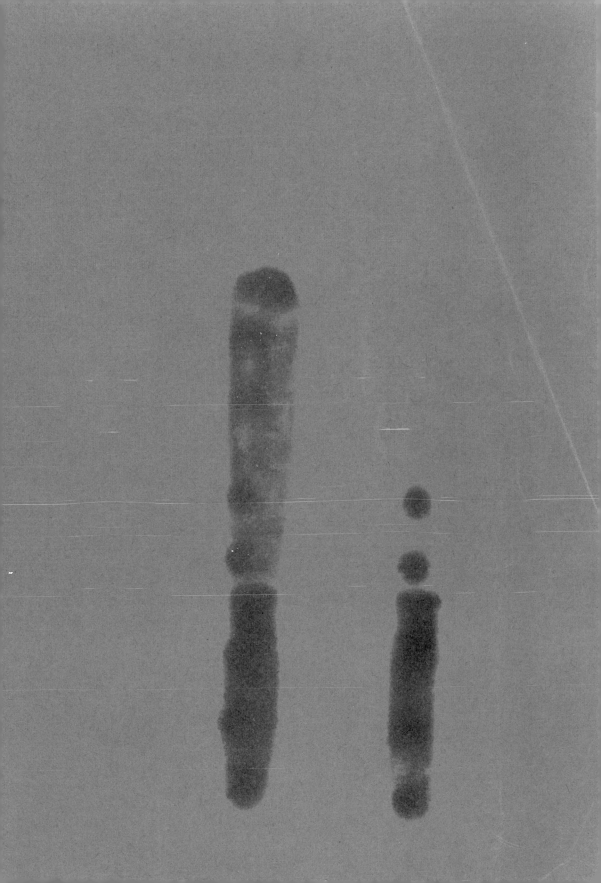